REF

QB
68
.D59

Dixon, Don.

Universe

DATE			

UNIVERSE

UNIVERSE

DON DIXON

Houghton Mifflin Company Boston 1981

For Chesley Bonestell,

who imagined what might be;

and for Thomas Tregarthen Dixon,

whose generation will know.

Library of Congress Cataloging in Publication Data

Dixon, Don.
  Universe.
  Includes index.
  1. Astronomy — Pictorial works.   I. Title.
QB68.D59   523   81-1621
ISBN 0-395-31290-6   AACR2

Printed in the United States of America

H 10 9 8 7 6 5 4 3 2 1

Book design by Edith Allard, Designworks, Inc.

BST

CONTENTS

ACKNOWLEDGMENTS

IT IS A PLEASURE TO THANK THE MANY people who helped with this project. Richard Childers elicited initial interest in the book from several publishers, and it was subsequently placed with Houghton Mifflin by my agent Harold Moskovitz. My editors there, Frances Tenenbaum and Clay Morgan, deserve thanks for their encouragement and patient instruction.

At the University of Hawaii's Institute for Astronomy, Ginger Plasch was invaluable in providing photographic materials and arranging meetings with David Morrison, Tom McCord, Duncan Chesley, and Jeff Bosel, who generously shared their time and expertise. I'm particularly grateful to Dale Cruikshank for inviting me to an observing session at Mauna Kea Observatory, and to Leon Milberg of Ocean Adventures in Kaneohe for his gracious hospitality.

Eugene Shoemaker, at the U.S.G.S. in Flagstaff, kindly shared some of his ideas on planetary formation, and Jody Swann provided the planetary maps. Helen Horstman, at Lowell Observatory, and Connie Rodriguez, Ellen Kemper, and Agnes Paulesen, at Kitt Peak Observatory, supplied additional photography.

I owe a great deal to Barry Friedman, president of Creative Associates, not only for his industrious promotion of my work but for his friendship and help during a difficult time. Tom Heppenheimer gave similar support, and, in his professional capacity as a planetary scientist, prepared the solar system data tables, helped track down source materials, and arranged interviews with other scientists, such as Peter Goldreich, Andy Ingersoll, and Jurie Van der Woude.

Mike and Martha Standlee, of Michael Standlee Design in Newport Beach, California, are to be complimented for the excellent diagramatic art and also for their patience in dealing with the worst possible client, a fellow artist. I also want to thank Gwyn Standlee, who typed part of the manuscript and offered cogent criticism as well as encouragement.

Many other friends and colleagues helped in various ways. Among them are Gail Selinger, Harrison Rose, Kerry O'Quinn, David Houston, Don Piccolo, George Van Valkenberg, Frank De Vino, Mary Ann Fischer, Mrs. F. H. Kline, Roxanne and Albert Morales, Douglas Arnold, Jim Harrod, Linda Mahru, Manuel Mazivers, Mike Brodie, Betty Jean Cunningham, Rick Sternbach, and Asenath Hammond. I also want to thank the many "Spacescapes" customers who made it possible for me to pursue an art career. My debt to Chesley Bonestell, who was painting realistic astronomicals in the days when everyone "knew" space flight was impossible, is acknowledged in the dedication.

Irvine, California
October 15, 1980

I BEGINNINGS

ONE THE DISTANT PAST

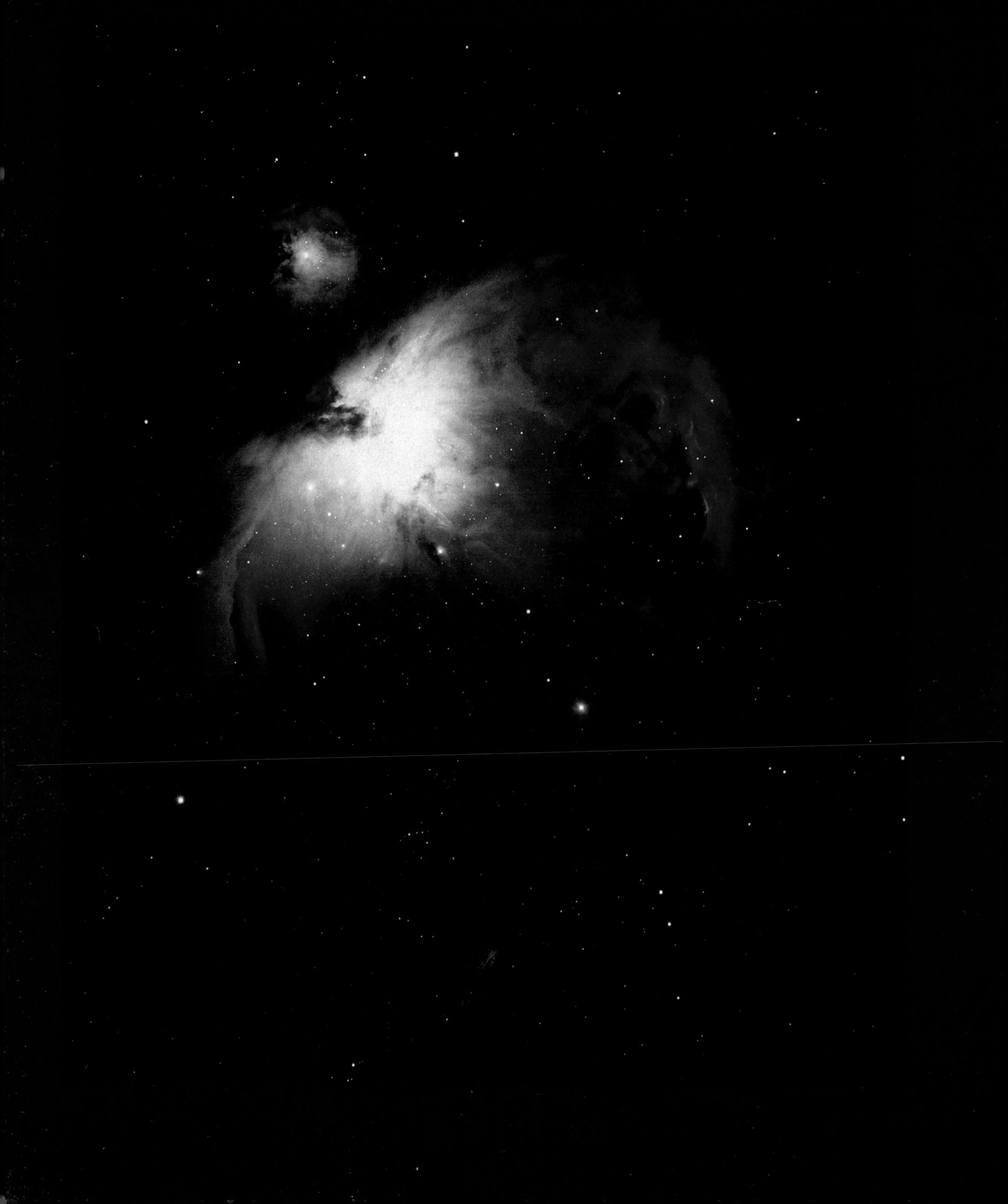

IN EXPLORING THE DISTANT PAST, WE MUST bear in mind that we are like the short-lived insects in the Chinese parable: we spend but a day in the forest, so we cannot watch the trees grow. We can, however, find seeds, saplings, mature individuals, and fallen hulks, and through imagination and logic we can deduce the life pattern of a tree. The same is true with the grander, more ponderous cycles in nature. Even the most short-lived star endures through a million human lifetimes, but by examining a number of stars in various stages of their development, we can understand the cycle of stellar birth and death. Creation is a continuous process that we can observe.

We are reluctant to acknowledge that an immense span of time has preceded our own existence; it threatens our sense of self-importance. Western religions in particular have fostered the belief that the universe is little more than a clockwork toy, with man as the central gear. This is unfortunate, for by so reducing the scope of creation, we limit our appreciation of its grandeur. Perhaps the greatest contribution of modern astronomy is that it has not only revealed a universe full of pulsing energy, ethereal beauty, and great mystery but has also given us a perspective on our ultimate origins. And that perspective is a soul-satisfying one: we may be dust, but we are star dust. The fading echoes of creation still whisper in our radio telescopes, and their surprising message is that the ancient poetry was correct: we, and all that we behold, were indeed born in a burst of light.

Prior to a moment approximately 16 billion years ago, the universe did not exist in any sense that we can understand. Darkness was indeed upon the face of the deep — except that there was no deep, for there was neither time nor space, but only an incomprehensible nothingness.

Something happened. Perhaps a previous universe collapsed and rebounded, or there may have been some sort of interdimensional leakage from another "megauniverse." We have no information beyond a certain point, so perhaps the question of prime cause is best left to theologians. What we do know, or at least strongly suspect, is that at a unique instant of time, all the matter and energy that now comprises our universe was concentrated in a very small volume of space.

There was an explosion of sorts. Unlike conventional explosions, however, it had no center. To locate a center, one would have to stand outside the universe, which is impossible by definition. For purposes of discussion, however, we can think of the newborn universe as an expanding globe of virtually pure energy.

The space containing the fireball grew at many times the speed of light, and as it grew, it cooled. The fundamental physical forces — gravitation, electromagnetism, strong and weak nuclear interactions — shaped the primordial stuff into elementary particles: photons, neutrinos, electrons, and positrons. Particles of matter and antimatter met, annihilated one another, and were reborn. The battle for supremacy between the two incompatible types of matter continued until one type, through a slight initial numerical advantage, won out.

A Cosmological Mandala. The bright central region represents zero time, the moment of creation. Proceeding radially, we move toward the present day: the universe cools, groups of galaxies form and then move apart, impelled by the initial explosion. *(Art by author)*

Facing page
The Orion Nebula. Within such clouds of dust and gas, creation continues, and over the course of time we can observe the formation of new stars. *(Photo © Association of Universities for Research in Astronomy, Inc., The Kitt Peak National Observatory)*

Primordial clouds of gas and dust abound in space, and one gave birth to our solar system approximately 4.5 billion years ago. Stars are born in litters, and the Sun's newborn siblings shone through immense but tenuous clouds of hydrogen. The pressure of their light, and eddies within the galactic gravitational field, caused a local concentration of gas to form in one part of the nebula. This gas took shape as a dark globule, hundred of billions of kilometers across, that slowly collapsed upon itself as it was squeezed by its own gravitational field. *(Art by author)*

The universe continued to cool, dropping billions of degrees each second. Within 0.01 second, photons — the basic quanta, or "particles," of light — no longer had enough energy to produce protons and neutrons. After ten seconds, their energy was insufficient to give rise to electrons and positrons through pair production. It was still too hot for atoms to form, however. For at least 700,000 years the universe was mostly energy — that is, more mass-energy was present in photons and neutrinos than in the hydrogen, deuterium, and helium nuclei that had been formed in the moments following creation, when fusion processes had been possible. As the universe expanded, photons continued to lose energy, however, and the balance shifted. Matter became dominant. At this point, the universe became transparent, and photons were able to travel great distances in space, and, ultimately, in time. And these same photons comprise the cosmic background radiation that causes an ineradicable hiss in the most sensitive radio receivers today.

By now the basic chemical composition of the universe was established. Immense clouds of hydrogen and helium gas condensed out of the fireball. Mutual gravitation within these clouds caused them to fragment into even smaller clumpings. The fireball began to break up. Discrete clouds of incandescent gas, tens of millions of light-years across, drifted apart from one another. Each of these clouds in turn broke up into smaller clumps.

Now gravity, weakest of the fundamental forces, began to play a dominant role. Every particle of matter in the expanding fireball exerted a weak but continual attraction

on every other. This not only began to slow the general expansion but also caused the smallest clumps of gas to collapse. As the radiation density of the universe decreased, these clouds, or protogalaxies, cooled. Just as cooling a rain cloud causes water droplets to form about condensation nuclei, such as dust particles, so did cooling the protogalaxies cause "droplets" of hydrogen to form in the vicinity of yet smaller, random inhomogeneities. These new clumps of gas, which were only a few light-months across, were on the order of a million times smaller than the parent protogalaxy, and they were the seeds of stars.

Gravity continued to hold sway, and these dark globules of gas began to collapse. As the density within the protosuns increased, collisions between gas molecules became more frequent and energetic, causing the protosuns to heat up. When the central temperature reached approximately 10,000,000° Kelvin (K), nuclear processes began and the protosuns became stars.

We can imagine this moment in cosmic history. The universe was in chaos, and the dying fires of creation still flashed sporadically behind darkening rivers of gas. Suddenly, a tiny spark of light glimmered redly against the darkness. It flickered, died, and then flared into diamond brilliance, shining with a steady light. This first star was soon joined by others, of varying sizes and luminosities, and the universe began to assume the form we know today.

It was a barren universe, however, like a rocky field bereft of soil, for only various forms of hydrogen and

Birth of the Sun. As the solar nebula collapsed, it began to rotate. Centrifugal force flattened it into a disk. Near the center, compression of the gas caused temperatures to soar, and a slow-motion explosion, the T-Tauri wind, rippled outward, blowing the lighter gases into space and exposing the belt of orbiting matter that would one day become the planet Earth. *(Art by author)*

helium had been created at the beginning. The heavier elements, including those present in living things, such as oxygen, nitrogen, carbon, and phosphorus, did not yet exist. The creation of these atoms required no less a sacrifice than the death of suns, for only in the hearts of stars can the chemicals of life be born.

Gravity was once again the driving force. If the nuclear furnace at the core of a star doesn't produce enough pressure to counteract the immense weight of the star's outer layers, the star will collapse upon itself. The most massive stars that originally populated our galaxy quickly exhausted their nuclear fuel, became gravitationally unstable, and exploded, spewing their chemical-rich interiors into space. Just as plants fertilize the soil when they die and decompose, so the corpses of the first population of stars enriched the interstellar medium.

The cycle of stellar birth and death continued for 10 billion years. Groups of galaxies, vast conglomerations of stars, dust, and gas, some spherical, others elliptical or irregular, drifted apart from one another. Some galaxies, advanced in their evolution, assumed lovely spiral forms, spinning slowly like celestial pinwheels. In one of these, a wave of slightly higher gravity rippled through a particularly rich cloud of interstellar gas. The resulting compression caused a scattering of protosuns to form. Nearly half of these protosuns were in pairs, and later became binary stars, waltzing gracefully about a common center of mass. Such systems were too turbulent, gravitationally, to allow smaller, colder bodies to form in their vicinity. Other protosuns were too massive, and the stars into which they evolved burned fiercely for a few million years and then died in cataclysmic explosions. Some of the protosuns,

Accretion of the Earth. Within the belt, gravity continued inexorably to draw matter together. Ice-coated pebbles assembled into swarms and collapsed to form boulders. Somewhere in the belt, the interplay of gravitational fields caused a major concentration, which soon swept up the remaining planetesimals. *(Art by author)*

however, were of an intermediate size, and solitary. While their larger, more profligate siblings raced toward early extinction, these protosuns contracted. One of them was destined to become our Sun.

The presolar nebula was, by industrial standards, a good vacuum; it probably had fewer than 100 atoms per cubic centimeter. This was dense enough, nonetheless, to maintain the cloud's gravitational integrity against external forces that would tend to disperse it, such as its own internal motion and the shear effect of differential orbital velocity within the galaxy.

Over the course of several thousand years, the cloud contracted.* At first an amorphous blob, it initially collapsed toward a spherical shape, but the net angular momentum — that is, the impetus of all those particles that were not falling directly toward the center, but rather at angles to it — caused the cloud to rotate. The centrifugal force of this rotation made the cloud bulge at the equator. Just as a pirouetting figure skater spins faster when she pulls in her arms, so did the cloud rotate more quickly as it collapsed. The increased centrifugal force flattened the cloud even more, so that it assumed a disk shape, rather like that of a classic flying saucer, with a central bulge and thin edge.

Within this accretion disk, tiny grains of iron, silicon, aluminum, and other heavy elements no thicker than human hair collided gently and adhered to one another. These specks fell slowly through the primal nebula, toward the plane of the disk, becoming larger as the result of chance collisions with similar particles. As they fell through the thickening cloud, they were caught up in the general swirling motion of the accretion disk, so that by the time they reached the central plane they were moving in roughly circular paths about the central condensation.

If some ancient spacefarer had visited the solar system at this time, he would have beheld a scene of wintry majesty. In the distance was the protosun, shining a somber red through roiling clouds. Glowing with the heat of gravitational collapse, its nuclear furnace not yet ignited, it gave little warmth to the outer reaches of the solar system. Indeed, in every direction our mythical traveler looked, he would have seen glistening constellations of ice-coated grains, few larger than pebbles, floating like dust motes in a quiet room, weightless, drifting randomly, stirred occasionally by gentle breezes from the embryonic sun. It would have been difficult for anyone floating in the midst of this slow-motion blizzard to believe that within a few centuries the quiescent scene would be replaced by one of literally world-shattering violence.

The billions of tiny, icy granules drifting in the accretion disk were the seeds of planets. As they floated in counter-

---

* The peculiar ratio of certain isotopes found within meteorites has led some astrophysicists to suggest that the formation of the Sun was triggered by the shock wave from a nearby supernova. Also, it is of interest to note that an unusual concentration of xenon was found within the Murchison meteorite that fell on Australia in 1966. Since xenon is thought to be produced within red-giant stars, such a star may have contributed to the matter that eventually formed our solar system.

clockwise paths about the forming sun, some of the particles collided gently with others, and stuck together. Because of their increased cross-sectional area, these aggregate particles grew even faster, like snowballs rolling downhill. Eventually they attained the size of boulders, and then small mountains that were kilometers across.

Up to that point, unions between particles in the cloud had been generally nonviolent, since neighboring chunks tended to move with similar velocities. As the planetesimals grew in mass, and the gas in the nebula thinned, condensing as ice on the planetesimals, however, that weakest of forces, gravity, once again came into play. Collisions became more energetic. Imagine a kilometer-wide conglomeration of rock and frozen gases, plowing along at 30 kilometers per second. In its path, moving in a slightly different orbit at lower speed, is a boulder-sized planetesimal. They collide, and the boulder is shattered. Instead of drifting away into space, however, half the fragments rise slowly away from the giant planetesimal and then fall gently back to the surface. The planetoid grows by a tiny amount. After thousands of such encounters, the planetoid has doubled its mass, and also its gravitational field. The swath the planetoid cuts through the accretion disk is no longer restricted to its physical cross section, but extends beyond its surface, so that particles that earlier might have survived a near miss are now swept in. Like a whale grazing on celestial plankton, the planetoid grows larger.

Collisions of planetesimals within the solar nebula became less frequent as material was swept up by the forming planets. *(Art by author)*

But it is not alone. Elsewhere in the solar cloud are similar bodies, kilometers wide. The orbits they follow are sometimes highly elliptical, inclined to the plane of the disk, and they occasionally intersect. It is only a matter of time before two planetoids arrive at the same place at the same time. When they collide, one of several things can happen. If the two bodies are in very different orbits, they may impact head-on, with a closing velocity of tens of miles per second, shattering into thousands of fragments. Their careers as would-be planets are nipped in the bud, and they once again become fodder for larger cows in the solar pasture.

Their deaths are not entirely in vain, however. Such collisions over the course of tens of thousands of years had a damping effect on the accretion cloud. The average orbit became more nearly circular and co-planar, and the solar system as a whole became more orderly. Within this less turbulent accretion disk, collisions between large planetoids no longer necessarily resulted in disaster. If the two bodies were moving in similar orbits, so that their closing velocity was only a few hundred feet per second, they usually shattered one another, but, instead of scattering throughout the solar system, the fragments stayed together as a conglomerate, bound by gravity and moving in a new orbit. Over the course of centuries, gravity collapsed the mass into a new, larger planetoid. Thus the planets grew.

At the end of this stage of planetary formation, there were probably thousands of planetesimals orbiting the Sun. Warmed by the new star, the volatiles of the innermost planetesimals, such as ammonia and methane ices, were boiled and evaporated into space, leaving behind the stony silicates and metals. The latter formed the cores of the terrestrial planets — Mercury, Venus, Earth, and Mars. A fifth group, disturbed by Jupiter, remained unaccreted. The planetesimals in the cold outer regions of the solar system retained their icy volatiles and eventually formed the giant worlds of liquid hydrogen — Jupiter, Saturn, Uranus, and Neptune.

Computer simulations of planetary formation suggest that at first the planetesimals followed orbits that were nearly circular and relatively close to one another, but as they collided and the differences in their masses became more pronounced, the orbits became more elliptical and spread farther apart. Collisions were then less frequent but more energetic. After perhaps 30 million years, the planetesimals were assimilated into a much smaller number of bodies, some the size of small planets. One of these latter, a rocky sphere some 6000 kilometers in diameter, was destined to form the nucleus of Earth.

During its peak period of accretion, Earth was growing by 30 billion tons every day. This means that any given patch of Earth's surface with an area equal to New York's Central Park would have been struck daily by the equivalent of a house-sized boulder. Such rocks were moving so rapidly, with speeds sometimes in excess of 10 kilometers per second, that upon impacting they released as much energy as the Hiroshima blast. The early environment must have been Dante-esque. Geophysicist D. L. Anderson has suggested that the heat of accretion may have melted the

The nucleus of Earth was probably cool and homogeneous, but as its mass increased, pressures within its interior caused rock to melt and flow. A process of sedimentation, or differentiation, began: heavy materials, such as metals, sank to the core, while lighter, rocky material rose to form a crust. During the last stages of accretion, most of the Earth was probably molten, including its surface. *(Art by author)*

Facing page
Evolution of the Atmosphere. The dynamic forces developing within the Earth produced many volcanoes. Vast quantities of carbon dioxide, water vapor, and other gases were added to the original atmosphere of hydrogen, methane, and ammonia that had been retained from the primordial solar nebula. *(Art by author)*

forming Earth to a depth of 500 kilometers. The surface would have been an utterly flat sea of molten lava, crusted over by a thin gray scum of lighter rock much like that which forms on the lava lakes of Kilauea today. But like pack ice in a thaw, this would-be crust was continually shattered by the waves and splashes resulting from nearby impacts, and could not grow to any great thickness. Gradually, though, over the course of perhaps 100 million years, the bombardment eased, permitting Earth to cool and allowing a true crust to begin to form. The 3.8-billion-year-old ironstones found in the Isua Formation in western Greenland are thought to be remnants of this original crust.

Earth's surface continued to cool. While its crust grew thicker and more solid, the heat of radioactive decay in the interior drove new fires to the surface. Volcanoes erupted everywhere. Clouds of steam, carbon dioxide, nitrogen, sulfur dioxide, and other gases gushed from the vents and were incorporated into the atmosphere that contained methane, ammonia, and water vapor left over from the preplanetary ices.

The oceans formed quite early in Earth's history, but the source of our planet's plentiful water is uncertain. Until recently the consensus among geologists was that volcanic steam provided most of the water. If this was the case, then the ocean basins filled gradually, fed by intermittent rainfall over the course of tens of millions of years. But there were other sources of water available to the young Earth.

The heat of radioactive decay deep within
Earth's core drove fountains of gas, molten rock,
and metal to the surface, enriching the crust
and atmosphere. *(Art by author)*

An alternative explanation of the origin of the
oceans and the atmosphere has recently been
proposed by Eugene Shoemaker. In this model
of the Earth's accretion, differentiation takes
place within the solar nebula as well as inside
the forming planets. Within the hottest portion
of the solar nebula, only iron and other heavy
metals condense to form planetesimals and,
ultimately, the cores of the terrestrial planets.
As this material is swept up, and the nebula
cools, more volatile silicates condense and are
assimilated by the proto-Earth. Finally, all the
material in the inner solar system is depleted,
and the only new material to impact Earth
comes from the outer solar system, where cooler
temperatures have permitted the formation of
"snowballs" of frozen water, methane, and
ammonia. It may be that these late-arriving
planetesimals contributed more mass to the
oceans and atmosphere than did outgassing
from the interior. Earth is shown in cross-
section at the upper right of the diagram, and
its rate of growth in the solar nebula is defined
by the radial lines. For example, this particular

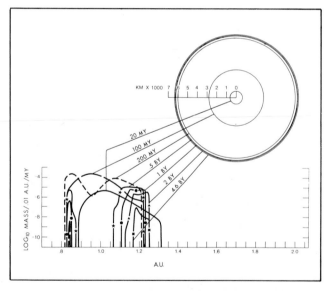

model suggests that Earth required 100 million
years to grow to a radius of 3000 kilometers,
and that most of this core material came from a
part of the solar nebula approximately 1.0
astronomical unit from the Sun. After 1 billion
years, Earth had grown to a sphere more than
6000 kilometers in radius, depleting the
reservoir of nearby-orbiting planetesimals, and
was now assimilating material that had been
formed in the cooler region approximately 1.2
astronomical units from the Sun. Graph above
indicates the amount of matter required to
make each shell.
(Diagram courtesy of Eugene Shoemaker)

The planetesimals themselves probably contained significant amounts of chemically bound water that was released upon impact, and studies of the pattern of cratering on Saturn's moons suggest that the bulk of Earth's water came not from the interior of the planet but from the frigid depths of the outer solar system, in the form of a final barrage of icy comets that were diverted Earthward during the formation of the giant planets Uranus and Neptune.

The early ocean was stirred twice daily by tides, but the Moon was much closer then, and its tidal effect greater. Since the young Earth rotated on its axis approximately every ten hours, high tides occurred only five hours apart. The ocean must have been in constant turmoil. At ebb, a shallow sea might have retreated beyond the horizon, only to return in a series of mountainous waves a few hours later. This agitation may have been instrumental in bringing life to our planet. Though biologically sterile, the early ocean was a rich broth of dissolved atmospheric gases and minerals leached from the land. When waves broke over hot volcanic rocks, organic molecules, such as amino acids — the building blocks of proteins — were formed. Tidal action quickly distributed these chemicals throughout the ocean, where they continually combined and recombined to form ever more complex molecules.

Sunshine, lightning, volcanic heat, and tidal stirring transformed the early ocean into a nutritious chemical soup. If we consider the volume of ocean that is currently displaced by living organisms, we can gain some idea of

The first lunar tides must have been awesome indeed, if in fact the Moon 3.5 billion years ago was one-third its present distance from Earth. Mountainous waves crashed against the early continents, and friction within Earth's crust may have raised ocean temperatures substantially. In this seething chemical cauldron, complex organic compounds were continually being created. Eventually, one arose that had the ability to replicate itself.
(Art by author)

the wealth of food molecules that must have originally filled the sea. A living cell, turned loose in such a fertile medium, would have prospered mightily.

It has been suggested that the first organism drifted to Earth as a spore, blown by interstellar winds from "elsewhere." This theory merely places the origin of life farther back in time; it doesn't explain it. Laboratory experiments designed to simulate the Earth's early environment suggest that life probably arises through quite natural chemical processes and will occur anywhere conditions are right.

The carbon atom is unique in that it is capable of forming molecules of virtually infinite complexity. Some of these molecules are more stable than others, and will survive to combine with other equally stable molecules, forming molecular structures of ever-increasing complexity. Thus adenine, a purine base that constitutes one of the four molecular building blocks of the DNA (deoxyribonucleic acid) molecule — the basis of all terrestrial life — can be regarded as an isomer of a polymer of five hydrogen cyanide molecules. This process of chemical evolution is so inevitable that many of the steps leading to life may have taken place within the parent bodies of a certain type of carbon-rich meteorite even before Earth had oceans.

Given that the early oceans were rich in the chemical forerunners of life, we are still faced with the problem of explaining the transition from nonlife to life. The dilemma is simplified if we assume that there is no clear, abrupt boundary between the living and nonliving world. Modern viruses, although generally regarded as living organisms, are quite inert outside a host cell; only when they commandeer the nuclear machinery of a cell can they reproduce. But even the simplest virus is much more complex than any compound that might have been found in the primordial soup. The odds against molecules drifting randomly in the ancient sea spontaneously assembling to form a virus are astronomical. Not even proteins or nucleic acids can be made in this way. The evolution of the first organism was probably a gradual process consisting of many intermediate steps, each with a fair probability of occurrence, and it required the evolution of molecules that were stable and complex, some of which could ultimately develop the ability to reproduce portions of their own or other molecular structures.

Such partial replicators could have been amazingly simple. In experiments designed to simulate the early environment, David White and other researchers from NASA's Ames Research Center and the University of Santa Clara have shown that a simple amino acid chain can produce chains of another amino acid, glycine, up to 6 links long. The process is aided by the presence of a catalytic molecule, histidyl-histidine, which functions like a primitive enzyme, enabling the replicating process to continue up to 50 times. Because such molecular entities can be produced in a test chamber in a limited amount of time, most scientists feel safe in assuming that in the vastness of the ancient sea, given millions of years, even more sophisticated replicating processes evolved.

Some scientists suggest that such organic structures could be defined as "living" once they became able to synthesize proteins and perhaps primitive nucleic acids, since these very complex organic molecules could not arise by chance combinations. The gulf between a replicator molecule, passively growing and reproducing, and a living cell able to reproduce at will is immense, however, and it was probably bridged through a kind of chemical symbiosis. Animal cells contain a number of tiny bodies called mitochondria, which produce the cell's energy. It has been plausibly argued that mitochondria evolved from primitive bacteria that established a symbiotic relationship with larger cells.

The first cells may have been the product of a similar kind of teamwork. As complex organic structures filled the sea, those that developed membranes in which to isolate themselves from the environment had a significant advantage, as did those that developed the ability to absorb nutrients from simpler and more readily available molecules. The first such team to join forces was destined to be our ultimate ancestor. It was living on borrowed time, however, for like modern animals and fungi it depended for its survival on energy-rich compounds that were plentiful in the environment. As these compounds became depleted, there was evolutionary pressure to find new ways of making a living. Some cells, proceeding in evolution, developed the ability to store or manufacture certain pigments similar to chlorophyll. These pigments had the ability to trap energy from sunlight, storing the energy and in time using it to manufacture energy-rich substances such as sugars and other carbohydrates essential for life. One of the waste products of this process was oxygen, a gas so reactive that it cannot remain long in the free state. As descendants of the first plant cells spread through the sea, they dumped huge quantities of oxygen into the environment. For the first few hundred million years of photosynthesis, most of the oxygen served only to rust the abundant supply of iron that was dissolved in the sea. Once the iron was oxidized, oxygen could then be released to the atmosphere, but it first had to combine with the abundant ammonia and methane before it could build up. Over the course of time, these humblest of organisms changed the environment of their planet, producing the oxygen-rich atmosphere that sustains us today.

These first plants may have resembled cyanobacteria, formerly known as blue-green algae. Rocks dating from 3.5 billion years ago have curious laminated structures, as if they had been formed by the deposition of thin films of tiny, uniformly sized particles. Mats of algae growing in tidal marshes exhibit a similar structure when they are sliced, suggesting that these ancient rocks may be fossilized algal mats; and these "stromatolites" are so regarded by geologists. Unicellular life apparently arose quite early, perhaps in the first half-billion years. Although evolution probably produced a great many species of one-celled organisms, an immense span of time was required to produce more complex multicellular varieties, for the earliest

Top
The first continents were lifeless and desolate slabs of granite strewn with lava, but the inexorable action of wind and tide forced simple aquatic plants to establish tentative footholds on the land. *(Photo by author)*

Bottom
The primeval Earth, seen from space, appeared very different in its youth. The protocontinent Pangaea had not yet fragmented into the land masses we know today. *(Art by author)*

Facing page, left
The Inner Solar System
(Diagram by Michael Standlee Design)

Facing page, right
The Terrestrial Planets. Diagram shows the relative sizes and comparative internal structures of the inner planets. The thickness of the planetary crusts has been greatly exaggerated to show relative differences. On this scale, Earth's crust would be a line too thin to print.
(Art by Michael Standlee Design)

fossil evidence of multicellular creatures possessing hard bones or shells is but 580 million years old, suggesting that perhaps more than half of biological history was given over to one-celled life.

This period of time was very productive, though. The build-up of oxygen in the atmosphere made more energetic biological processes possible. Some organisms became motile, for instance, seeking and feeding off the simple plants. Another epochal innovation — sex — increased the diversity within populations, thereby improving the odds that there would be individuals able to cope with changes in the environment. Evolution proceeded even more quickly.

The Moon was once again a driving force. Now more distant, having robbed Earth of a certain amount of rotational energy, it still raised respectable tides. Each high tide stranded millions of organisms on the surfaces of coastal rocks. Most died when exposed to the desiccating effect of the air. Some, however, perhaps one in a million, had qualities that enabled them to survive the harsher environment, and their offspring colonized the land, inching inland with each generation. The first pioneers were probably simple mosses, and these prepared the way for more complex life forms, breaking rocks into soil and fertilizing the soil with their remains. Soon there were inland plants with tough cell walls that allowed them to store water between showers, making them independent of the sea. Animals, possibly the remote kin of today's crabs, scavenged on coastal rocks, and stranded fish made desperate overland crossings to return to the sea. Only those with some land tolerance survived to pass on their strength.

Details are of necessity hazy, but the fossil record gives us a picture of the tortuous evolutionary path that eventually led to man. The transition from fish to amphibian to reptile to mammal was accompanied by ever-increasing control over the environment, both internal and external. Nervous systems became more complex, and so did the range of intellectual/emotional responses. A scant 100 million years intervenes between the "eat-fight-run-mate" syndrome and Maxwell's equations and Beethoven's Sixth Symphony. An understanding of cosmic and biological evolution, far from belittling us, allows us to appreciate how truly marvelous the universe is, and how intimately connected we are to the rest of nature. The ancient sea still pulses in our veins, and we are made of the atoms of long-dead suns. In the 16 billion years since creation, energy has become matter, and matter, mind. The universe has become aware of itself.

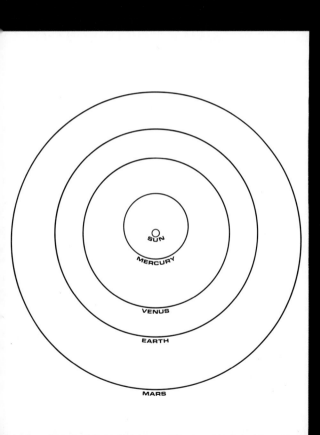

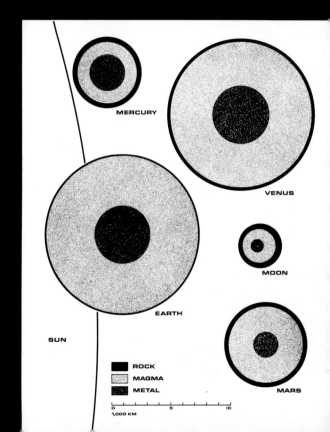

SUN
MERCURY
VENUS
EARTH
MOON
MARS

ROCK
MAGMA
METAL

0   5   10
1,000 KM

IN THE BLACK AIRLESS SKY OF MERCURY, the Sun appears three times larger than it does from Earth, and shines with a merciless intensity capable of heating the battered surface to 700°K. The chaotic landscape is colorless; shadows are pitch black, and sunlit slopes are painfully bright. Only when the long night descends can we find beauty in this wasteland. As the last chord of the Sun's disk sets in the west, the scene is transformed. Rays of gold, green, and blue play above the now-dark horizon. These are streamers of the corona, the Sun's outer atmosphere. As our eyes adjust to the darkness, we notice that the corona blends gradually into a softly luminescent band of light that fans nearly to the zenith. This is the zodiacal light, the tenuous mist of dust and gravel remaining from the solar accretion disk, visible only because we are looking through a billion-mile thickness at maximum illumination. The raw landscape is softened by this diffuse glow; the harsh shadows and contours have vanished. As this tiny world continues slowly to turn its face away from the Sun, the corona fades from the sky, but two new lights appear in the east: Venus shines with diamond brilliance, casting long, subtle shadows, and it is accompanied by a bluish double star only slightly less bright — the planet Earth and its faint daughter, Moon.

For centuries, Mercury, the planet nearest the Sun, appeared to be little more than a fuzzy patch of light in telescopes, visible for only a few days at a time in the dawn or evening sky as it raced in its tight orbit. When the

Facing page
Mercury, innermost of the Sun's planets, as imaged by *Mariner X*. (NASA photo)

Mercury. The Sun blazes fiercely in the black sky of its closest planet. Mercury's surface has been shaped by a combination of volcanism and impacts, so a thermally eroded volcanic plain is shown here. (Art by author)

Facing page, top
The Caloris Basin, so named because it is near the subsolar point at which Mercury passes perihelion. It is therefore one of the hottest places on the planet. This basin was formed when a body at least tens of kilometers in diameter fractured the crust, permitting magma to reach the surface. It is 1300 kilometers in diameter. *(NASA photo)*

Facing page, bottom
Terrain far rougher than the Moon's is depicted in this *Mariner X* photo of Mercury. *(NASA photo)*

Mercury was first photographed in detail by the spacecraft *Mariner X*. *(Art by author)*

spacecraft *Mariner X* flew within 750 kilometers of its surface, on March 29, 1974, the onboard cameras took photographs revealing a battered, crater-pocked world very much like the Moon in general appearance. Mercury's bulk composition is very different from the Moon's, however. It is the densest of all the planets. Since Mercury is so close to the Sun, it was intensely heated by the protosun during its accretion period, and most of its lighter materials were vaporized and driven into space. The T-Tauri solar wind that blew out of the embryonic sun not only stripped proto-Mercury of its gases and primordial ices but also dispersed the heavier grains of silicate, rocklike material. The stuff left behind after this baking and blowing process was mostly metal, which accounts for Mercury's high density. Mercury's metallic core comprises more than two-thirds of its volume, and the planet is deficient in the light rocks that comprise Earth's crust and mantle.

Although Jupiter's satellite Callisto is the most heavily cratered body yet found in the solar system, Mercury runs a close second. And unlike Callisto's icy crust, which cannot support great differences in elevation, the surface of Mercury is rough — far rougher than that of the Moon. Like the Moon, Mercury is blanketed by a thick layer of pulverized rock dust, but the radar-scattering properties of its surface suggest that it has a greater number of large boulders strewn across its most cratered areas. The population density of Mercury's craters is greater than that found

on the Moon, but Mercury's craters tend to be smaller. And Mercury's higher gravity would tend to reduce the range of impact ejecta. Like the Moon, Mercury has a number of dark, relatively smooth lava plains, or *maria,* caused by the upwelling of magma following particularly violent impacts, but these have been found to occur in high elevations as well as low-lying regions — a situation that has recently been found to obtain on Venus as well, but not on the Moon.

One of *Mariner X*'s surprising discoveries was that Mercury has a magnetic field. Such fields are thought to be dynamo effects generated by a rapidly spinning, molten metallic core, such as Earth's, but Mercury spins very slowly on its axis, rotating every 59 days, and is so small that it should have long since cooled and solidified to a great depth below its surface. Nevertheless, this "fossil" magnetism suggests that Mercury's interior was once in a molten state. The *Mariner* photographs show a number of long scarps, 500 to 1500 meters high and hundreds of kilometers in length, which seem to mark distinct divisions between high and low-lying regions. These scarps, like the ridges that appear in the skin of a dehydrating apple, are believed to be evidence of a still-shrinking crust. In addition, Mercury has a somewhat ellipsoidal shape, with its long axis perpendicular to its axis of rotation.

By rights, this bulge should have become locked toward the Sun, so that Mercury's rotation period would equal its orbital period of 88 days. Such is the case with all other close satellite systems we have observed: the satellite always keeps one hemisphere turned toward its primary, and the other turned eternally toward space. Before the 1960s, this was thought to be the case with Mercury.

The actual situation is more complicated. Mercury's rotation is related to its period of revolution, but the ratio is 2:3 rather than 1:1. Mercury completes two rotations every three "years." If Mercury's orbit were a perfect circle, this spin-orbit coupling would have little consequence, but in fact Mercury is nearly 24 million kilometers farther from the Sun at aphelion (greatest distance from the Sun) than it is at perihelion (least distance from the Sun). Since Mercury's axis has virtually no tilt, the annual variation in the amount of solar energy received at a given point on the surface is dependent on longitude rather than latitude. Meridians at 0 degrees and 180 degrees receive more than two-and-a-half times as much light as points along 270 degrees and 90 degrees. Because Mercury is moving quickly during perihelion, the apparent shifting in position of the sun eastward, due to parallax, is greater than the 6-degrees-per-day eastward rotation of the planet, with the result that Mercury's surface briefly overtakes the terminator (the great circle between day and night). Observers at meridians 90 degrees and 270 degrees would see the Sun rise partially above the horizon, set briefly, and then rise once again to continue its normal course across the sky.

Because Mercury is hot and small, it would not be expected to retain much of an atmosphere; but it does have a very thin atmosphere of helium that is continually replenished by the solar wind.

Map 1

SHADED RELIEF MAP OF MERCURY

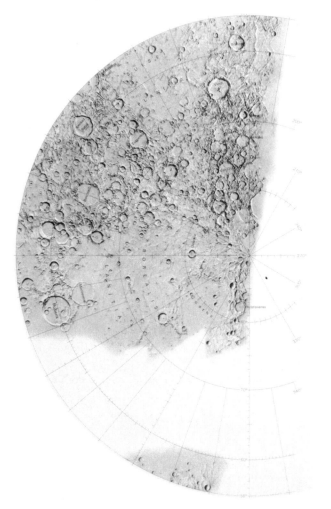

NORTH POLAR REGION

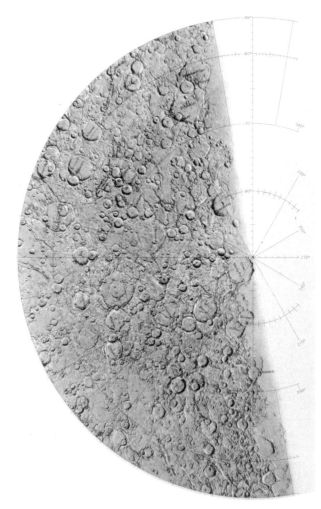

SOUTH POLAR REGION

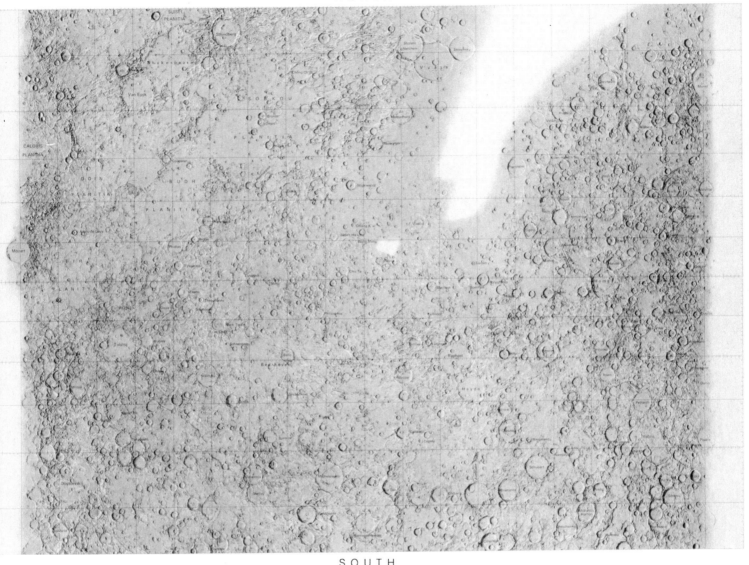

A reluctant Sun rises, sets, and rises again over the walled plain Matisse at 90 degrees west longitude. Mercury rotates at a constant rate, but moves more quickly in its orbit during the time of perihelion passage, permitting surface features to overtake the terminator. *(Art by author)*

*A dungeon horrible, on all sides round
As one great furnace flam'd; yet from those
    flames
No light, but rather darkness visible . . .*
                    Milton, Paradise Lost

AT ITS BRIGHTEST, VENUS APPEARS AS A dazzling silver star in the evening or predawn sky, outshone only by the Moon and Sun. Because of its brightness, and the fact that atmospheric refraction can cause it to sparkle through the full spectrum of colors when it is near the horizon, Venus in early cultures was almost universally associated with the prevailing goddess of beauty. To the Chinese, she was Tai-pe, the Beautiful White One; to the Babylonians, she was Mistress of the Heavens, Nin-dar-anna. The Greeks originally had two names for the planet: Hesperos, when seen in the west, and Phosphorus ("light bearer"), when rising at dawn. The Latin name *Venus* is that of the Roman goddess of love and spring, equivalent to the Greek Aphrodite.

The problems attendant to telescopic study of Mercury also apply to Venus: When the planet is nearest, it appears as a thin crescent close to the Sun and must either be observed high in the turbulent daytime sky or through a dense air mass near the horizon. Still, Venus approaches closer to the Earth than any other planet and one would expect that four centuries of telescopic study would have gleaned a wealth of information about this sister world. Such is not the case, however. In fact, before the early 1960s it wasn't even possible to determine Venus's period of rotation. The problem is that Venus is completely shrouded with clouds. This cloud cover is unbroken and virtually featureless in the visible range of the spectrum. Only with deep blue or ultraviolet filters can any atmospheric features be seen, and these are transitory, making it difficult to determine the speed, or even direction, of rotation. Pre–space-age discoveries concerning Venus may be summarized quite briefly.

In 1610, Galileo observed that Venus undergoes changes in phase like those of the Moon, thereby proving that Venus does indeed circle the Sun on an orbit interior to that of the Earth, in accordance with the Copernican theory. In 1761, Venus transited the solar disk and gave evidence of an atmosphere: a thin ring of refracted sunlight outlined the dark hemisphere just before and after the transit. This lent credence to the argument that astronomers were seeing clouds rather than topography. In 1931, a precise determination of the length of the astronomical unit allowed a computation of Venus's diameter, which proved to be about 95 percent of that of the Earth. Since Venus has no moon (although there were many spurious "discoveries" of such a satellite), a determination of its mass had to be made by analyzing the perturbations it caused in Mercury's orbit. It was determined that Venus's mass was about 80 percent of that of the Earth. This gross physical resemblance led

Facing page
Venus, showing its typical atmospheric features as they appear in ultraviolet light. *(NASA photo)*

many to think of Venus as Earth's "twin," and possibly an abode of life. After all, the argument went, Venus was only 20 percent closer to the Sun, and its clouds were highly reflective. And while it might be expected that Venus would be somewhat warmer than Earth, it should not be intolerably so. Indeed, the presence of dense clouds seemed to point to a tropical environment. Models of an Earthlike Venus ranged from steaming carboniferous swamps to planetary oceans. Prior to 1962, there was even talk of someday sending big-game hunters to Venus to bag the Venusian analogue of *Tyrannosaurus rex*.

The bad news started coming in when the first radio telescopes were turned toward the veiled planet. A portion of the energy reradiated by Venus fell in the radio end of the spectrum, indicating that most of the energy was in the infrared range.* Venus was hot — far hotter

Supercritical Refraction. Just what does the surface of Venus really look like? It is now established that the Venusian atmosphere is composed mainly of carbon dioxide, and has a temperature of 500°C and a pressure 90 times greater than Earth's — equivalent to that at an ocean depth of 1 kilometer. A transparent medium of this density should cause light rays to follow curved paths, with the result that no matter where we stood on Venus's surface, it would seem as if we were in the middle of a vast basin, with landscape curving up impossibly all around. But pictures transmitted by the *Venera* spacecraft showed no such effect. The horizon line was close and quite distinct against a bright, featureless sky. The supercritical refraction that should have been apparent, according to the laws of optics, was not. Why? (*Art by author*)

* When discussing the spectral distribution of radiant energy from a source, scientists use the theoretical model of a "black body" — a mass that absorbs and emits radiation with perfect efficiency. A black body at a temperature of, for example, 5000° — the temperature of the Sun's surface — emits some radiation at all wavelengths along the electromagnetic spectrum, from very short ultraviolet rays to very long radio waves. But most of the energy at this temperature is in the form of visible light. A black body at Venus temperature of 500° will not be hot enough to emit much visible light; the peak energy will, instead, be in the longer, infrared wavelengths. A certain, smaller, percentage of the radiation will be in the form of still

than the boiling point of water. By bouncing radio waves off Venus and measuring the distortion of the faint but detectable echo, it was possible to determine the planet's rotation rate. Previous estimates had ranged from approximately 24 hours to 224 days (the planet's orbital period). Radar observations showed that Venus not only rotates retrograde — that is, contrary to the general direction of solar system movements; counterclockwise, when viewed from solar "north" — but takes 243 days to do so. Its "day" is longer than its year. Venus began to seem increasingly less like Earth, despite their similar dimensions. When *Mariner II* flew by the planet in 1962, it recorded surface temperatures of 500° Celsius (C), or 900° Fahrenheit (F) — hot enough to melt lead. Subsequent missions confirmed indications that the atmosphere was very dense; surface pressure was found to be nearly 100 times that of Earth — the equivalent of that found at an ocean depth of 1 kilometer.

One of the most important problems in planetary science is explaining how a planet of roughly the same size, mass, and — presumably — internal composition as Earth should have evolved so differently. Does Venus represent a normal stage in the evolution of Earthlike worlds, or did something go terribly wrong? It seems

---

longer radio waves, which can be detected from Earth, and by measuring the amount of energy that falls in this range we can deduce the amount that must be present in the infrared.

The *Venera* images raised other questions. The rocky landscape surrounding the two landing sites resembled nothing so much as a terrestrial sea bottom (minus the tons of biological detritus that blanket Earth's seabeds). It seems possible that Venus's hot, dense atmosphere acts rather like an ocean, shaping the landscape with currents instead of winds, rolling house-sized boulders across the surface. *(Art by author)*

Inferno. Venus could not retain its original supply of water in the liquid state long enough for dissolved calcium to remove the ever-increasing supply of atmospheric carbon dioxide released by volcanoes, so its surface temperature rose above the boiling point, dooming the planet forever. *(Art by author)*

reasonable to suppose that Venus acquired the bulk of its atmosphere in the same way Earth did, through volcanism. There is no obvious reason why Venus should have been geologically more active than Earth, producing more gas. The more likely explanation is that Earth and Venus started with about the same amount of atmosphere, but that some mechanism reduced the amount of air Earth ultimately ended up with.

The major constituent of the Venusian atmosphere is carbon dioxide, which is fairly transparent to visible radiation but highly absorbent of infrared radiation — radiant heat. This effect is what keeps the inside of a greenhouse warm on a chilly but sunny winter's day, and it also seems to be responsible for Venus's hellish temperatures. Even though 80 percent of the Sun's light is reflected back into space by Venus's clouds, a small percentage reaches and warms the surface, and this reradiated heat is trapped by the carbon dioxide in the atmosphere. The result has been a runaway greenhouse effect. The dense atmosphere permits Venus to store an astonishing amount of heat, and a complex system of "conveyor belt" layers within the atmosphere permits this heat to escape only slowly back into space.

The principal reason Venus, rather than Earth, experienced a runaway greenhouse effect is that for some reason not yet understood, Venus began its career with a dearth of water. On Earth, most of the carbon dioxide in the original atmosphere was dissolved in the ocean and chemically bound into solid carbonates, such as limestone. Venus, which had no large bodies of water, was unable to remove the carbon dioxide that was outgassed from its interior, with the result we see today. It

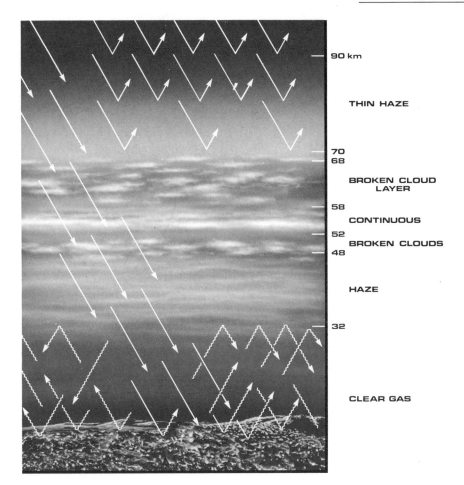

90 km

THIN HAZE

70
68

BROKEN CLOUD
LAYER

58

CONTINUOUS

52

BROKEN CLOUDS

48

HAZE

32

CLEAR GAS

is of interest to note that any increase in the Earth's average temperature — such as will occur when the Sun begins to exhaust its hydrogen fuel some billions of years hence — could reverse the carbon-binding cycle; warmer oceans would dissolve more carbonates, releasing carbon dioxide into the atmosphere, which in turn would trap more heat and warm the oceans further, accelerating the process until a situation similar to that now found on Venus could result. The oceans would begin to boil, and life would end.

Inhospitable as Venus is, its atmosphere provides a meteorological model much simpler than Earth's, and study of it may ultimately prove helpful in the formulation of a general theory of climate. Our weather systems are complicated by Earth's rotation, axial inclination, and the differing thermal capacities of land and water. Venus has no oceans, virtually no axial tilt, and rotates very slowly. It is a near-ideal comparative example.

The subsolar point on Venus's equator is most strongly heated by the Sun, and the resulting warm air mass spreads out in a characteristic Y-shaped pattern toward the poles, cooling, falling, and ultimately returning to the equator in a classic convection pattern. This pattern was predicted even before *Mariner X*'s ultraviolet "movie" of Venus's atmosphere showed it. What was not expected — although it may have been observed by Bernard Guinot in the early 1960s — were the extremely high winds in the upper cloud layers. Their

The Greenhouse Effect. Some sunlight penetrates to Venus's surface, but its infrared component (wavy lines) is trapped and recirculated by the atmosphere, raising temperatures to 500°C.
(Diagram by Michael Standlee Design)

speed is on the order of 200 meters per second, causing weather systems in Venus's upper atmosphere to circulate the globe in only 4 days, in contrast to the 30 days required on the more quickly rotating Earth. This could be understood if there were a large temperature difference between the night and day hemispheres of Venus, but there is not; the planet is uniformly hot. Analysis of the paths of probes that have descended to Venus's surface show that this wind is an upper-atmosphere phenomenon; near the surface the dense atmosphere behaves more like an ocean current, moving at a ponderous rate of 1 meter per second. It appears that the wind is driven from a level midway in the atmosphere by a combination of surface and solar heat. A better understanding of this complex effect may be useful in future weather predictions on Earth.

The cloud cover of Venus is unbroken, preventing direct observation of the surface in visible wavelengths of light. By using large radio telescopes to bounce microwaves off the planet, however, scientists in the late 1960s were able to determine that the surface of Venus bears the ubiquitous impact basins found elsewhere and has a wide range of elevations and textures. The most powerful tool for the study of Venusian topography is the *Pioneer-Venus Orbiter,* whose radar has been observing narrow slices of the planet since 1978, gradually building up a detailed picture of most of Venus's surface. This radar mapper, in concert with other instruments, has at last begun to part the Venusian veil, revealing a world that has some geological similarities to Earth as well as unique characteristics of its own.

Venusian Caldera. Planetary scientists have been able to map some of the larger features of Venusian topography by bouncing radar signals off the planet. It seems that Venus may be at least as geologically active as Earth. Radar maps have revealed not only the ubiquitous impact craters and lava plains of the Moon and Mars but also great rift valleys and vast volcanic craters that may still be active. *(Art by author)*

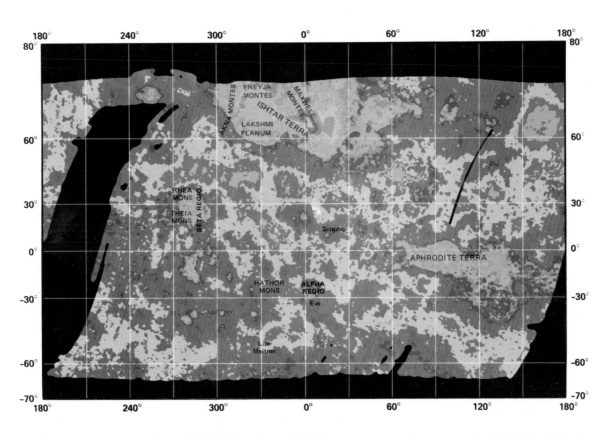

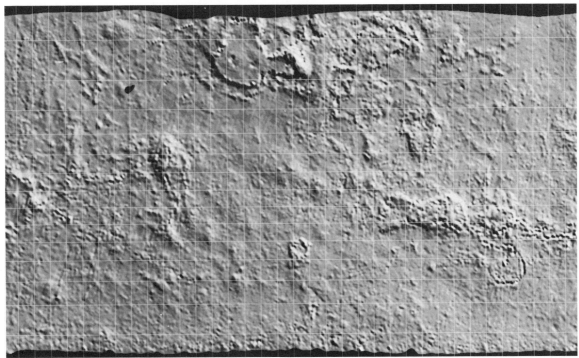

Venus's crust appears to be much thicker than Earth's and seems to comprise a single tectonic plate, while Earth's is fractured into six major and several minor plates. This thickness prevents magma from welling up along fault lines to form new crust, so most of Venus's surface is quite old, although there is evidence of isolated instances of massive volcanism. The lower level of the crust is probably composed of basalt, which is the original crustal material found on the Moon and Mars, and in the oceanic basins on Earth. Above this is a planet-girdling crust of continental granite that covers 84 percent of Venus.

Since Venus has no seas, differences in elevation are expressed relative to a reference radius of 6050 kilometers from the planet's center. Some 60 percent of the topography consists of flat, rolling plains at this level. The lowest features are 2.9 kilometers deep, while the highest peak is 10.8 kilometers above the mean — a range somewhat greater than that found on Earth. Only about 16 percent of Venus's surface is below the average elevation, compared to nearly 67 percent on Earth. Most of Venus's surface is less than 1 kilometer high; only about 8 percent is highland terrain.

Because Venus is the only planet named after a goddess, the International Astronomical Union's Committee on Nomenclature has decided that the names of large-scale features on the planet will be drawn from female mythological figures, while smaller features, such as impact basins, will be named after famous women in history. To establish this tradition, the two "continents" of Venus have been named Aphrodite Terra and Ishtar Terra.

ANCIENT TERRAIN AND HIGHLANDS

There appear to be abundant primordial impact craters, like those on Mars and the Moon, scattered over the surface of Venus.* These craters have diameters exceeding 75 kilometers (45 miles) — large enough for *Pioneer* to observe. Most of Venus's surface (and hence crust) appears to be ancient terrain. Atmospheric heating, water loss, and crust formation apparently took place during the first 1 billion to 2 billion years of the planet's history.

Venus's two continent-sized highland areas, Ishtar and Aphrodite, may be remnants of the last tectonic-plate collisional zones, which existed before crust formation choked tectonics off completely. Alternatively, they may result from local lifting forces, such as those that created California's Sierra Nevada range.

ISHTAR TERRA
The highest and most dramatic continent-sized highland region on Venus is the northern highland, or Ishtar Terra.

---

* This description of Venusian features is based on research by Harold Masursky and G. B. Pettengill, "The Surface of Venus," *Scientific American*, August 1980.

A high plateau containing several mountain ranges, it is about the size of Australia or the continental United States.

The western part of Ishtar (named for the Assyrian goddess of love and war) appears to be a smooth plateau. This area is called Lakshmi Planum and is about 3300 meters (10,000 feet) above average level. Lakshmi is bounded on the west and north by mountains ranging upward from 2300 to 3300 meters (7000 to 10,000 feet) above the plateau, and 5700 to 7000 meters (17,000 to 20,000 feet) above average level. The western mountains have been tentatively named Akna Montes, and the northern range is called Freyja Montes. The Ishtar plateau is approximately the same height as the Tibetan plateau, but twice as large. The central area of the plateau is smooth in the radar images and may be covered with relatively young lavas. The huge escarpments around the plateau's edge are quite steep.

MAXWELL MONTES

Venus's highest known point, a mountain massif higher than Everest, has been named Maxwell Montes. This huge area of uplifted terrain occupies the entire east end of the Ishtar Terra highlands. Its highest point is 11,800 meters (35,300 feet) above average level and 9000 meters (27,000 feet) above the adjoining Lakshmi plain. The highest parts of the massif run northwest-southeast, with lower projections extending both east and west. Observations from both Earth and *Pioneer* suggest that the mountain region itself is the roughest part of the planet, with jumbled terrain that changes abruptly from the smooth plateau west of it. The radio reflectivity of this feature indicates that the steep slopes of this Mount Everest of Venus are covered with rocks larger than 10 centimeters (2.5 inches) in diameter. *Pioneer* photographs indicate a dark, circular feature, some 100 kilometers (60 miles) in diameter and more than 1000 meters (3000 feet) deep, on the east flank of Maxwell Montes.

APHRODITE TERRA

The largest continent-sized highland region on Venus has been tentatively named Aphrodite. It is as large as the northern half of Africa, and consists of two mountainous areas separated by a somewhat lower region. Situated almost on Venus's equator, Aphrodite Terra runs almost directly east and west for 9600 kilometers (6000 miles).

Unlike Ishtar, a relatively level plateau with high mountains, the Aphrodite highland region rises to various heights above the mean planet surface. The western mountainous area rises 8000 meters (23,000 feet) above the surrounding terrain, 9000 meters (26,000 feet) above Venus's mean surface. The eastern mountains of Aphrodite rise 3300 meters (10,000 feet) above the surrounding terrain, 4000 meters (13,000 feet) above the mean surface. The terrain of these Aphrodite mountains, like those on Ishtar, appears to be quite rough. Because Aphrodite does not appear to contain uplifted plateaus or volcanic mountains, it may be older and more degraded than Ishtar Terra.

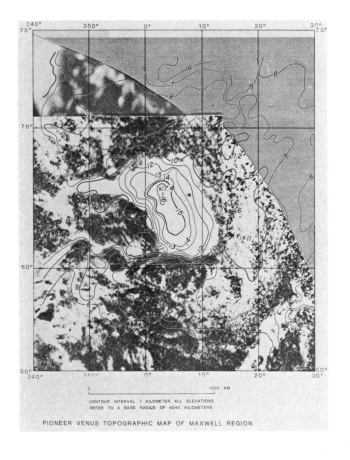

CONTOUR INTERVAL 1 KILOMETER ALL ELEVATIONS REFER TO A BASE RADIUS OF 6045 KILOMETERS

PIONEER VENUS TOPOGRAPHIC MAP OF MAXWELL REGION

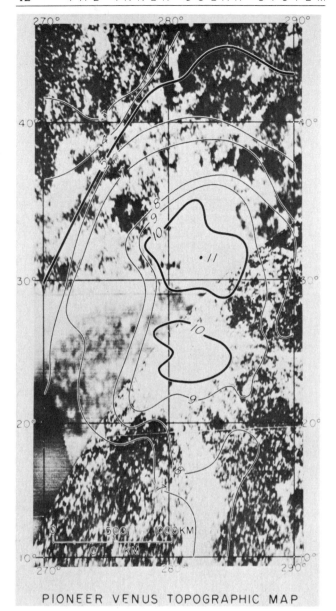

PIONEER VENUS TOPOGRAPHIC MAP

BETA REGIO

Located at about 30 degrees north latitude on Venus is Beta Regio, which apparently consists of two huge shield-shaped volcanoes larger than the Hawaii-Midway chain. Beta Regio appears to be situated on a fault line that runs north and south, from 40 degrees north latitude to 50 degrees south latitude. This long fault zone connects several other highland features, which may be volcanic, south of Beta Regio. Beta Regio's two huge adjoining mountains, which are smooth on the surface and shaped like the very wide-based Hawaiian volcanoes, run north and south for about 2100 kilometers (1300 miles). The rocks making up the twin Beta mountains appear to be basaltic and hence are very likely of volcanic origin. (The Soviet spacecraft *Venera IX* and *Venera X* landed just east of Beta and found the rocks there to have radioactive element concentrations similar to those found in basalts.)

The two shield-shaped mountains making up the Beta region have been named Theia Mons (the northerly mountain) and Rhea Mons (the southerly mountain). Both rise out of Venus's great planet-spanning plains, and both are about 4000 meters (13,000 feet) above the plain — that is, above Venus's mean surface.

ALPHA REGIO

The fourth notable highland feature on Venus is Alpha Regio, a rough region lying about 1800 meters (6000 feet) above the Venusian Great Plain. Alpha Regio is about 25 degrees south of the equator and 6400 kilometers (4000 miles) west of Aphrodite. Radar imaging shows that it has extremely rough terrain with parallel fractures throughout the whole feature. Alpha Regio may combine old and new geologic forms, and resembles the basin and range structure of the western United States.

VENUS'S GREAT PLAIN

As we have already noted, a relatively flat, rolling plain covers 60 percent of Venus's surface. Radar imaging shows that this plain has dark, circular features with bright central spots. These apparent craters, which have diameters of 400 to 600 kilometers (250 to 320 miles), characteristically have depths of only 200 to 700 meters (650 to 2300 feet). The bright central areas could be the central peaks that typically exist in impact craters.

The very shallow depths and the very large diameters of these apparent craters / compared with those on the Moon and Mars / can be explained by "surface rebound" like that found on Jupiter's planet-sized moons. (The apparent widespread cratering suggests that Venus's heavily cratered ancient crust still covers much of the planet.)

LOWLANDS

The largest low area so far found on Venus is located west of Ishtar at 70 degrees north. At its deepest point, this great basin is about 3000 meters (9000 feet) below Venus's Great Plain region. This low area, like others on the planet, is smooth and lacks large crater forms. It may be relatively young geologically, like Earth's ocean basins, and is perhaps filled in by basaltic lava flows. This area is about the same size as the North Atlantic ocean basin.

The lowest point on the planet appears to be in the rift valley just east of Aphrodite. Slightly lower than the Northern Hemisphere basin, it is about 2.9 kilometers (9500 feet) below Venus's mean surface. This trench is deeper than the Dead Sea rift, but only one-fifth the depth of the Marianas trench in the western Pacific. It is roughly the same depth as Valles Marineris, the great canyon on Mars. While Venus apparently has no plate tectonics, this rift valley and another running parallel to it, both in the region east of Aphrodite, seem comparable to tectonic rifts on Earth. Here, new rock material wells up out of the molten interior.

In general, the jumbled region east of Aphrodite is characterized by high ridges and deep valleys. There is a similar region east of Ishtar.

EARTH IS THE ONLY PLANET KNOWN TO have extensive supplies of liquid water, and it is this distinction more than any other that enables it to harbor life.

There are many reasons why Earth is an aqueous planet. First, the conditions prevailing during the formation of Earth may have been slightly different from those during the formation of, for example, Venus. Whereas the T-Tauri solar wind stripped Venus of its lighter gases, Earth, possibly because of its slightly larger mass or its greater distance from the Sun, was able to retain most of its water. Plant life evolved in the early oceans at a critical instant, just before the Sun's radiation reached its full intensity, and dissolved calcium absorbed most of the original carbon dioxide from the atmosphere, thus forestalling the runaway greenhouse effect that now obtains on Venus. Perhaps the most important factor was that Earth's nearly circular orbit was neither too close nor too far from the Sun. It has been calculated that a change in the semimajor axis of Earth's orbit of only a few percent either way would have resulted in the oceans either boiling or freezing solid. In short, we Earthlings have consistently been in the right place at the right time.

Water is one of the most efficient heat-absorbing compounds known. As Earth turns in the sunlight, the 70 percent of its surface covered by ocean soaks up and retains more solar energy than does the land. Because the distribution of land masses is irregular, the uneven heating of Earth's surface results not only in the most complex and unpredictable weather patterns in the solar system but also in the widest range of environments. While environmental conditions on the other terrestrial planets can be characterized in a few words (Venus: hot; Mars: cold), no such generalization can be made about Earth. Air temperatures range from $-65°C$ at the poles to $59.4°C$ in desert areas such as Insala, near Algiers. Regions such as the Amazon Basin may receive 2500 millimeters of rainfall annually, while others, such as Calama, in northern Chile, may receive none.

Earth is also unique in that its atmosphere is chemically unstable and is maintained only by the continuing action of living things. It is primarily composed of nitrogen (78 percent) and oxygen (21 percent), gases that are merely trace constituents in other planetary atmospheres. Were life to suddenly cease, most of the Earth's oxygen would eventually combine with the iron in crustal rocks. Without ozone, the trimolecular form of oxygen, the Sun's ionizing ultraviolet radiation would penetrate deep into the atmosphere, breaking down molecules of water vapor into their constituent atoms. These would combine with gases released from volcanoes to form a plethora of noxious compounds, including, perhaps, sulfuric acid.

Distinctive as Earth's biosphere is, in comparision to the bulk of the planet it is no thicker than the layer of moisture produced by breathing on a ball bearing. Earth is, of course, the archetypical terrestrial planet, and although it must rank behind Jupiter's satellite Io in geological activity, its internal fires, unlike those of Mars, are by no means extinct. The decay of heavy radioactive elements within

Facing page
Earth, the Water Planet. This cloud-swirled world has just enough air at just the right temperature to maintain water in the liquid state over most of its surface, making carbon-based life forms possible. *(NASA photo)*

Although they seem worlds apart, the verdant island Kauai, *top,* and the barren summit of Mauna Kea are within 500 kilometers of one another, demonstrating the wide range of earthly environments. *(Photos by author)*

Earth's metallic core produces enough heat to keep all but the upper 10 kilometers of the planet in a state of slow, glacierlike motion. Since Earth's crust is not a solid shell but is fragmented into plates, the slow movement of the mantle causes the plates to move about the surface of Earth, rubbing against each other. This phenomenon of plate tectonics, or continental drift, is the cause of earthquakes, and it is responsible for the fact that today's continents seem to be pieces of a jigsaw puzzle that has broken apart. Early in the history of Earth, all the continents were gathered together in a single land mass that geologists have dubbed Pangaea. It is probable that the youthful Earth exhibited the same surface dichotomy that we find on Mercury, the Moon, and Mars; indeed, the Pacific Basin may be a remnant of this. If Earth's internal fires hold out, the Americas may ultimately circle the globe, rejoining Asia on the eastern coast. This will take hundreds of millions of years, however; careful measurements of the changing separation between the continents (made possible by laser reflectors left on the Moon by astronauts) reveal that the average rate of movement is less than 10 centimeters per year.

One consequence of Earth's metallic core is its magnetic field, which shields us from high-energy particles that stream from the Sun, by trapping them in radiation belts thousands of miles above the equator. There is evidence that the magnetic field declines in strength and reverses polarity on an irregular basis, perhaps every 80,000 to 100,000 years. During these periods of magnetic reversal, Earth's surface may be exposed to much higher levels of radiation, and it has been suggested that this may explain such watershed events in evolutionary history as the extinc-

Earth's atmospheric blanket shields us from most dangerous radiation and moderates surface temperatures. *(NASA photo)*

tion of the dinosaurs some 60 million to 70 million years ago and the explosive growth of the human brain 1 million years ago. If a polarity shift were to occur today, we would expect to see an increase in radiation-related diseases such as cancer and congenital defects.

There are other cycles that influence Earth's environment. Earth rotates on its axis like a spinning top, and just as a top precesses, or wobbles, when it is nudged, so does Earth. The gravitational tug of the Moon causes the polar axis to describe a cone in space once each 25,725 years, so although the North Pole now points toward the star Polaris, in 5000 years it will have swung toward Vega. If Earth's orbit were a perfect circle, this precession would have little or no effect on the climate, but in fact Earth is approximately 5 million kilometers closer to the Sun in January than it is in July. At present, this only serves to slightly moderate seasons in the Northern Hemisphere, and if land were uniformly distributed on the surface of Earth, the effect would be negligible. A cursory examination of the globe, however, reveals that most of Earth's

Planet Earth, September 2, 1974. These computer-reconstructed weather-satellite images show typical circulation patterns in the Northern *(below)* and Southern hemispheres *(facing page)*. Note how coriolis effects cause storm systems to spiral in opposite directions in the two hemispheres.
(National Oceanic and Atmospheric Administration photo)

heat-sink capacity — the ocean — is concentrated in the Southern Hemisphere. At present, the Southern Hemisphere acts as a kind of thermal battery, charging up when Earth is nearest the Sun. The extra thermal energy stored there helps keep the northern land masses from getting too cold in winter. As the orientation of the axis changes, however, this situation will reverse: the Southern Hemisphere will tilt away from the Sun when Earth is most distant, and there will be a general cooling. This effect, combined with variations in solar output and a long, cyclical change in the eccentricity of Earth's orbit, has produced ice ages in the past, and, barring human intervention, will likely do so again in the future.

Viewed from space, Earth presents a fascinating range of colors and features. Martian astronomers would doubtless refer to Earth as the Blue Planet. Its distinctive color is due to the fact that light of short wavelength has a high probability of interacting with molecules in the atmosphere, and hence is scattered in all directions, while light of longer wavelength is not. This phenomenon, known as

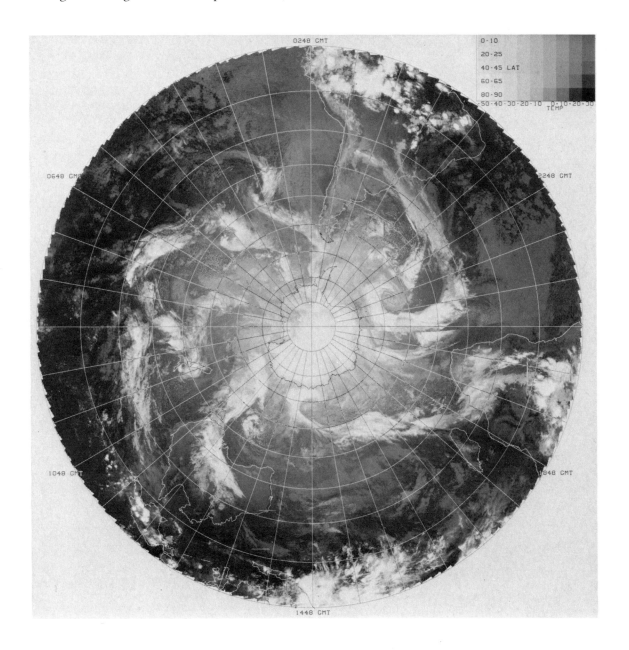

The United Kingdom and northern Europe (*top*), seen from a point 600 miles above the Bay of Biscay. The contrast between clouds and surface is decreased in this painting, to show more clearly the contrast between sea and land. (*Art by author*)

Laser Ranging from Haleakala Observatory. By bouncing laser beams from reflectors left on the Moon by *Apollo* astronauts, we can make such accurate determinations of the separation between distant observatories that the centimeters-per-year continental drift can be observed. (*Photo by Paul Ely, University of Hawaii, Institute for Astronomy*)

Rayleigh scattering, gives the sky its blue color. Although most of the royal blue coloration of the deep ocean is merely a reflection of the sky, shoal water in shallow, transparent seas, such as the Caribbean, scatters sunlight directly and can assume a magnificent hue of turquoise. The blueness of the atmosphere tends to rob the land of much of its color, so that the continents are generally brownish gray, but desert areas such as the Sahara can be distinctly orange, and lush vegetation gives tropical lands a blue-green hue. Contrasting beautifully with the azure globe are the dazzling white streamers of cloud that curl out from either pole and ply along the equator.

Earth shows a greater variety of geologic features than any other planet; but because of its dynamic atmosphere and biosphere, these features tend to be short-lived. Although no one can say what features lie preserved beneath the kilometer of silt on the ocean floor, the continents retain only a few highly eroded impact basins; there are no ancient, highly cratered surfaces like those found on the other terrestrial planets. There are, however, some large, circular features, such as the eastern edge of Hudson Bay, that are reminiscent of lunar *maria* (dark, roughly circular plains; *maria* is Latin for "seas"). Most large-scale features on Earth are the direct result of plate tectonics. The Himalayas, for example, are huge wrinkles in the crust that were formed when the plate bearing the Indian subcontinent rammed into southern Asia. All volcanic activity occurs along the faults, or cracks, between the plates. Small-scale features are primarily the product of water erosion, in the form of rainfall or glacial movement.

THE MOON

Earth's single natural satellite is distinctive in that it is, in proportion to its primary, the largest satellite in the solar system.* While Jupiter's moon Ganymede and Saturn's Titan are both more than twice as big as the Moon, their respective primaries are on the order of twenty times larger than they are. The Earth:Moon ratio, on the other hand, is approximately 4:1, making the two bodies virtually a binary planet system. The Moon's comparatively large size has led some scientists to suggest that it may have evolved elsewhere in the solar system, as an independent planet, and was subsequently captured by Earth. In support of this idea is the fact that the Moon's bulk composition is unlike Earth's. The Moon is deficient in volatile materials, such as lead, sodium, and potassium, suggesting that it may have accreted in a hotter part of the solar nebula. The problems with the capture hypothesis seem so overwhelming, however, that there is a marginal consensus in favor of the idea of dual formation, which holds that the Moon's volatiles

---

* Excluding the system of Pluto and its satellite Charon, which have a closer size ratio of about 3:1 but are believed by some astronomers to be renegade satellites of Neptune, rather than an independently formed planet and moon.

The Moon, seen from space (*photo above*). The dark, circular basin Mare Crisium is near the center of the disk, and the bright-rayed crater Tycho is near the lower limb. (*NASA photo*)

Earth and Moon virtually comprise a double-planet system. (*NASA photo*)

Following page, top
Formation of the Crater Tycho. One of the most spectacular lunar features is Tycho, which dominates the Southern Hemisphere of the full Moon with its dazzling impact basin and ejecta rays. Formed perhaps as "recently" as 50 million years ago, Tycho is the result of a disagreement over right-of-way between our satellite and an asteroid perhaps 5 kilometers across. Impacting with a speed of tens of kilometers per second, the kinetic energy of the asteroid may have been equal to that of 1000 hydrogen bombs. (*Art by author*)

Following page, bottom
Moon rocks are chunks of the Moon's crust blasted out by asteroid impacts that occurred as much as 4 billion years ago, and are generally older than any rocks found on the more geologically active Earth. (*NASA photo*)

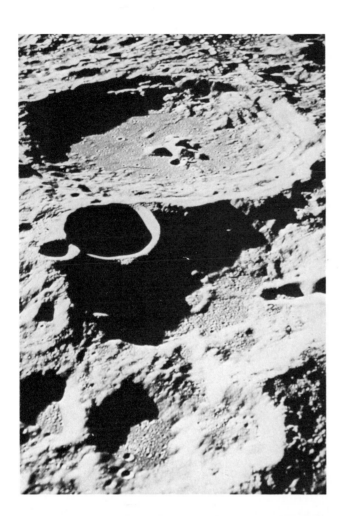

Central Peak in a Far-Side Crater. Lunar mountains differ from their terrestrial counterparts in that they are primarily formed by external, as opposed to internal, forces. Mountains on Earth are raised by the pressure of magma below the crust, or by buckling along colliding tectonic plates. Lunar mountains are essentially "splash" effects caused by asteroid bombardment. (NASA photo)

Below
The Moon and Earth probably formed together from the same accretion disk, but the immense heat of Earth's formation may have driven the lighter elements away from the lunar accretion cloud. (Art by author)

The Moon appears dazzling white in the night sky only by contrast to empty space, and is actually quite dark, reflecting only 7 percent of the sunlight that illuminates it. In other words, it is about as black as slate. Its color index is toward the red, which explains why, from under certain Sun angles, it appeared brownish to some members of the *Apollo* expeditions, though most reported it as gray. At night, however, the Moon is illuminated by the blue Earth, which appears four times bigger and eighty times brighter to us than the Moon does at a corresponding phase. (Earth and Moon phases are complements of each other at any given moment: an observer standing on a nearly full Moon would see a slender crescent Earth, and vice versa.) The first image presented here is a painting showing Earth as it might appear from the crater Tycho, two days past full phase. The Pleiades cluster to the right of Earth would be occulted in another two hours. The image at right shows that the Moon can also borrow color by moving through Earth's shadow. Sunlight refracting through the backlit atmosphere is reddened, and the Moon reflects the glow from all the sunrises and sunsets taking place on Earth at the time. *(Art and photo by author)*

were driven off by the intense heat radiated by the proto-Earth during its accretion. Generally discounted today is the earlier hypothesis that the Moon was somehow spun out of what is now the Pacific Basin.

While the origin of the Moon is still in doubt — even after six *Apollo* expeditions to its surface — the processes that formed its features are well understood. Toward the end of the first phase of its accretion, 4 billion to 4.5 billion years ago, the Moon was molten. Because of its

small mass (approximately one-eightieth Earth's), however, the Moon quickly radiated its heat into space. As it cooled, the upper 200 kilometers of lava solidified to form a crust about 60 kilometers thick, composed of lightweight anorthositic rocks, predominantly plagioclase feldspar ($CaAl_2Si_2O_8$). Beneath this anorthositic crust was a foundation of heavier rocks, comprising the Moon's lithosphere. Toward the end of the accretion period, the crust was continually battered by asteroidal bodies. The smaller ones, only a few kilometers across, merely excavated typical explosive-impact craters, scattering rays of bright, fresh rock across the lunar surface. The larger bodies, however, which were on the order of tens to hundreds of kilometers in diameter, blasted such deep craters that the isostatic balance — the balance of the weight of crustal rock against the pressure of compressed magma in the mantle — was destroyed, and lava filled these huge depressions, thereby creating maria.

Thus the Moon presents two general types of terrain: bright, heavily cratered, and presumably quite ancient highlands; and dark, low, relatively smooth maria. It also has a number of small volcanic domes and rills, but none of the huge volcanic mountains found on Earth and Mars. It is still a mystery why the lunar Far Side, turned eternally away from Earth, has a crust nearly twice as thick as that of the Near Side.

Eclipse Seen from the Lunar Surface. When Earth eclipses the Sun in the airless sky of the Moon, more detail can be seen in the corona than is apparent during a terrestrial eclipse. The fan-shaped band of light behind the Earth is the zodiacal light. *(Art by author)*

Map 2

LUNAR CHART

POLAR STEREOGRAPHIC
PROJECTION
(Polar areas 45° to 90°)

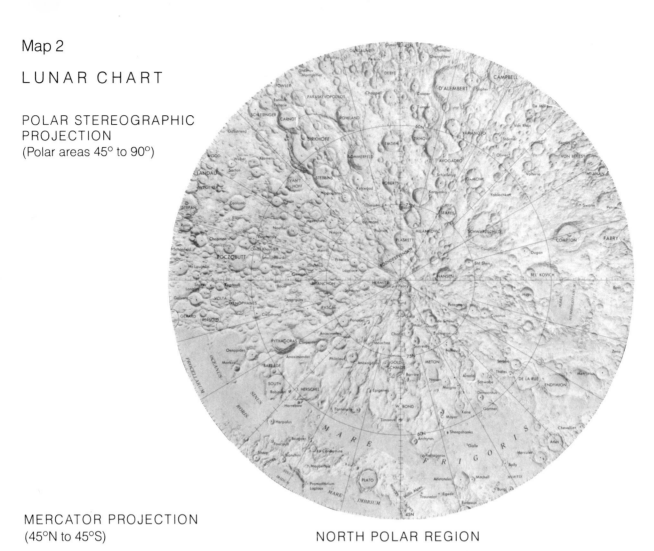

MERCATOR PROJECTION
(45°N to 45°S)

NORTH POLAR REGION

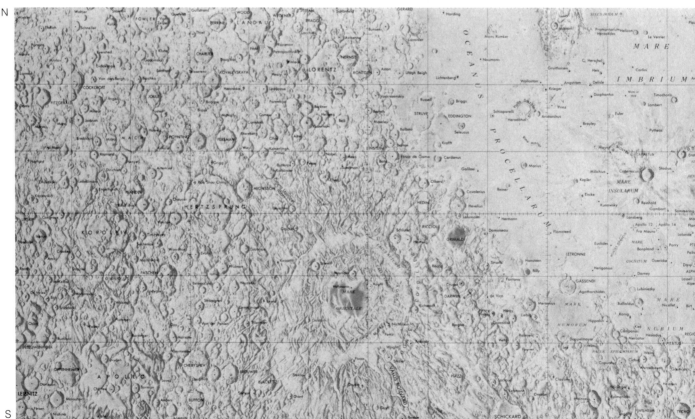

SOUTH POLAR REGION

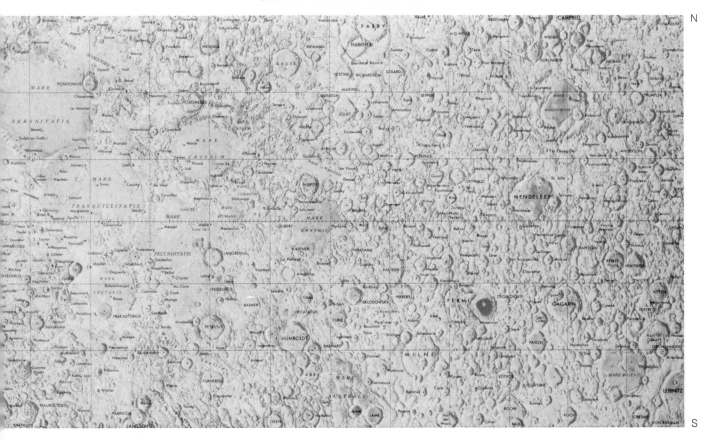

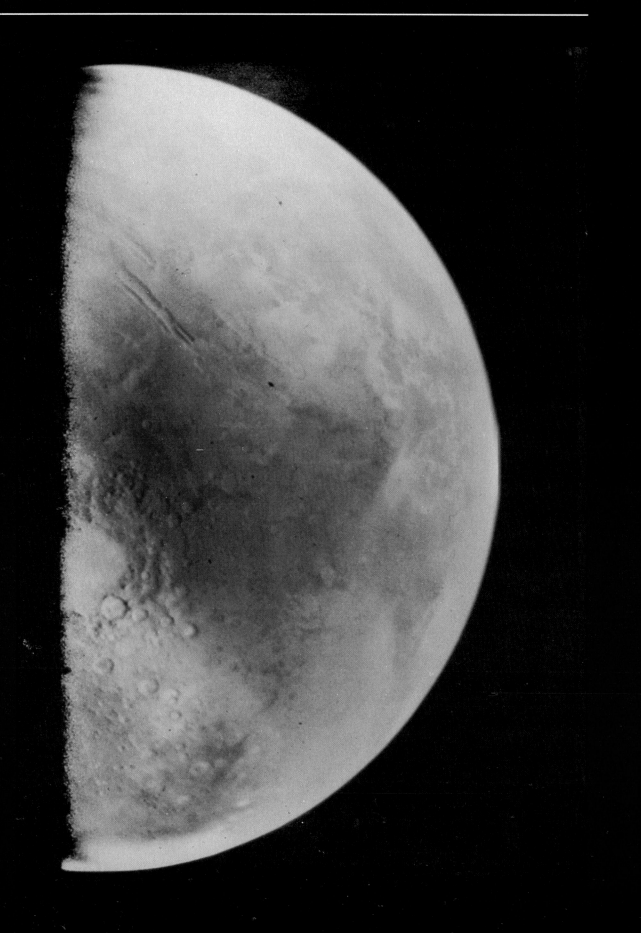

IT IS LATE AFTERNOON. THE WESTERING
sun shines brightly in a salmon sky, casting soft shadows
on the rusty desert. The warm colors are deceptive, for the
air temperature is a brisk 16° below zero, Celsius, but this
is normal for late spring. A 20-miles-per-hour southwest-
erly breeze sighs over the rocky plain, adding to the chill.
The wind has little force in the thin air, however, and its
only effect is to disturb an occasional precariously perched
grain of sand, or to nudge a wisp of cirrus cloud over the
horizon. All is quiet and still. In every respect this is a
typical, uneventful day on the Plains of Gold.

Suddenly there is a flash at the zenith, a metallic glint of
reflected sunlight. A sparkling, starlike object is falling in
from space. It grows at an alarming rate, and soon reveals
itself to be a strange insectoid entity — squat, gray, its
voice an angry, crackling hiss. It gropes toward the ground
with three extended legs and kicks up billowing clouds of
dust with its fiery breath. A padlike foot touches ground.
There is sudden silence. The object bounces slightly and
then nestles comfortably into the soft red soil. After a
moment of stillness, a drift of sand collapses and buries one
of the pads, as if to hide this ungainly alien. Unmindful,
the invader shakes itself and extends several feelers, testing
the air.

Twenty light-minutes away, at the Jet Propulsion Laboratory in Pasadena, California, several hundred technicians, scientists, and journalists wait tensely. It is shortly
after 5:00 A.M., July 20, 1976, and although most of the
people assembled in Von Karman Auditorium have been
keeping vigil throughout the long night, no one seems
tired. There is an electric air of expectation among the

Facing page
Mars Photographed from a Distance of 300,000
Kilometers. *(NASA photo)*

Ten Feet Above Mars. *Viking Lander I* becomes
the first spacecraft to successfully land on the
Red Planet, on July 20, 1976. *(Art by author)*

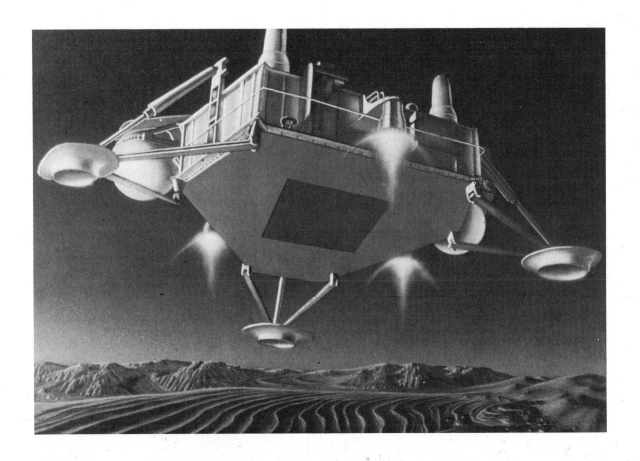

members of the international press corps, and a sense of fraternity. Not only is there an ample story for everyone here tonight, but also a universal hope for success. Even those critical of the space program find themselves caught up by the sheer magnitude of what is about to happen, and, for the small coterie of science-fiction writers and astronomical artists assembled, it is Christmas morning.

Minutes pass, palms begin to sweat. Whatever is happening out there in space has *already* happened twenty minutes ago; the radio signal, crawling along at 186,000 miles per second, takes that long to reach us. There is a curious alteration in our perception of time, a sense of being in two places at once. If our distant emissary was doomed, disaster has already occurred, and no amount of urging can rescue it. Still, we clench our fists and hope.

Finally, at 5:12:07 A.M., the word comes: "Touchdown. We have touchdown." There is cheering and applause, followed by a collective sigh of relief. Everyone is grinning. Strangers slap one another on the back in passing. We've done it!

After a brief break to attend to long-neglected biological functions, the journalists in the auditorium engage in a sort of Brownian motion, picking their way over what seem to be miles of coaxial cable, in search of *the* monitor, the one with the clearest picture. At last it is located, on the right side of the room, and a pecking order is established in front of it. The screen remains dark until 5:54, and then a sliver of light appears on the left-hand edge. There are murmured exclamations. As the picture builds, we see small pebbles embedded in soft-looking soil, and then . . . the edge of a saucer-shaped footpad. It's really true. We've landed on Mars!

The landing of the *Viking I* spacecraft that morning — not coincidentally, the seventh anniversary of the first manned lunar landing — was the culmination of a century-old dream. The very name *Mars* conjures up all the romance of space travel and symbolizes our hope of someday finding extraterrestrial life. No other world is so like Earth and yet, in our imaginations at least, so weirdly different, so full of delicious mystery. A modern-day equivalent of the medieval quest for the Grail, *Viking*'s search for life on the Red Planet was fueled by a similar blend of spiritual longing and rich tradition, lightly seasoned with fact. Just as the legend of the Grail provided a motive for early European explorations, so the romance of Martian lore has been a significant driving force in our exploration of the planets.

HISTORICAL OBSERVATIONS

Because its reddish tint suggested the colors of fire and blood to the ancients, Mars has traditionally been associated with the god of war. Indeed, when Mars shone with particular brilliance every two years, a war was usually in progress somewhere, so the presumption of a correlation is understandable. It is easy to imagine a Chaldean astronomer-priest noting the rising of Nergal, the warrior chief,

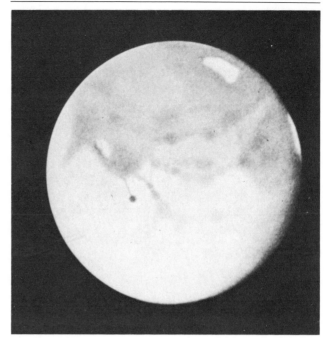

opposite the setting Sun, and hastening to warn the authorities of impending hostilities. Mars at its closest is outshone in the night sky only by the Moon and Venus, and it must have figured strongly in early religions.

This association of Mars with war has persisted throughout history. To the Egyptians, Mars was Horus the Red, the flaming hawk (later Hellenized to *Ares*). The Romans adopted the god, the "star," and the symbol — a shield and spear — and gave the planet its modern name, from whence derive words such as *martial* and the French *mardi* ("Tuesday"). Even after Mars's nature as a small, rather Earthlike world was established in the mid-nineteenth century, the stigma persisted. In H. G. Wells's 1898 novel, *The War of the Worlds,* the inhabitants of the planet Mars were naturally the ones who "slowly and surely drew their plans against us."

Bad press notwithstanding, Mars has played a significant role in the history of astronomy. It may be assumed that Mars's sinister reputation lent zeal to the observational and record-keeping activities of the first astronomers. Such records were of value to the Alexandrian astronomer Ptolemy when he compiled his *Almagest* in the second century A.D. In an effort to predict, if not explain, the seemingly erratic motions of the planets, Ptolemy resurrected and refined a theory that the Greek scholar Hipparchus had propounded more than two centuries earlier — namely, that Earth was located at the center of the universe and that all other bodies orbited around it. Mystical tradition required that all bodies follow "ideal" circular paths, so, in order to explain the retrograde loop that certain planets, including Mars, had been observed to perform in their journeys among the "fixed" stars, Ptolemy had to invent a complex system of small circles (epicycles) within larger circles (deferents).

This "Ptolemaic" system worked fairly well. It could be used to predict the approximate positions of the planets years in advance. It was not perfect, however; corrections were constantly necessary. One planet in particular refused to conform to predictions: Mars. This deviation from theory was galling to astronomers. Imperfection could be tolerated on Earth, but the heavens were the eternal domain of the gods, and therefore perfect. The minor deviations that the other planets exhibited could reasonably be attributed to observational error. Such was not the case with Mars. Something was wrong with Ptolemy's theory.

One astronomer who was intrigued by this problem was the Danish nobleman Tycho Brahe, whose "mural quadrant" at Uraniborg allowed him to measure a star's altitude above the horizon to a small fraction of a degree, thus greatly reducing the possibility of error over earlier efforts. During his short but productive career, from about 1569 to his death at 54 in 1601, Tycho made many thousands of positional observations. The data he obtained allowed him to devise a theory of planetary motion that was just an intuitive leap away from the correct one. While retaining Ptolemy's concept of the Earth as a pivotal center, Tycho adapted part of the Copernican theory, which had been published in 1543. According to Tycho's theory, the Moon and Sun orbited the Earth, while the rest of the planets orbited the Sun. Orbits were still assumed to be circular, although Tycho's observations of the comet of 1577 led him to suspect that its path might be somewhat oval. This speculation marked a deviation from tradition and was a tribute to his scientific honesty.

Tycho's assistant, Johann Kepler (1571–1631), apparently accepted the basic Sun-centered system of Copernicus quite early in his career. He assumed that all the planets, including Earth, revolved about the Sun, and that the driving force of their motion came from the Sun. Thus the closer planets, such as Mercury and Venus, would move faster in their orbits than did Jupiter and Saturn. This was a departure from earlier theory, which attributed the difference in orbital periods merely to the size of the planets' orbits. Tycho too felt that Copernicus's circular epicycles and deferents were a contrivance, and that the planets moved along a simple, continuous curve. Using the wealth of observations left by Tycho, Kepler set about finding that curve. In 1609, the year before Galileo first turned a telescope toward the heavens, Kepler published *De Motibus Stellae Martis* [On the Motions of Mars], in which he announced that Mars, and, by extension, every planet, moved in an elliptical path, with the Sun at one of the foci.

Kepler's choice of Mars as a subject was logical as well as fortuitous. Mercury, being so close to the Sun, was too difficult to observe (indeed, Copernicus is said never to have seen it). The motions of Venus and Jupiter differed too little from circular paths, so they could fit either the Ptolemaic or Copernican models. Saturn moved too slowly in its orbit for Tycho to have collected data through a full revolution. The only planet left was Mars, which had steadfastly refused to be predictable. This was because Mars's orbit is highly elliptical; its perihelion is only 83 percent of its aphelion.

This variation in distance has interesting consequences. Earth, on its inner orbit, overtakes the slower-moving Mars

every 780 days. At that time, known as *opposition,* the two
planets are closest, and observations are most fruitful. The
rest of the time, Mars is too far away to be seen very
clearly. Since Earth's orbit is nearly circular, while Mars's
is highly eccentric, the amount of separation at opposition
varies greatly. At the most favorable oppositions, which
occur at intervals of about 15 to 17 years, Mars is only 56
million kilometers away — 140 times farther than the
Moon. At unfavorable oppositions, the gap widens to 101
million kilometers, almost twice as far. By the time serious
telescopic studies of Mars commenced late in the seventeenth century, it was understood that Mars was a planet
that had to be observed on the fly, so to speak. Useful
observations could be made only during the couple of
months of opposition, and an astronomer could expect to
see only three or four good oppositions in his lifetime. This
tantalizing behavior has contributed much to the Martian
mystique.

Even at its closest Mars is difficult to observe, for it
subtends an arc of only 25 seconds.* This is the apparent
size of a quarter seen from a distance of 0.15 kilometer. Its
saving grace is that it is the only planet whose surface can
be charted effectively from Earth. All the others are either
covered with clouds or, in the case of Mercury, unfavorably
located. The first recognizable drawing of Mars was made
by the Dutch mathematician and physicist Christian Huygens in 1659. It depicts the dark, wedge-shaped area that
later became known as Syrtis Major. By timing the appearance of such markings, Huygens was able to determine
that Mars rotated on its axis approximately once every 24
hours. In 1666, the Italian Gian Cassini made a more
accurate estimate of 24 hours, 40 minutes, which is about
2.5 minutes longer than the actual rotation rate. Cassini
also seems to have been the first to glimpse the white polar
caps of Mars. His nephew, Giacomo F. Maraldi, noticed in
1719 that the ice caps were not quite centered on the poles
(which is also the case on Earth), and observed that Mars's
appearance seemed to change from one night to the next.
It is possible that he was seeing dust storms or other cloud
formations.

Sir William Herschel, personal astronomer of King
George III of England, determined in the early 1780s that
Mars's axis of rotation was tilted about 30 degrees toward
the plane of its orbit. Since Earth's similar tilt of 23.5
degrees is responsible for the seasons, Herschel concluded
that the Martian environment might be rather like our
own. He also noted that the polar caps almost entirely
disappeared in summer, and hence might not be very
thick.

It is of interest to note that once the planets were
recognized as material bodies, much like the Earth, it was

---

* In astronomy, the apparent size of an object is measured in degrees
and fractions of degrees. A degree is an angle 1/360 the circumference
of a circle (such as the horizon line). To measure smaller angles, each
degree is divided into 60′ (minutes of arc, not time), each of which is
in turn divided into 60″ (seconds). Thus the apparent size of the full
Moon is 0.5590° or 0°33′32″, which is 80 times the apparent diameter
of Mars at opposition.

automatically assumed that they were inhabited. An influential book by Bernard de Fontenelle, published in 1688, argued that there was a "plurality of worlds." (He used the phrase not in its traditional sense — that there are, philosophically speaking, a multitude of world-models — but literally; he suggested that there was life on other planets.) The Church was still reeling from the Reformation, and such unorthodoxy was in disfavor. Nevertheless, these ideas persisted. There was already rich literary ground to nourish their growth. Nearly a century earlier, Kepler himself had written a speculative book entitled *Somnium* [The Dream], in which he described living conditions on the Moon. Mindful of the fact that life must adapt to its environment (in itself a noteworthy insight, for the time), Kepler attempted to create a plausible scenario. Because of the low gravity, "everything . . . is monstrously large in size. Growth is very rapid." To avoid the two-week-long lunar night, "[The Moon's inhabitants] have no safe and secure established dwelling, but instead wander about their world in troops . . ." Point by point, Kepler suggested how the unique properties of the Moon's environment would determine the form and behavior of its inhabitants.

The Moon was known to be very different from Earth, so it was expected that its inhabitants would tend to be rather bizarre, having little in common with humankind. Mars, on the other hand, seemed rather Earthlike, with its four seasons and 24.5-hour day. It seemed plausible that not only exotic animals, but people, rational beings, could be found there, and that they might even reveal their existence across the interplanetary gulf. When Mars drew unusually near during the opposition of 1877, astronomers turned their telescopes toward the Red Planet with this possibility in mind.

During a century of Martian cartography, a reasonable if misleading interpretation of the planet's features had been established: the white areas were snow, the orange areas were land, and the dark, gray patches were seas. All designations of Martian features followed this convention. Hence Richard Proctor's 1867 map bears names such as Herschel Continent, Copernicus Land, and Beer Sea (after the German banker, not the beverage). When Father Angelo Secchi charted some broad, gray streaks connecting two of the "seas" in 1869, it was reasonable for him to refer to them as *canali,* or channels. He saw them as purely natural waterways. A compatriot, Giovanni Schiaparelli, director of the Brera Observatory in Milan, was at this time preparing his own map of Mars. He was determined not only to place features far more accurately on the geodesic grid but also to give them prettier names. Schiaparelli drew on mythology and geography to find names such as *Elysium* and *Utopia* for Martian "lands," and assigned such euphonic appellations as *Meridiani Sinus* [Meridian Bay] and *Solis Lacus* [Lake of the Sun] to the "water." When, in 1877, he observed a number of dark linear features crossing the light areas, he naturally adopted Father Secchi's term *canali* to identify them, since the word fit his own nomenclature scheme so well. He, too, assumed that they were natural channels.

Western culture was then in the midst of a technological boom, and people were eager to discover new marvels. An inexact translation of the word *canali* by the press sparked the following line of reasoning: If there are canals, there must be (or at least must have been) canal builders; therefore Mars is inhabited. The idea of a planetwide irrigation system dovetailed neatly with what was then known about Mars. For a century, it had been suspected that there was a dearth of water on the planet. And since the polar ice caps shrank to almost nothing during summer, they must be quite thin. As the ice caps receded, there seemed to be a corresponding expansion and darkening of the "seas," suggesting that they were being fed by melting snow and that coastal vegetation was benefiting from the increased moisture. The planet's smaller size and lower gravity implied a thin, weakly held atmosphere, such as that found at high elevations on Earth, and the general clarity of the Martian atmosphere, together with the tenuous nature of those clouds that did occasionally appear, supported the idea that Mars was a planet in the process of drying up, and was possibly older than Earth. What could be more natural than for intelligent Martians to build a network of canals to transport the precious polar runoff to equatorial farms?

One man who was captivated by the poignant scenario of an advanced people uniting to conserve and equitably distribute their world's dwindling water reserves was Percival Lowell, wealthy scion of the influential Boston Lowells. In 1894, he established an observatory under the clear skies of Flagstaff, Arizona, for the express purpose of studying the canals of Mars. He was quite successful. While other astronomers complained that they couldn't even see the canals, Lowell charted hundreds of them. His canals, furthermore, were not the fuzzy streaks drawn by Schiaparelli, but geometrically thin lines that arced hundreds of kilometers across the Martian desert, intersecting at "oases." He observed the curious process of "gemination," or twinning, that Schiaparelli had described, whereby a canal seemed to manifest a companion running parallel to it, 50 to 600 kilometers away, as if Martian engineers had opened valves on an alternate branch of the network. Lowell drew canals across the "seas," concluding that these were actually arable lowlands, rather than open bodies of water. These Lowellian farms were as neatly bounded as any on Earth, although Martian surveyors apparently had a penchant for triangles and trapezoids, disdaining the less avant-garde rectangle. One could only conclude that the canals, as drawn by Lowell, were the product of intelligence. The only question is, as Carl Sagan has observed, which end of the telescope the intelligence was on.

To be sure, not everyone who accepted the existence of the canals believed them to be engineering works. Schiaparelli himself maintained that they were probably geological features. Alternative explanations ranged from cracks in a shrinking crust to ridges raised by the gravitational pull of atmosphere-grazing asteroids. Many astronomers, moreover, believed that the sharp, linear features drawn by Lowell simply did not exist, that they were optical illusions

The Canals of Mars. A globe based on thousands of drawings made at Lowell Observatory near the turn of the century shows the network of fine lines that was believed to cover the planet. *(Courtesy of Lowell Observatory)*

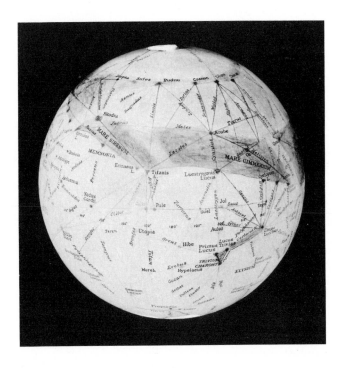

created by the distortions of Earth's atmosphere and the mind's tendency to abstract patterns from randomly distributed features on the Martian surface, in much the same way that we learn to see constellations.

In fairness to Lowell, observing Mars through a telescope is a tedious business calculated to set spots, if not canals, dancing before one's eyes. Even at opposition, a magnification factor of 300 or more is required to resolve detail on the surface, and such a degree of enlargement also magnifies the tremulous distortions caused by small variations in the density of Earth's atmosphere as it moves through the light path. On even the best nights, the planetary disk blurs and shimmers, and an observer must sit with eyes glued to the eyepiece, waiting for those rare moments of perfect "seeing" when the image steadies and features assume crystalline sharpness; then he must frantically sketch what he sees. Under such conditions, there is a natural tendency to sketch what one expects, or hopes, to see, and Lowell had strong motivation to see canals. Because of the limitations of Earthbound observatories, the existence or nonexistence of the canals was an issue that could not be resolved until the space age, and even then more than seven years would elapse between the first close-up photograph of Mars and the final word on the canals.

Following Lowell's death in 1916, study of Mars entered a hiatus, primarily because the thrust of astronomical research had turned away from the planets to the distant realm of stars, nebulae, and galaxies. A few astronomers, notably V. M. Slipher of Lowell Observatory, carried on exhaustive photographic studies of Mars, confirming the existence of a seasonal "wave of darkening" that was thought to be evidence of vegetation if not intelligence, but attempts to spectroscopically observe water or free-oxygen in the Martian atmosphere indicated that Mars was even drier and more inhospitable than anyone had thought. An effort to detect chlorophyll turned up negative, suggesting that the dark patches on Mars were probably not covered with plants. The dream of Martian life began to fade. When the spacecraft *Mariner IV* was launched toward Mars on November 5, 1964, few space scientists expected to find evidence of Lowell's planetary engineers, but most still believed that Mars harbored simple, hardy plants, such as lichen.

The exploration of Mars by instrumented spacecraft provides an object lesson on the dangers inherent in generalizing from insufficient data. Like blind men examining an elephant, space scientists were forced, with each new mission, to reevaluate their conclusions regarding the nature of the beast they were studying. A true picture did not emerge until 1971, when the entire planet was surveyed by an orbiting spacecraft.

On July 14, 1965, the spacecraft *Mariner IV* flew within 10,000 kilometers of Mars, transmitting 15 useful pictures of the planet. Although the probe's trajectory carried it over several charted canals, none were apparent in the photographs. Instead, *Mariner*'s camera revealed a heavily cratered surface reminiscent of the Moon, indicating to

Bleak, frost-rimmed craters were photographed by *Mariner IV*, suggesting to many that Mars was a Moonlike planet. *(NASA photo)*

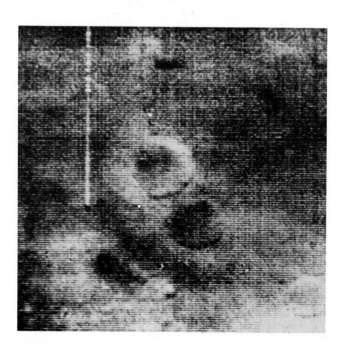

The horizon is 19,000 kilometers from *Viking Orbiter I* in this oblique view across Argyre Planitia, a region of ancient, cratered terrain. *(NASA photo)*

Below
Between Two Worlds. Thirty-six minutes after launching, *Viking* separates from the Centaur stage of the *Titan III-C* vehicle. Already 16,000 kilometers from Earth, the spacecraft is now a miniature planet, following an orbit about the Sun that will bring it to Mars one year later. *(Art by author)*

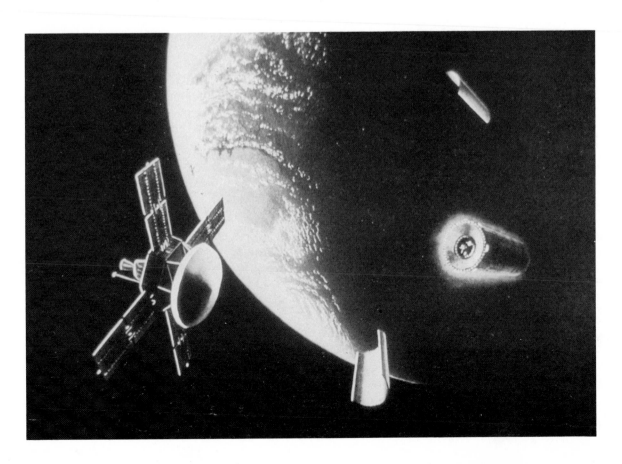

Facing page, top
Rugged Martian Terrain. This photomosaic was taken by *Viking Orbiter 1* near the eastern end of Valles Marineris, the 5000-kilometer-long equatorial canyon system. The large, ancient crater Galilaei dominates the top third of the frame. Its floor is peppered by dozens of later impact craters. The cracked surfaces in the bottom half of the picture may be collapse features produced by the melting of subsurface ice. The resulting water flowed in channels, seen near the center of the picture, and possibly flowed into Galilaei. *(NASA photo)*

Facing page, bottom
Valles Marineris. The great rift valley of Mars, seen from its upper slopes. *(Art by author)*

Arriving at Mars. The combined *Viking Orbiter-Lander* fires its engines to establish a parking orbit. *(Art by author)*

most scientists that Mars, like the Moon, was geologically dead, and had changed very little in billions of years. To the general public, the following syllogism seemed reasonable: The Moon has craters and is lifeless; Mars has craters, therefore it too must be lifeless. Results of the radio occultation experiment, which measured the density of Mars's atmosphere, seemed to support this bad logic: surface air pressure was less than 10 millibars, the equivalent of a terrestrial altitude of 30 kilometers. The Martian atmosphere was a near-vacuum. In a single day, *Mariner IV* toppled the Lowellian dream. Gone was the mysterious world of master engineers, and in its place was a desiccated, barren wasteland.

This was not the last word on Martian biology, however. Questions still abounded. The seasonal darkening was a real effect; it had been photographed. Experiments designed to simulate the Martian environment — thin carbon dioxide atmosphere, low temperatures, ultraviolet radiation—in so-called "Mars jars" indicated that a plethora of terrestrial organisms, ranging in complexity from anaerobic bacteria to turtles, could survive exposure on Mars. It seemed reasonable to suppose that if life had arisen during an earlier, more clement epoch, it would have adapted to the present harsh conditions. In addition — and this is a fact that was largely overlooked at the time — *Mariner IV*'s photographs covered only 1 percent of the planet. Had a similar mission been launched from Mars to Earth, what generalizations might Martian investigators have drawn from a photographic pass over the Pacific Ocean or the Sahara Desert? Clearly, more missions were necessary.

In February and March of 1969, twin spacecraft, *Mariner VI* and *Mariner VII,* were launched on fly-by missions to Mars. Improved communication and television systems permitted the spacecraft to take more pictures at greater resolution than had *Mariner IV*. On July 30, 1969, *Mariner VI* recorded 25 near-encounter pictures of Mars. These were followed on August 4 by *Mariner VII*'s 33 close-up photos, which included coverage of the South Polar Cap. The smallest surface details that could be photographed were 300 meters across, but less than 20 percent of Mars was imaged at this resolution.

The 1969 missions revealed a Mars that was as geologically fascinating as it was biologically hostile. There were more craters than expected, some fresh and Moonlike, others eroded and filled with windblown dust, and there was terrain that geologists characterized as "chaotic" — possibly the result of the surface slumping into basins left by melting permafrost. The ultraviolet spectrometer detected none of the ozone that shields Earth's surface from most of the Sun's ultraviolet radiation, and observed that the South Polar Cap was reflecting nearly the full solar ultraviolet flux, indicating that the Martian surface was blasted by this sterilizing radiation. Most discouraging of all, the infrared radiometer indicated that the South Polar Cap had the same temperature as dry ice — frozen carbon dioxide — and might have very little water ice after all. Mars seemed drier, colder, and more barren than ever before, and there was definitely no evidence of canals.

On November 18, 1971, *Mariner IX* fired its braking rocket and became the first spacecraft to orbit Mars (or,

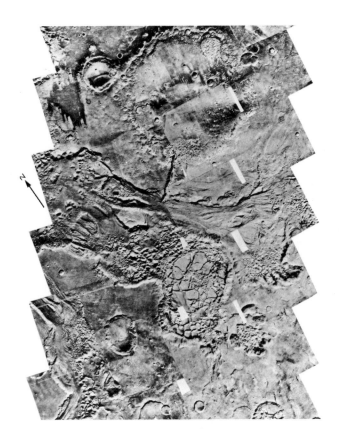

indeed, any other planet). During the weeks preceding its arrival, long-range photographs had revealed a fascinating if frustrating phenomenon on the planet: a dust storm. Such storms had been observed previously, and generally occurred around the time of perihelion, which this was. Usually, some details could be seen through the dust clouds. But this time the storm was planetwide and completely opaque. It was as if Mars, confronted with a spacecraft capable of unveiling its secrets, was making a last-ditch effort to avoid scrutiny.

Gradually the dust settled, and a planet as intriguing as any Lowellian fantasy was revealed. The first features to emerge were huge volcanoes, far larger than any on Earth, bespeaking internal fires in Mars's past. Photos and instrument data showed the residual North Polar Cap — the tiny remnant that persists through summer — to be a fascinating structure that was probably composed of water ice and exhibited many of the features characteristic of glaciers, suggesting that it was probably quite thick. The case for extensive water on Mars was strengthened by the discovery of dozens of long, sinuous valleys meandering through the desert. These ancient riverbeds were certainly "canali" if not canals, and were identical in appearance to terrestrial arroyos caused by flash flooding in arid land. This suggested to some that it might have rained recently on Mars, at least by geologic standards.* Evidence for plate tectonics — continental drift — also came to light: There was a huge gash near the equator, a "grand canyon" 5000 kilometers long, 150 kilometers wide, and 10 kilometers deep. It had fluted edges characteristic of rain-and-wind-eroded valleys on Earth, and a central ridge similar to that found in the Great Rift Valley in eastern Equatorial Africa. Clearly, this was not the dead, moonlike planet earlier missions had described.

During the course of 1972, *Mariner*'s wide, looping orbit allowed it to completely map Mars and observe the planet for more than half a Martian year. The mystery of the wave of darkening was explained by the discovery of seasonally shifting winds that altered the distribution of fine sand or dust on the dark, rocky surface. A full global survey revealed that Mars has two geologically disparate hemispheres, apparently a quality common to all terrestrial planets. One side is characterized by extensive volcanism and faulting, while the other is ancient and cratered. Earlier missions had photographed only the cratered side, giving rise to the Moonlike model of the planet. The *Mariner IX* data gave rise to the two new models of Mars that were much more exciting from a biological perspective.

The "precessional spring" model supposed that Mars is currently in the grip of a global ice age, much as Earth was more than 10,000 years ago. Because of the present orientation of its rotation axis, Mars experiences winter in its Northern Hemisphere near the time of aphelion. On Earth,

---

* Although it is unlikely that these sinuous valleys are observable from Earth, in 1939 Edison Pettit reported seeing dark "veins, as in a mineral" during moments of perfect seeing. This would aptly characterize the appearance of the valleys, had he actually glimpsed them.

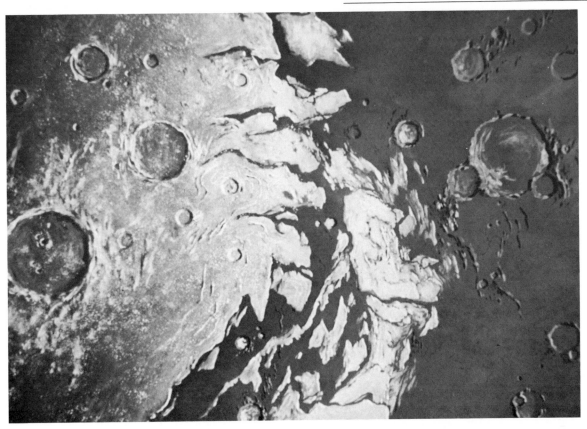

The typical melting pattern of the frozen carbon dioxide snows that blanket the South Polar Region of Mars in winter is shown in this view from 300 kilometers above the planet's surface. (*Art by author*)

Left
Martian Canyons. Probably the most photogenic feature on Mars is the enormous canyon — Valles Marineris — that cuts deeply into the surface and stretches nearly a third of the way around the planet. This photomosaic was made from pictures taken August 23, 1976, by *Viking Orbiter I* from an average range of 4200 kilometers (2600 miles). The principal canyon crosses the bottom half of the picture. North is to the top. The far wall of the main canyon shows several large landslides, which probably formed in episodes and perhaps were triggered by Mars quakes. Along the near wall, another widening process appears to have occurred: a series of branch channels cuts into the plateau at the bottom. These may have formed either by slow erosion as a result of the release of ground water, or by mass wasting processes in which rock debris moved slowly downhill as ground ice froze and thawed. Other branches of the canyon are visible at the top of the picture. (*NASA photo*)

a similar effect serves only to slightly moderate Northern Hemisphere seasons and to mildly exacerbate those in the Southern Hemisphere. As a factor in heating efficiency, the very slight deviation from circularity in the Earth's orbit is far less important than the angle at which sunlight impinges on a given area of the surface. Because of the highly elliptical nature of Mars's orbit, however, its distance from the Sun strongly affects its temperature. Currently, the North Pole of Mars is tilted away from the Sun when the Sun is most distant, making for extremely cold northern winters and summers that are mild at their warmest. If most of Mars's water is bound up in the vestigial Northern Ice Cap, as appears to be the case, this means that the water never thaws, and that, unlike the carbon dioxide on Mars, it does not circulate seasonally between the poles.

Proponents of this model suggested that since Mars's axis precesses, like that of a spinning top, every 178,000 years, the situation was different approximately 50,000 years ago. The seasons were milder then, and the water circulated between the hemispheres. It was at this time (and at similar periods throughout Mars's history) that the Martian rains fell. If this theory is correct, then we are now observing Mars during the Great Winter, when it is a frigid, dry, nearly airless world. Fifty thousand years ago, our late Pleistocene ancestors may have seen Mars as a blue star in their sky. During Mars's Great Spring, advocates of this theory suggested, rain clouds scudded over the Martian desert, filling the canyons and arroyos with life-giving water. Since airborne seeds frozen for millennia in Antarctic ice can be thawed and germinated, why shouldn't Martian organisms lay dormant during the Great Winter, and spring into life when the rains finally come?

Martian Topography. A wealth of diverse geological features can be found on the Red Planet: impact craters, some fresh and sharp, others filled in with drifting sand; volcanoes, 10 kilometers high, with "lee" waves of ice crystals streaming from their flanks; and, most intriguing, dry riverbeds that course through the desert for hundreds of kilometers.
(Art by author)

This is an appealing theory, but it has faults. Planetary scientists generally assume that the last wave of impact-crater formation ended approximately 4 billion years ago, and that from then on, erosional processes began to erase the craters. The proportion of young, fresh craters to old ones is therefore considered to be an indication of the relative age of a given area. When geologists studied those features that apparently bespoke an active, still-evolving Mars, such as the volcanic mountains and the river valleys, they found craters; and this was enough to convince them that most such features were billions, rather than thousands, of years old. The post–*Mariner IX* consensus was that Mars was planetary fossil that died in its geologic infancy and had remained in more or less its present state throughout the history of the solar system. *Requiescat in pace, Marti,* was the prevailing sentiment.

Hope springs eternal in the exobiologist's breast, however. Mars was once Earthlike, after all; there was liquid water in the planet's history. If Mars was wet for even a few million years, life may have developed; and if the planet dried up gradually, Martian organisms might have adapted to the present conditions. To test this supposition, two *Viking* spacecraft, equipped with marvelously ingenious automated biology labs, were dispatched to Mars in 1976. Both spacecraft were sterilized, to avoid contaminating Mars (and the life-detection instruments) with terrestrial organisms, and landing sites that were relatively "low, warm, wet and safe" were chosen after a month's orbital surveillance. *Viking I* landed at 22.5° N, 48.0° W, in the region known as Chryse Planitia, on July 20, 1976; *Viking II* touched down on the temperate plain of Utopia, at 48°

Viking Lander II. The boulder-strewn field of red rocks reaches to the horizon, which is nearly 2 miles from the spacecraft on Mars's Utopia Plain. Fine particles of red dust, which give the Martian sky its salmon color, have settled on spacecraft surfaces. Color calibration charts for the cameras are mounted at three locations on the spacecraft. Note the blue starfield and red stripes of the flag. The circular structure at top is the high-gain antenna, pointed toward Earth. *Viking II* landed September 3, 1976, some 4600 miles from its twin, *Viking I,* which touched down on July 20, 1976. *(NASA photo)*

N, 226° W, an area believed to be an ancient river delta, on September 3, 1976.

The color photos transmitted by the landers showed a surprisingly terrestrial landscape, reminiscent of the bleaker areas of the American Southwest, and even the orange sky (tinted by fine iron-oxide dust permanently suspended in the atmosphere) was familiar to smog-ridden Southern Californians. The red, rich-looking soil seemed a likely place to find microorganisms.

The *Viking* spacecraft were equipped to conduct four life-detection experiments. In the *gas-exchange experiment,* nutrient solution was added to a sample of Martian soil, and the changing composition of gases in the test chamber was monitored over several Martian days. A surprising amount of oxygen was evolved, but since the sample was kept in total darkness, it is unlikely that any biological mechanism, such as photosynthesis, was responsible. The water in the nutrient was probably reacting with peroxide compounds in the soil. In the *pyrolytic-release experiment,* Martian soil was exposed to radioactive carbon dioxide, the supposition being that any microorganisms present would incorporate the radioactively labeled atoms into their bodies during metabolic processes. After an incubation period, the gas was drained off and the soil was heated to 175°C. A small amount of radioactive gas was indeed driven out of the soil by heating, suggesting that biological processes

Facing page
The Tharsis Ridge is the youngest volcano field on Mars. Note the area of intense crustal faulting at the bottom of this *Viking Orbiter I* photo, and the cluster of volcanic mountains at the right, ranging in width from 65 to 400 kilometers. The flanks of these mountains bear volcanic crater chains, channels, and lava flows. The ejecta rays from meteorite impacts fall across the volcanoes, which suggests that they are millions of years old. A prominent channel connects the summit of one volcano with an impact crater near its base. This may indicate that the last eruption was triggered by the fall of a meteorite. *(NASA photo)*

A river valley in the Rasena region of Mars snakes through the desert for 600 kilometers, ending in branching tributaries. At one point, it appears to cut through solid rock, forming a natural bridge. Any ice that might be preserved within the cavern would be an ideal place to search for evidence of past life. *(Art by author)*

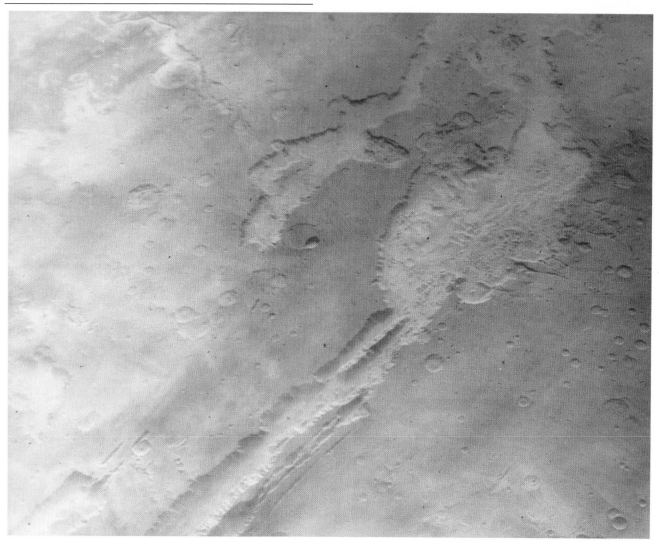

Two Views of Martian Canyons. In the *Viking Orbiter I* photo above, Mars's "Grand Canyon," Valles Marineris, is imaged near local noon, and the tenuous, clear atmosphere permits us to see details on its floor, which is 2 kilometers below the upper desert. *(NASA photo)*

As the Sun rises over Noctis Labyrinthus (the labyrinth of the night), bright clouds of water ice can be observed in and around the tributary canyons of this high-plateau region of Mars. Scientists are not sure why the clouds cling to the canyon areas, spilling onto the plateau surface only in certain areas. One possibility is that water that condensed during the previous afternoon, on shaded east-facing slopes of the canyon floor, turns to vapor as the early morning sunlight falls on those same slopes. *(NASA photo)*

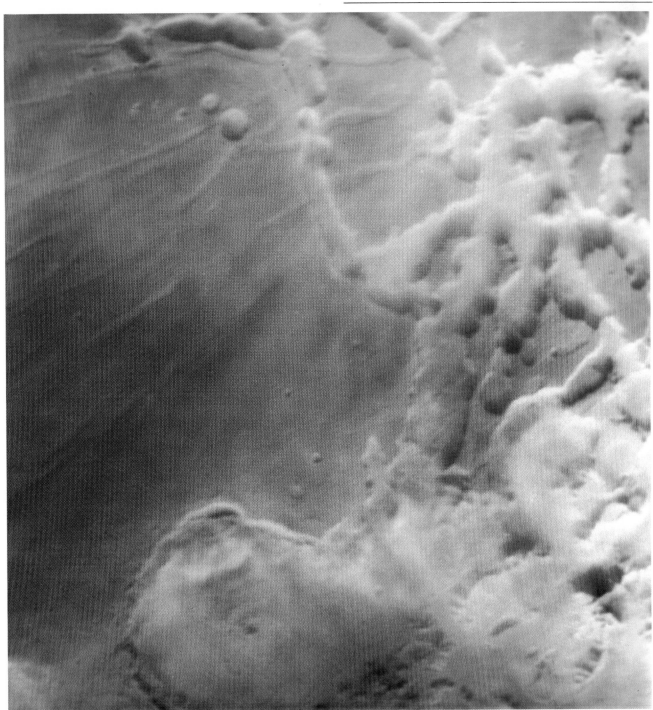

Martian Landslides. Aprons of debris on the canyon floor indicate how Valles Marineris enlarges itself. The walls appear to collapse at intervals, forming huge landslides that flow down and across the canyon floor. Linear striations on the landslide surface show the direction of the flow. In the picture, it appears that on the canyon's far wall, one landslide has ridden over a previous one. Streaks on the canyon floor, aligned parallel to the length of the canyon, give evidence of wind action. Layers in the canyon wall indicate that the walls are made up of alternate layers of lava and ash or wind-blown deposits. *(NASA photo)*

could be taking place. A second sample, heat-sterilized prior to incubation, incorporated less radioactive gas — a reaction that was to be expected, if microorganisms were responsible. In the *labeled-release experiment*, radioactively tagged nutrients were added to a soil sample, and radioactive gases indeed evolved from it.

The pyrolytic and labeled-release results seemed to suggest that Martians did exist, albeit tiny ones; but a test of soil chemistry indicated that there were *no* complex organic compounds. On Earth, all life is made up of long-chain, carbon-based molecules, and the fact that none were detected on Mars — with the exception of those found in a weak residue of cleaning fluid in the equipment — bodes ill for the prospect of Martian biology. Either the population of microorganisms is extremely small, or "fancy chemistry" took place when liquid water was introduced into the bone-dry, highly oxidized soil. Laboratory simulations using synthetic, biologically sterile Martian soil suggest that the latter is the case.

The fourth life-detection experiment was the *facsimile-camera* system. While no trails of footprints appeared in any of the *Viking* photographs, recent studies of "stretched," highly exaggerated color images suggest that the surfaces of Martian rocks have patches on them that change shape and color during the year. Whether this is due to exotic chemistry, biology, or some other process is unknown.

In many respects, the quest for life on Mars was a longshot. There are places on Earth, such as the high valleys of the Antarctic, that barely sustain even microbial life, although the environment there is infinitely more hospitable than any found on Mars. Still, the Antarctic environment is a geologically recent one, and it might be argued that there has not been sufficient time for many organisms to have adapted so as to fill that particular niche. It is often difficult to prove a negative, and the final answer to the question of life on Mars may come only after the entire planet has been systematically explored by automated roving vehicles or, eventually, by astronauts. Indeed, the answer may never be found. Who can say that there is not, deep within some hidden, steaming vent on the slopes of Olympus Mons, a small patch of organized matter, survivor of a bygone age, desperately clinging to existence? We can only wish our Martian cousins well; real or imaginary, they have led us out of our planetary cradle.

THE MOONS OF MARS

Mars has two moons. Deimos, the smaller, outer satellite, orbits in Mars's equatorial plane, 23,490 kilometers from the center of the planet. This position is just above synchronous orbit, and the resulting rotational period of 30 hours, 18 minutes is so close to Mars's rotational period of 24 hours, 37 minutes, that Deimos moves very slowly across the Martian sky, requiring 59 hours and 33 minutes to journey from the eastern to western horizon. Seen from a point on Mars's equator, Deimos would wax and wane

Martian snow is depicted in this *Viking Lander II* photo taken on the Plains of Utopia, May 18, 1979. At the onset of winter, tiny grains of dust, suspended in the atmosphere, adhere to ice crystals. Solid carbon dioxide condenses on the aggregate particles, making them heavy enough to fall to the surface. The early morning sunlight thaws the frozen carbon dioxide, leaving behind a film of water ice perhaps no more than 0.001 inch thick. *(NASA photo)*

Sunset over Chryse Planitia, photographed by
Viking II on August 20, 1976. As the Sun
drops below the horizon, it illuminates the thin
upper atmosphere above the reddish dust layer.
Rayleigh scattering provides an uncharacteristic
blue sky over Mars at this time. *(NASA photo)*

Phobos. The larger, innermost Martian satellite
appears here in a photomosaic of *Viking Orbiter I*
images, taken when the spacecraft was
maneuvered within 480 kilometers of the
approximately 20-kilometers-wide moon. The
South Pole is near the bottom, where the
pictures overlap, in the crater Hall (named after
the discoverer of Mars's two moons). Features of
interest include striations, crater chains, a linear
ridge, and small hills, believed to consist of
material ejected from the craters. A long linear
ridge starts near the South Pole and extends to
the upper right-hand part of the picture. A
sharp ridge at the intersection of two kilometer-
sized craters is apparent near mid-terminator. A
horizontal line of crater running parallel to the
orbital plane of Phobos is visible near the top of
the picture. Such crater chains are commonly
associated with secondary impacts from ejecta
thrown out by primary impacts. *(NASA photo)*

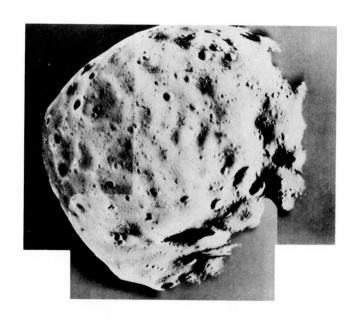

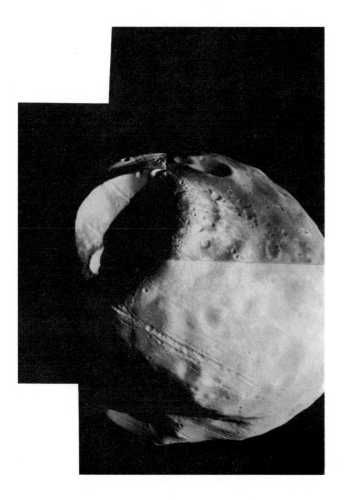

Another Side of Phobos. This photomosaic shows the side of Phobos that always faces Mars. Stickney, the largest crater on Phobos (10 kilometers, or 6 miles, across), is at the left, near the morning terminator. Linear grooves coming from, and passing through, Stickney appear to be fractures in the surface, caused by the impact that formed the crater. Kepler Ridge, in the Southern Hemisphere, is casting a shadow that partially covers the large crater, Hall, at the bottom. *(NASA photo)*

Mars's Outer Satellite, Deimos. Deimos is about half the size of Phobos. Craters in this picture are less than a kilometer across. *(NASA photo)*

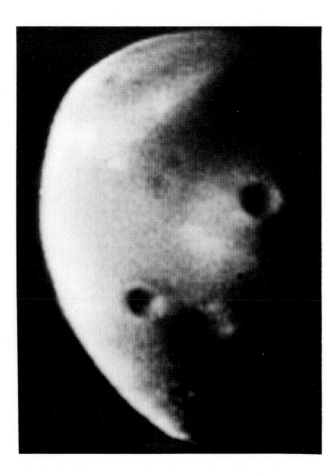

Map 3

TOPOGRAPHIC MAP OF MARS

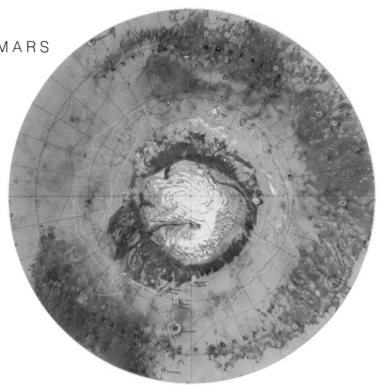

NORTH POLAR REGION
Polar cap as it appeared on August 4, 1972

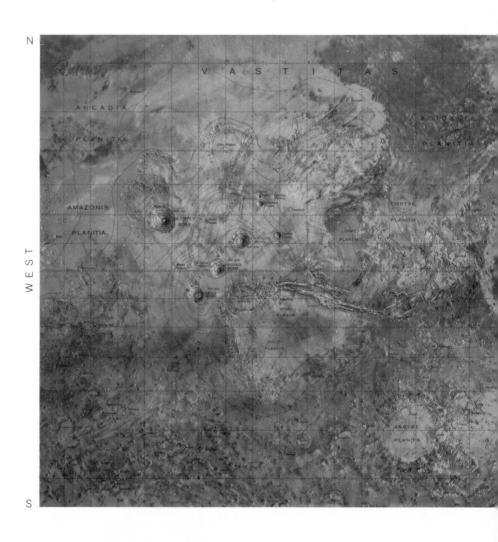

SOUTH POLAR REGION
Polar cap as it appeared on February 28, 1972

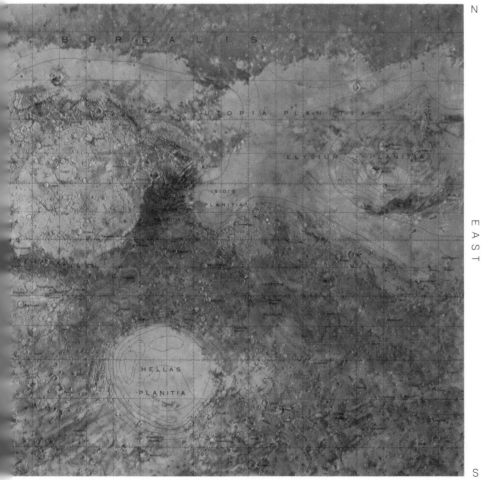

In the sky of Deimos, Mars's outer satellite, the Red Planet appears nearly 20 times larger than the full Moon. The dark fork of Meridiani Sinus is near the center of Mars's disk, and Hellas, the Martian dust sea, is on the sunset terminator. (*Art by author*)

through more than two-and-a-half phase cycles between rising and setting. While it might be romantic for future colonists to watch the tiny satellite wax from new to full during the course of a single night, the spectacle would probably be best appreciated with telescopic aid, since Deimos at its closest would subtend an arc of only 2 minutes, which is one-fourteenth of the apparent diameter of the full Moon. Through a telescope, however, the play of shadows across Deimos's cratered surface should be fascinating.

Phobos orbits Mars at a radius of 9350 kilometers, a scant 5955 kilometers above the surface of the planet. With an orbital period of 4 hours, 17 minutes, it actually overtakes the Martian surface, so that it rises in the West and sets in the East, in the manner of artificial satellites. Because it is so close, there must be a noticeable change in its apparent diameter during its 5 hour, 32 minute journey across the sky. Seen from the Martian equator, Phobos would subtend an arc of 7 minutes, 9 seconds at rising, growing to 12 minutes, 3 seconds when it crossed the zenith. Still, this is less than half our Moon's apparent size.

Both Martian satellites are more or less potato-shaped, so irregular that three axial diameters are required to describe them. Phobos, the larger moon, has a long axis of 27 kilometers that is tidally locked toward Mars, so its rotation about its North-South axis (19 kilometers) is the same as its orbital period. Its minimum equational diameter is 21 kilometers. Deimos has a long axis of 15 kilometers, and its polar and equational diameters are 11 and 12 kilometers, respectively. It too is tidally locked. As is the

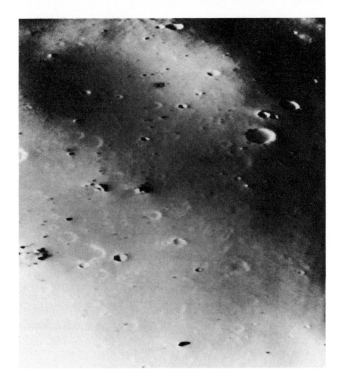

Above
The *Orbiter* Mission. On October 15, 1977, *Viking Orbiter II* was maneuvered within 50 kilometers of Mars's outer satellite, Deimos, in order to obtain the photograph below, which shows surface features as small as 3 meters across. (*Art by author*)

Left
Dusty Deimos. The smaller Martian moon is covered with a thick layer of dust that seems to blanket any crater smaller than 50 meters across, making it appear smoother than Phobos. House-sized boulders, probably ejected from nearby craters, cast long shadows across the surface. The relative velocities of the spacecraft and Deimos were so high that the *Orbiter* had to rotate to pan with Deimos, in order to prevent smearing of the image. (*NASA photo*)

Landing on Deimos. Data transmitted by the *Viking Orbiters* suggest that Mars's two tiny satellites, Phobos and Deimos, may be asteroids of the type known as carbonaceous chondrites. Such bodies contain complex organic (carbon-based) molecules that could be of great value in space manufacturing and colonization programs. An industrial facility on a carbonaceous Martian moon could be virtually self-sufficient, and during the next century could serve as a base for manned exploration of Mars. *(Art by author)*

case with our own Moon, each satellite has a hemisphere turned eternally toward space, hidden from its primary.

Because the satellites are so small, it has been suggested that they are captured asteroids. While this is possible (and certainly the Martian moons may be described as asteroidal bodies), the mechanisms of capture are such that it seems unlikely that two independent asteroids would end up occupying such nearly circular, co-planar orbits above Mars's equator. An alternative explanation is that the satellites are remnants of the proto-Mars accretion disk. Phobos orbits well inside Roche's limit and is slowly spiraling in toward Mars. Should it sustain another impact like the one that formed the crater Stickney, near its North Pole (this may have fractured Phobos internally; a system of parallel rills seems to radiate from Stickney), Phobos could shatter, forming a ring about Mars. Over the course of time, ring fragments would spiral into Mars, adding a few million tons of mass to the planet. The slow descent of Phobos may represent the final stage of Mars's formation.

Facing page
The Outer Solar System
(Diagram by Michael Standlee Design)

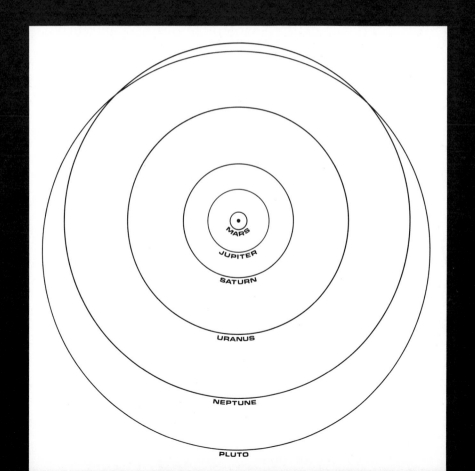

MARS

JUPITER

SATURN

URANUS

NEPTUNE

PLUTO

IN JUNE 1908, AN EXTRATERRESTRIAL object struck the Tunguska taiga in Siberia with a force of such magnitude that the resulting blast leveled every tree within a radius of 10 kilometers. Eyewitnesses compared the brightness of the descending object to that of the Sun, and many suffered temporary hearing impairments as a result of the concussion. In fact, the explosion was heard hundreds of kilometers away.

There is reason to believe that the object that struck Tunguska was the nucleus of a small comet, one of a class of small bodies left over from the creation of the solar system. Although the last great wave of asteroidal bombardment ended approximately 3 billion years ago, the meteoric rain continues, albeit at a drizzle; on any clear moonless night, an observer can expect to see an average of seven meteors per hour. Most meteors are no larger than a grain of sand, and particles of this size comprise the greatest percentage of the unassimilated material in space. Larger bodies, however, are not uncommon; several meter-wide objects may survive passage through Earth's atmosphere each year, and perhaps once each century an object strikes that is big enough to do damage. In prior ages, the odds were that such impacts would occur in unpopulated areas; but our numbers have more than tripled in this century, and most people in the civilized world live near large cities. It is sobering to note that had the Tunguska object arrived just a few hours later, it could easily have devastated Moscow. In an era concerned about ICBMs, we would be wise to learn as much as possible about the smaller bodies wandering our solar system.

ASTEROIDS

When the asteroid Ceres was discovered in 1800, it was thought to be the planet many astronomers had felt must occupy part of the huge expanse between Mars and Jupiter. But when three more asteroids were discovered within seven years, astronomers realized that they were dealing with a new species of solar-system body. With the advent of astrophotography in the 1890s, lengthy time-exposures of star fields near the ecliptic were so often marred by the trails of uncharted asteroids that these minor planets were soon dubbed "vermin of the skies." At present, more than 2250 objects are listed in *The Ephemeris of Minor Planets*, and all of these are at least several kilometers in size. Undoubtedly, innumerable smaller, yet undetected bodies also exist.

At first it was thought that asteroids were the remains of a major planet that had somehow been destroyed, but this is improbable, since the mass of all known asteroids combined is far less than that of the Moon. It is more likely that asteroids are leftovers from the solar accretion disk that were prevented from accumulating into a single globe by the gravitational interference of Jupiter.

Of all the asteroids, probably only the largest assumed a spherical shape: Ceres (1000 kilometers in diameter), Pallas (600 kilometers), and Vesta (530 kilometers). Even these

Facing page
Sampling an Asteroid. To be independent of Earth, space colonies will obviously have to find resources of their own. Astronomical evidence is mounting that most of the materials needed for space manufacturing can be found as very pure ores in asteroids. Iron, nickel, and carbonaceous materials apparently abound in Earth-crossing asteroids such as Apollo and Amor, and these can be reached with comparatively low expenditures of energy. Depicted here is a mobile prospecting base on such an asteroid. (Mining activities are already in progress in the background.) Since the topography of smaller asteroids is shaped primarily by ancient impacts, rather than by gravity, the base is equipped with long, spindly legs, to level itself above the chaotic surface. (*Art by author*)

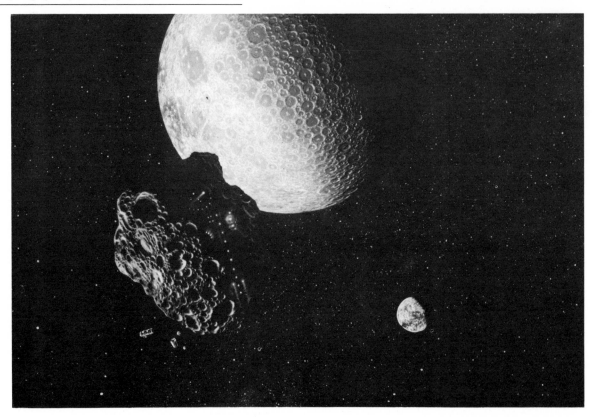

Asteroid Mining. Once a suitable ore-bearing asteroid is located, the problem of transporting it to the space manufacturing facility remains. It may be possible to transform the asteroid itself into a vehicle, by erecting a mass driver on it. The mass driver is essentially a long track with electromagnets spaced at intervals. The magnets accelerate buckets filled with rock to speeds of several kilometers per second, and then eject the rock, thus imparting thrust to the asteroid. *(Art by author)*

largest asteroids are too small and distant for astronomers to examine their surface details through a telescope, but it is possible that they are rocky, heavily cratered bodies similar in general appearance to the rough highland areas of the Moon. Features produced by volcanism are unlikely on such small bodies, and their gravity is far too weak to retain any atmosphere. It is possible, however, that all the large asteroids have been so battered by collisions that they are internally fractured and quite loosely packed. If so, they may retain little large-scale topography. The largest asteroid, Ceres, is of interest in this respect because its darkness and low density suggest that it is made of the same material as those meteorites known as carbonaceous chondrites. Such meteorites are rich in carbon compounds, very fragile and light, and comparable in appearance and hardness to charcoal. If Ceres is composed of this material, it is unlikely that its surface can support differences in elevation greater than 1 kilometer, so it may be comparatively smooth.

There are at least 100 asteroids whose diameters are within the 100–300-kilometer range, but the vast majority are little more than "flying mountains," on the order of 10 kilometers across. Like all other bodies in space, asteroids rotate. Since we cannot observe surface details, rotation periods are determined by observing the cyclical changes in brightness that are caused by variations in surface albedo or irregularities in shape. The larger, main-belt asteroids have characteristic rotational periods of about ten hours, but smaller ones with unusual orbits, such as Icarus — which ranges from within the orbit of Mercury to beyond that of Mars — rotate in only a few hours. Such rapid rotation rates and highly elliptical orbits could be expected, if

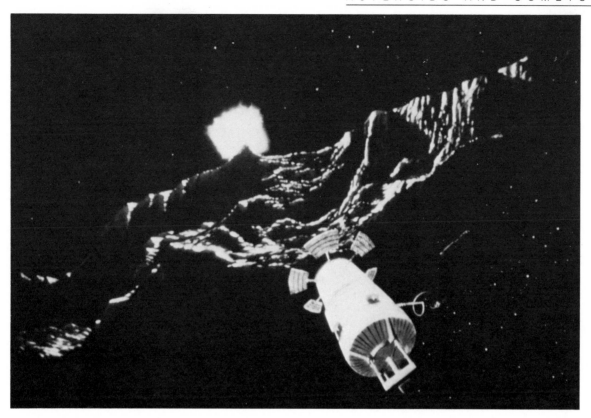

asteroids like Icarus were the remnants of burned-out comets or the product of particularly violent collisions between larger bodies. Such collisions were probably common during the first billion years of the solar system, but now they must be quite rare; most asteroids have already staked out their territories. The popular concept of a dense field of tumbling asteroids makes for exciting chase sequences in space operas but has little relation to reality. Though high population densities of asteroids may obtain in regions such as the rings of Saturn or Uranus, the main belt of asteroids, located between Mars and Jupiter, is still composed mostly of empty space. *Pioneer X,* the first spacecraft to cross this region, photographed only one asteroid, and that was at a distance of millions of kilometers.

The main belt of asteroids has a definite though tenuous structure. Just as Saturn's rings have gaps between them, such as Cassini's or Encke's divisions, so the asteroids orbit in a series of rings that are separated by what are known as the Kirkwood gaps. The gravitational field of Jupiter prevented asteroids from forming in these zones. There also seems to be an established geochemical variation within the belt: those asteroids in the sunward part of the belt are predominantly of the stony-iron silicaceous (S-type) variety, while farther out there are more of the carbonaceous, or C-type, asteroids.

In addition to the main belt, there is a family of perhaps 1000 small asteroids, of which 30 have been discovered, that travel in highly elliptical orbits which cross the Earth's. These are the Apollo-Amor asteroids, and it has been suggested that they could serve as a major source of raw material for future space-based industries, since they can be reached with a comparatively low expenditure of

In the shadow of Icarus, well inside the orbit of Mercury, a future manned mission sends a remote-control camera into the blazing light to obtain close-up photos of the corona. At this distance from the Sun, rocks could glow dull red, and a spacecraft's hull alone might not be adequate protection against solar radiation. *(Art by author)*

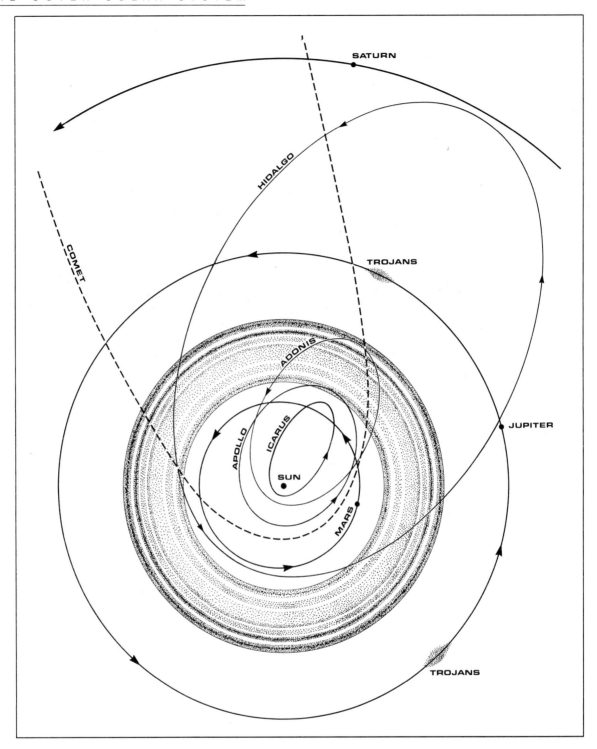

Asteroid Orbits
(*Diagram by Michael Standlee Design*)

energy. Another group of asteroids, the Trojans, trail and precede Jupiter in its orbit, clustering near two points 60 degrees from the planet.

Recently it has been speculated that some asteroids may have satellites. On June 7, 1978, when the 217-kilometer asteroid 532 Herculina passed in front of a faint star, the star seemed to blink twice, instead of disappearing only once, indicating that the asteroid may have a 45-kilometer companion. In December 1978, an occultation by Melpomene showed similar results. Such occultations are rare, however, so it is difficult to obtain confirming observations.

The discovery of Pluto's moon, Charon, does lend credence to the idea that relatively small bodies are fairly commonly attended by satellites.

The Icy Nucleus of a Comet. By the time a comet crosses the orbit of Mars, frozen gases have begun to sublime from the surface, and the pressure of sunlight and the solar wind causes them to stream away, forming a tail. *(Art by author)*

COMETS

When the planetesimals were forming in the solar accretion disk 4.5 billion years ago, a certain percentage of them were in slightly elliptical and inclined orbits. Although most of these were tamed by collisions and ultimately brought into circular orbits within the plane of the solar system, some managed to avoid this process and retained their unusual orbits until most of the solar nebula had been gathered up by the forming planets. If other influences had not been at work, their orbits would remain unchanged today. In 1950, however, J. H. Oort showed that the perturbations caused by the established planets, and by the slow removal of the solar nebula, gradually made highly elliptical orbits even more so, forcing their aphelia ever outward. This is what happened to the noncomformist planetesimals: their orbits were so stretched that they eventually ended up spending most of their time in the frigid emptiness far from the Sun. They are there today, in a roughly spherical halo 40,000 to 150,000 astronomical units from the Sun, half the distance to Alpha Centauri. This area is the Oort Cloud, where comets dwell in exile,

Comet West
(*Photo by Jack Harvey, Kitt Peak National Observatory*)

awaiting their summons back to the solar hearth. It is estimated that as many as 1 billion planetesimals inhabit this extraterrestrial Elba.

There on the fringes of interstellar space, the Sun is merely a bright star, a billion times fainter than it appears from Earth. Its gravity is so weak that a velocity of a hundred meters per second will keep a comet in a circular orbit. There are other suns farther away, however, and their gravity works over the course of millions of years to slightly alter the comets' paths. Each year, approximately one dozen comets are nudged in such a way that they begin to fall toward the Sun.

When one of these comets approaches within 4 astronomical units of the Sun, some of the frozen ammonia and carbon dioxide on its surface sublimes, forming a thin fluorescent halo around the solid central mass, or nucleus. Within about 2 astronomical units, the pressure of the solar wind pushes the gas away, forming a tail. Tiny grains of dust embedded in the subliming ice are freed, and the pressure of sunlight drives them away, but more slowly than the gas, so they tend to follow curved Keplerian paths. Whatever the comet's direction of motion, the tail always points more or less away from the Sun.

As a comet rounds the Sun and is most strongly heated, several interesting things can happen. The increased sublimation of gas can increase the brightness and length of the tail. Chaotic variations in the Sun's magnetic field can force streamers of the tail to twist and curl. Bubbles of particularly volatile frozen gas can erupt as jets, slightly altering the comet's course, and sometimes the nucleus of the comet can fragment, engendering two comets.

Seen from Earth, a very bright comet, such as Comet West in the spring of 1976, can provide one of nature's most magical spectacles. A few hours before dawn, the ghostly, often multiple tail begins to fan above the eastern horizon. An hour later, the hazy, blue-white head of the comet follows. As the comet climbs out of the mists at the horizon, a wealth of detail within the tail becomes apparent. Complex streamers curve toward the Northeast, and the dust tail has a distinct golden tint that nicely complements the blues and violets of the gas tail. As dawn begins to lighten the sky, the tail fades, but the position of the head, with respect to a nearby star, has changed visibly in just the few hours since the comet rose.

It is easy to understand how such a mysterious sight could have provoked fear and awe a few centuries ago. Indeed, when Earth passed through the tail of Halley's comet in 1910, there was a brisk market in "anti-comet" pills for a time. But comets have been described as the nearest thing to nothing that is still something; except for the icy nucleus, they are quite insubstantial. The matter comprising the head and tail of a comet could be packed into an average-sized house. Contact with the nucleus, however, is another affair: Ernst Opik has estimated that the blast from a maximum-energy collision with a comet nucleus 20 kilometers or larger could virtually sterilize an area the size of North America. Fortunately, actuarial tables suggest that strikes of this magnitude only occur at intervals of 1.5 billion years.

Following page, top
Comet West Rises Gracefully in the Predawn Sky in the Spring of 1975 *(Photo by author)*

Following page, bottom
Halley's comet is depicted here as it would be seen from an orbiting station in 1986, the year the famous comet is scheduled to return to the warmer regions of the solar system. The bright head of the comet is a million kilometers beyond the Earth. The prominent "spike" in the comet's tail is an effect of perspective, not a violation of the rule that a comet's tail always points away from the Sun. *(Art by author)*

Comet Halley as Photographed in 1910
(*Computer-generated color by Lowell Observatory and AURA, Inc.*)

It has been estimated that large comets impact Earth every 1.5 billion years, on the average, suggesting that our planet has sustained perhaps as many as three such blows in its history. Such collisions are far less likely today than they were in the early days of the solar system, which is fortunate. A blast like the one depicted here could virtually destroy life on Earth. There is reason to believe that climatic changes resulting from dust scattered through the atmosphere by lesser impacts may have caused several periods of "great dying" in the past, including the extinction of the dinosaurs. *(Art by author)*

Comets are of interest because they may constitute fairly accessible samples of the matter from which the planets formed. We know that some of the ices that compose them, such as water, methane, and ammonia, are common in various forms on the gas-giant planets such as Jupiter. In 1975, *Skylab*'s observations of Comet Kohoutek indicated the presence of exotic molecules such as methyl cyanide (CH_3CN) and hydrogen cyanide (HCN), which have also been detected in interstellar clouds. These findings further supported the idea that the comets represent original accretions from the solar nebula. Currently there are several proposals for rendezvousing with, and possibly "landing" an instrumented probe on, a short-period comet such as Tempel II or Comet Encke; but no comet mission has yet been funded. At present, the only direct means we have of investigating comets is by studying the meteoric dust that sifts down on high, snowcapped mountains. This dust is thought to be what is left after a periodic comet makes enough close passes of the Sun to exhaust its ice supply. A number of meteor showers occur annually when Earth crosses the orbits of long-dead comets.

A bright meteor from the Geminid swarm streaks past the constellation Orion (above center) and fades away near the right-hand edge of this two-minute time exposure, which was taken shortly after 2:00 A.M. PST, on the morning of December 13, 1980.
(*Photo by author*)

SOME RELIABLE METEOR SHOWERS

Name	Average hourly rate	Usual date
Quadrantids	40	January 3
Perseids	50	August 12
Orionids	20	October 15–25
Geminids	60	December 9–13

Note: Meteor showers draw their names from the constellation from which they appear to emanate. The greatest number of meteors can usually be observed after local midnight, when Earth is turning into the direction of its orbit.

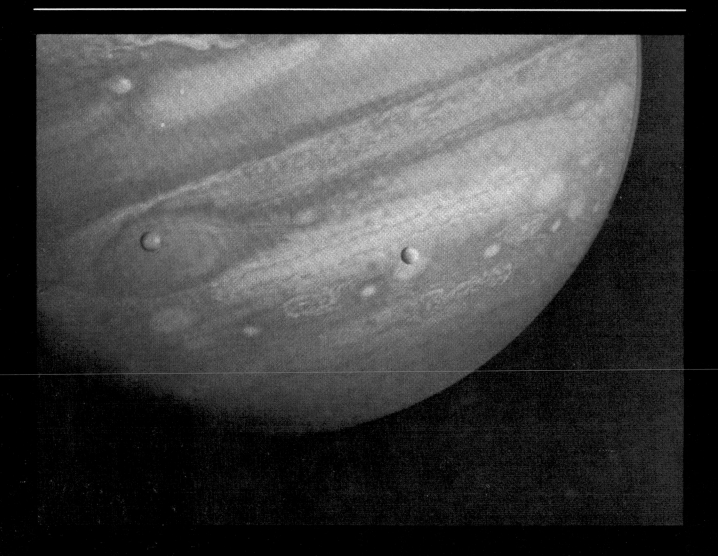

OUR PROBE HAS ENTERED THE ATMOSPHERE
on the night side of the planet, and we are enveloped by
darkness and the sound of rushing wind. Even though we
have jettisoned the heat shield, exposing the down-facing
windows, we can see little; our eyes are still dazzled by the
entry fireball.

Gradually, forms become discernible beyond the thick
viewports. We seem to be suspended above a sea of clouds.
At first the scene seems quite familiar; we could be in a jet
flying over a moonlit cloudscape back on Earth. But as
minutes pass and   we have fallen
nearly 100 '   rence in
scale: e. The
line   would
dwarf the   re than
2000 kilomete.

Suddenly the world below is transfixed by a searing,
blue-white flash. Through a rent in the cloud cover, we
glimpse several more lightning bolts. A storm is raging
below. We wait tensely for thunder. In a world this huge,
driven by such vast energy, it should be deafening. We
brace ourselves for a basso profundo roar, but the thunder,
when it finally arrives, is nothing more than a loud, high-
pitched crackle. The hydrogen atmosphere has robbed it of
its authority.

A jet stream carries our falling spacecraft past the storm.
The mountainous cloud tops are much closer now, and our
attention is riveted below. One crew member happens to
glance upward, however, and she gasps in delight: half-a-
dozen moons are clustered in the sky, and ghostly red
auroral curtains flicker about them. While we watch, two

Facing page
A Solar System in Miniature. One of the most
spectacular images of the space age is this one,
which shows the Galilean satellites Io *(left)* and
Europa floating before the dramatic backdrop of
their primary, Jupiter. Io appears directly in
front of the Great Red Spot, an immense
cyclonic disturbance that has been raging in the
Jovian atmosphere for at least 300 years. Dozens
of smaller, generally whitish spots of a similar
nature are also apparent, as are the dark belts
and light zones that girdle the solar system's
biggest planet. *(NASA photo)*

Exploring Jupiter. One scheme suggested for
manned exploration of the giant planet
involves the use of a vehicle combining the
characteristics of a spacecraft, a hot-air balloon,
a bathyscaphe, and a jet plane. After entering
the Jovian atmosphere via heat shield, and
using parachutes for further braking, the craft
would deploy a balloon filled with the one
substance lighter than Jupiter's hydrogen
atmosphere: *hot* hydrogen. After completing
their survey of the upper cloud levels, the
explorers would cut their craft loose from the
balloon and plunge into the denser air below,
gathering speed as the exterior pressure
mounted, until their nuclear ram-jet became
functional. Upon gaining thrust, the craft
would climb until the jet failed, at which point
rocket engines would be ignited to boost the
ship back into orbit. *(Art by author)*

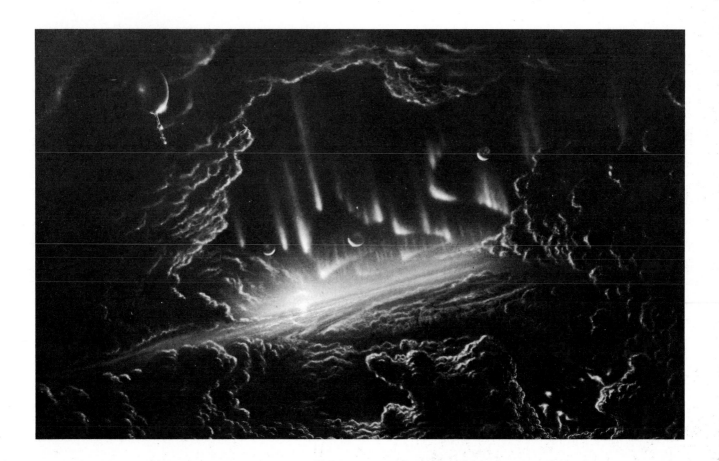

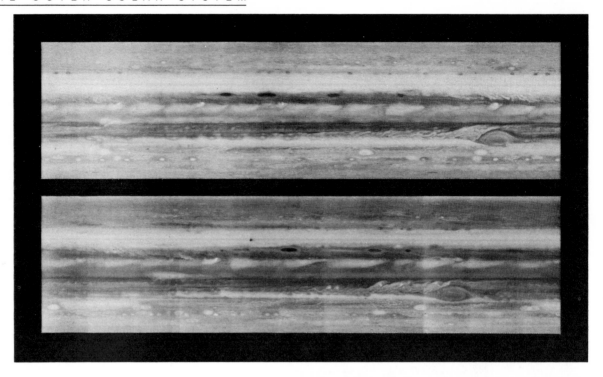

Changes in Jupiter's turbulent atmosphere are shown in these cylindrical projections of images taken by *Voyager I* during one ten-hour rotation of the planet *(top)*, in February 1979, and photographed again by *Voyager II* in June of that year. The Great Red Spot has moved westward, and the white oval features have moved eastward, during the interval between the two pictures. The regular plume patterns near the equator and the recirculating flows near the Great Red Spot have also changed. *(NASA photos)*

The tip of Jupiter's ring is clearly shown in the *Voyager II* photo at right. The thin haze of particles contained within the main part of the ring apparently continues into the cloudtops of Jupiter. *(NASA photo)*

Facing page
Jupiter's thin ring was imaged while the *Voyager II* spacecraft was over the night side of the planet. The rings appear orange, which is to be expected if they are composed of dust and rock that scatter sunlight. In this photograph, the rings disappear into Jupiter's shadow before arcing in front of the Near Side of the planet. *(NASA photo)*

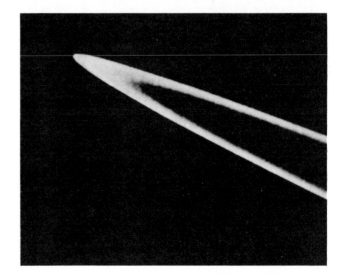

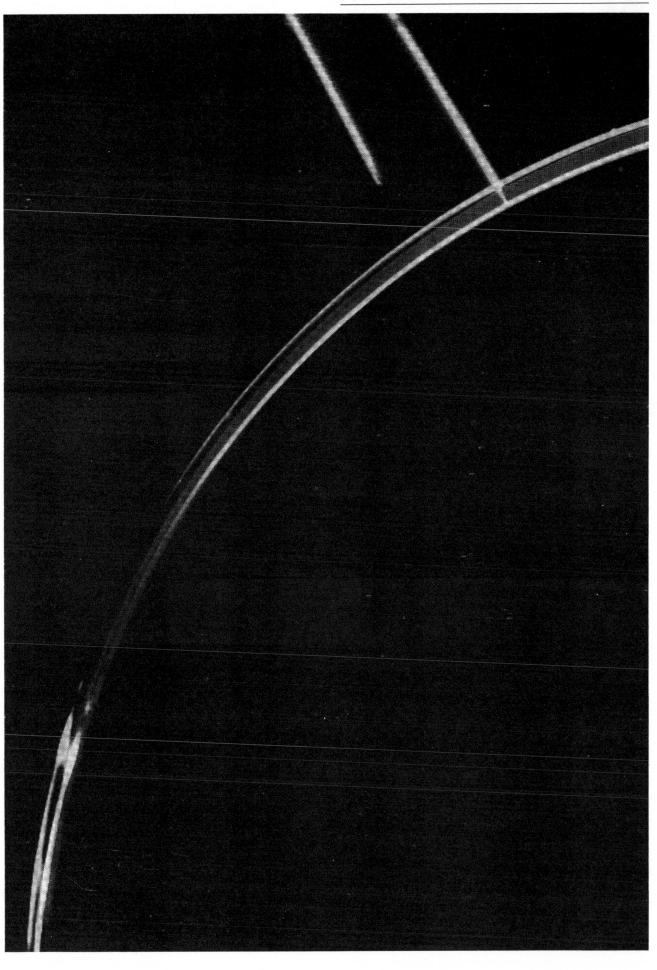

bright meteors streak across the scene. It is a spectacular light show; and as our craft slowly rotates toward the East, there is even more: above a horizon glowing blue with the promise of dawn, we see a golden sliver of light, arching toward the zenith. It is the Jovian Ring, catching the rays of the still-hidden sun . . .

It is appropriate that the fifth planet bears the name of the king of Roman gods. Jupiter is so huge that there is little in our experience with which to compare it. Its volume is more than a thousand times that of Earth, and its equatorial circumference is greater than the distance from the Earth to the Moon. If Jupiter had a solid surface, the horizon would be 17 kilometers from an observer of average height, compared to less than 5 kilometers on Earth. By itself, one of Jupiter's cyclonic storm systems, such as the Great Red Spot, is large enough to swallow Earth with hardly a splash. Jupiter is more than twice as massive as all the other planets combined, and it was instrumental in shaping the rest of the solar system. Its disruptive gravitational influence robbed Mars of the mass that could have made that planet Earthlike; prevented the asteroids from accreting into a single body; and cast the remaining planetesimals into the Oort Cloud. Jupiter controls a family of at least 17 satellites, 2 of which are the size of Mercury, and boasts a

Resembling an abstract painting, this photo taken by *Voyager 1* at a distance of 5 million kilometers shows Jupiter's Great Red Spot and the turbulent region immediately to the west. At the middle right of the frame is one of several white ovals that can be seen on Jupiter from Earth. The smallest details that can be seen in this photo are approximately 95 kilometers across. *(NASA photo)*

system of rings. Its liquid interior and rapid rotation create a dynamo effect, and the resulting magnetic field interacts with the solar wind and the innermost satellites in a complex manner, generating periodic radio emissions and some unique geochemical processes on its satellites.

In many respects, Jupiter is more like a star than a planet. It is a source of heat, radiating more than twice as much energy as it receives from the Sun. The additional heat is probably caused by Jupiter's slow, continuing gravitational collapse, and it is more important than solar radiation in influencing the weather systems on Jupiter. The planet is chemically similar to the Sun, consisting primarily of hydrogen. The relative abundances of the elements now found on Jupiter are thought to be identical to those extant in the solar nebula; unlike Earth and the other terrestrial planets, Jupiter was able to retain its original composition when the T-Tauri solar wind stripped the inner planets of their lighter gases.

Jupiter's low density, great bulk, and rapid rotational period (10 hours) combine to give it such a pronounced equatorial bulge that its polar diameter is nearly 5000 kilometers less than its equatorial diameter. Its nearly 23,000-kilometers-per-hour maximum linear velocity tends to smear the effects of solar heating, with the result that there is little temperature difference between the day and night hemispheres. Rotation also stretches out weather systems, giving Jupiter its banded appearance. The first evidence of Jupiter's nonsolid nature came when it was discovered, quite early in the history of telescopic study of the planet, that clouds at higher latitudes tended to lag behind those nearer the equator. In fact, Jupiter is essentially a huge ball of liquid hydrogen, and only the upper 500 kilometers of its atmosphere are directly observable.

Jovian winds constantly change the appearance of the planet. Although individual clouds in the atmosphere are long-lived, winds blow at greatly different speeds at different latitudes, causing the clouds to move independently and pass each other. The photo on the left was taken on January 4, 1979, while the one on the right was obtained on May 9, 1979. One of the white ovals, located southwest of the Great Red Spot, has drifted to a point 60 degrees east, permitting another feature, which was originally to the west, to move just below the Red Spot. The bright tongue extending upward from the Red Spot is interacting with a thin bright cloud that has traveled around Jupiter twice in four months. *(NASA photos)*

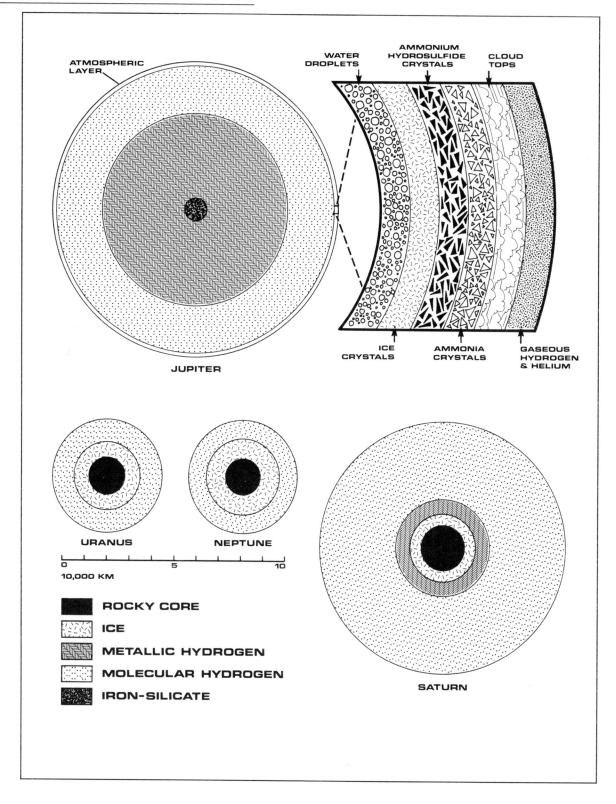

ATMOSPHERIC LAYER

WATER DROPLETS

AMMONIUM HYDROSULFIDE CRYSTALS

CLOUD TOPS

ICE CRYSTALS

AMMONIA CRYSTALS

GASEOUS HYDROGEN & HELIUM

JUPITER

URANUS

NEPTUNE

0   5   10
10,000 KM

ROCKY CORE
ICE
METALLIC HYDROGEN
MOLECULAR HYDROGEN
IRON-SILICATE

SATURN

The four giant worlds that orbit in the outer reaches of our solar system are gaseous and liquid bodies largely composed of hydrogen and helium. *(Diagram by Michael Standlee Design)*

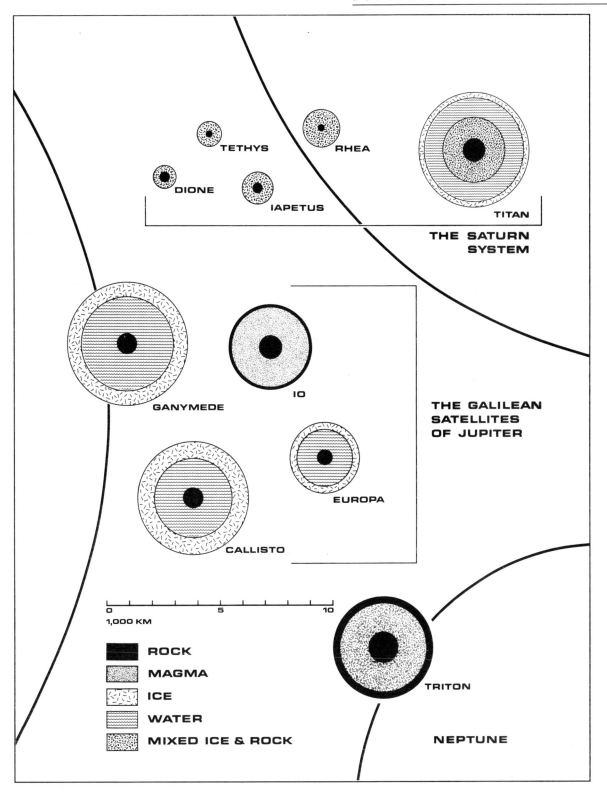

TETHYS

RHEA

DIONE

IAPETUS

TITAN

THE SATURN SYSTEM

GANYMEDE

IO

THE GALILEAN SATELLITES OF JUPITER

CALLISTO

EUROPA

0   5   10

1,000 KM

ROCK

MAGMA

ICE

WATER

MIXED ICE & ROCK

TRITON

NEPTUNE

Though outer satellites are comparable in size to the inner planets, they are very different sorts of bodies. Their crusts are generally composed of ice, which floats on a mantle of liquid water and ammonia.
(Diagram by Michael Standlee Design)

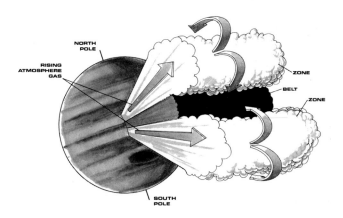

Convection Patterns in the Jovian Atmosphere. Warm air rises in the white zones, cools, and then falls back into the dark lower belts. (*Diagram by Michael Standlee Design*)

These clouds, revealed in all their spectacular color by the *Voyager* cameras, are primarily composed of ammonia ice crystals at high altitudes, and crystals of ammonium hydrosulfide at lower levels. While the white ammonia clouds are probably similar to the wispy cirrus clouds of Earth, the lower, dark-colored clouds seem to be more substantial. Such clouds cast distinct shadows when near the terminator, suggesting that they may be analogous to terrestrial cumulus or nimbus clouds. The alternating pattern of light zones and dark belts between the poles is caused by heat convecting out from Jupiter's interior. The atmosphere is, in essence, boiling, but rapid rotation imposes order on the process. Warm air rises in the light zones, lofting ammonia vapor high into the atmosphere, where it condenses as ice. As this ammonia cirrus cools, it falls into the neighboring dark belts. Operating like a series of fountains, the light zones provide the mechanism whereby Jupiter releases its heat.

Within the Jovian bands, there are numerous circular and oval features, most famous of which is the Great Red Spot. This feature has endured for at least 300 years, and appears to be an immense cyclonic storm towering above the surrounding clouds. Smaller spots, usually colored white or bluish gray, occur at regular intervals along each band. These are caused by standing waves in Jupiter's atmosphere.

The variegated colors of Jupiter's clouds bespeak a complex atmospheric chemistry. The range of warm colors — from yellow and brown to brick red — is probably attributable to the presence of a number of sulfur compounds, such as ammonium hydrosulfide (NH_4SH), ammonium sulfide ($[NH_4]_2S$), molecular sulfur, and a number of ammonium hydrosulfide polymers. At a depth of about 800 kilometers, there are probably clouds of water ice, and, below that, falling drops of liquid water. Because this level of Jupiter's atmosphere bears a striking resemblance to the mix of gases thought to have been present on the ancient Earth, it has been suggested that the prebiological stages of chemical evolution may be taking place on Jupiter. The continuous convection to lower, hot levels of the atmosphere, of any complex organics that might form, would tend to destroy them periodically, preventing further steps toward life. It is an intriguing possibility, however, that such chemical evolution might proceed further in the similar, but possibly less turbulent, atmospheres of the other gas giants, Saturn, Uranus, and Neptune.

At a depth of about 1000 kilometers below the cloud-tops, we encounter a boiling sea of liquid hydrogen. Perhaps half a Jupiter radius further in, the immense pressure would compress hydrogen into a metallic, liquid form. This metallic liquid probably gives way to a small, Earth-sized core of rock and metal.

THE MOONS OF JUPITER

When Galileo turned his homemade telescope toward Jupiter in the winter of 1610, he discovered four tiny "stars" circling the planet and concluded, correctly, that they were moons, bound to Jupiter as our own Moon is bound to Earth. This first evidence of nongeocentric motion provided support for the Sun-centered Copernican model of celestial mechanics. More than four centuries passed, however, before the Galilean satellites could be seen as anything more than small disks in the telescope. It remained for the twin spacecraft *Voyager I* and *Voyager II* to reveal these fascinating worlds.

The Jovian system has often been described as a miniature solar system. In addition to the fact that the Jovian system comprises a huge primary attended by a number of lesser satellites, Jupiter and its Galilean satellites present an interesting evolutionary parallel to the Sun and the terrestrial planets. The Galileans, like the inner planets, show a decrease in density as they orbit farther away from their primary, and for the same reason: both the Sun and Jupiter radiated immense amounts of heat during their

The Four Galilean Satellites of Jupiter. Io *(top left)*, Europa *(top right)*, Ganymede *(bottom left)*, and Callisto are shown in their correct relative sizes. Ganymede and Callisto are both larger than Mercury, while Io and Europa are about the same size as our Moon. Io is covered with active volcanoes and has a surface composed largely of sulfur. Europa is very different, and its icy crust is scored by hundreds of thin linear grooves. Ganymede and Callisto are primarily composed of water and have large quantities of ice on their surfaces. *(NASA photo)*

Map 4

PRELIMINARY PICTORIAL MAP OF IO

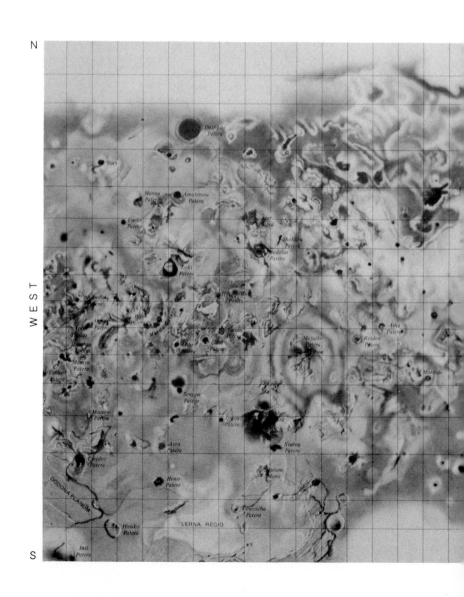

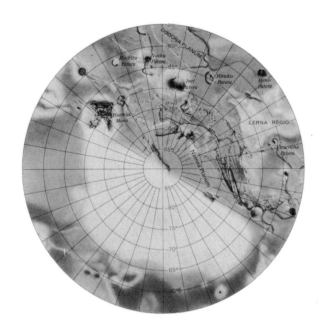

SOUTH POLAR REGION

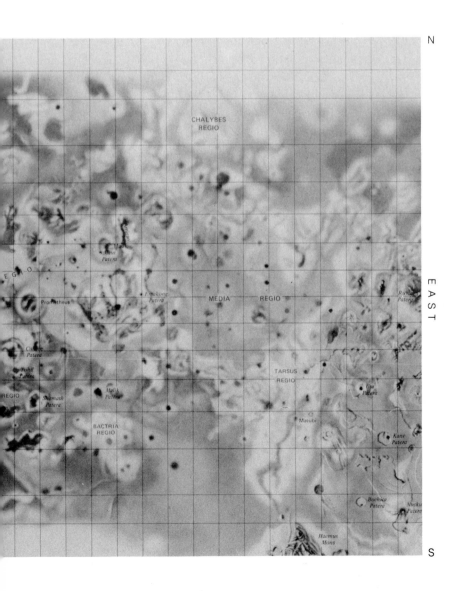

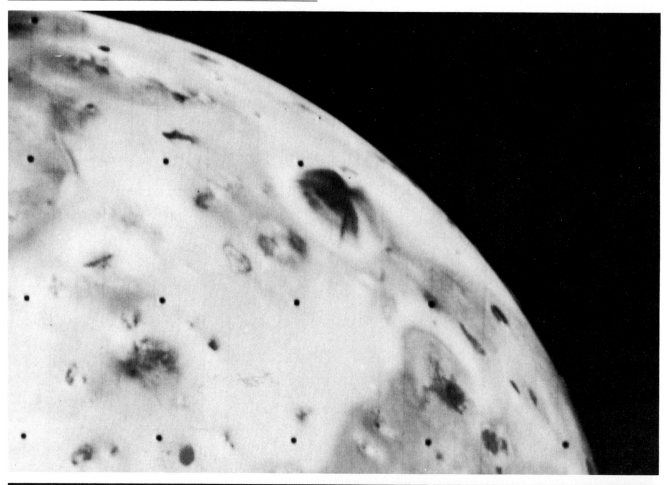

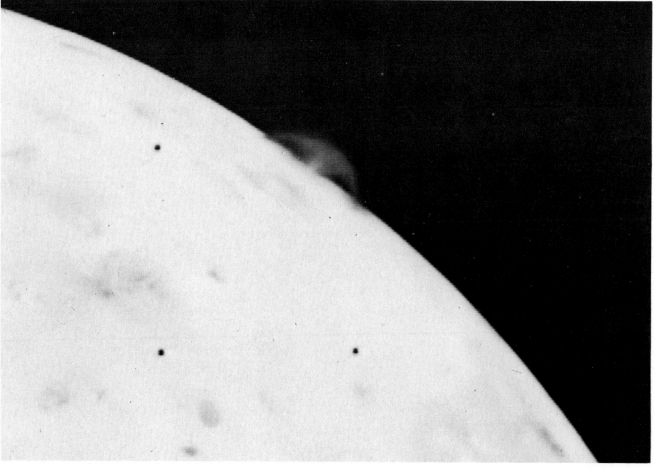

periods of accretion, and this heat baked out the lighter materials in their satellites. The closer a satellite orbited, the more likely it was to end up with a disproportionate amount of heavy materials. The main difference between the two systems is one of degree: whereas the Sun boiled Mercury's rocks, Jupiter generated only enough heat to boil Io's ices.

Even before *Voyager*'s cameras showed the explosive eruptions on Io, it had been predicted that Io would exhibit extensive volcanism. This prediction was based on the fact that the periodic gravitational tugging of the other satellites causes Io to move slightly, in and out, in its orbit. The resulting change in Jupiter's tidal effect causes Io to flex like an automobile tire. The tremendous heat produced by this flexing keeps Io's interior molten.

Io demonstrates a wide range of other fascinating phenomena. The gravitational flexing caused all the ice originally trapped within the satellite to melt and percolate to the surface. As the water evaporated into space, it left behind beds of dissolved minerals, especially sodium chloride, or table salt. Were it not for the fact that Io orbits near the most intense part of Jupiter's radiation belts, these salt flats would merely add some variety to the satellite's surface. But intense radiation breaks down the bonds within the crystals and causes sodium ions to sputter into space, where they form a halo around Io and along its orbit. The excitation of this cloud by solar and local radiation causes it to glow, so that to an observer on Io, the sky would be filled with flickering, golden auroras.

Facing page
These two photos represent the first evidence of active volcanism outside of Earth. The first picture shows an umbrella-like plume rising 100 kilometers above the surface of Io. The second, taken about two hours later, shows the same plume silhouetted against the black of space. Measurements made with the *Voyager* infrared radiometer indicate that this and similar features are several hundred degrees hotter than the surrounding terrain. *(NASA photos)*

Below left
Two volcanoes on a crescent Io flare a luminous blue in this *Voyager II* photo. *Voyager I* had observed both in eruption four months earlier. *(NASA photo)*

Below right
Illuminated by the light of a nearly full Jupiter, the night hemisphere of Io is faintly visible in this *Voyager I* photo. A volcanic plume rises 260 kilometers above the limb of the satellite, while another catches the rays of the rising Sun, just beyond the terminator. *(NASA photo)*

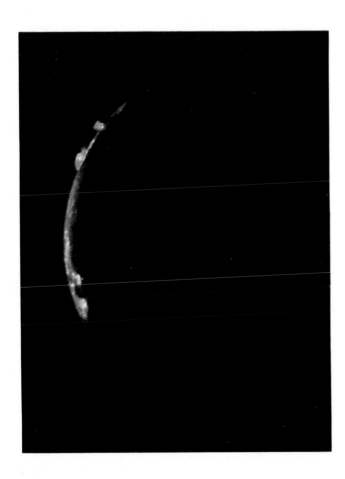

Io. A number of active volcanoes are apparent in this *Voyager I* image of Io. The circular, doughnut-shaped feature in the center is the expanding shell of gas surrounding a volcano. Io's volcanic activity is of two varieties: explosive eruptions that can spew material upward as far as 250 kilometers, and lava that flows from vents across the surface. *(NASA photo)*

This sodium-ion cloud produces other spectacular special effects. Just as moving a magnet through a wire loop causes a current to flow in the wire, so the sweep of Jupiter's magnetic field through Io's ionosphere causes a current to flow between Io and Jupiter. The potential across the loop is 200,000 volts, and the current is 5 million amperes, giving a power of 10^{12} watts. There was some fear that *Voyager I* might trigger some sort of discharge as it flew through this flux tube connecting Io and Jupiter, but fortunately nothing happened.

Moving outward from Io, we encounter the straw-colored satellite Europa. It bears a striking resemblance to Percival Lowell's drawings of Mars, for Europa's icy crust is fractured, and the resulting cracks sometimes run in straight, canal-like lines for hundreds of kilometers. There are few impact craters on Europa, indicating that the surface is young and that there is probably a combination of tidal and radioactive heating that keeps the crust in a plastic state. Unlike Io, Europa is unable to support high topographical features.

Ganymede, Jupiter's largest satellite, with its dark, circular plains and bright-rayed craters, bears some superficial resemblance to our Moon, but it is a world of an entirely different sort. Its thick crust of intermingled rock and ice

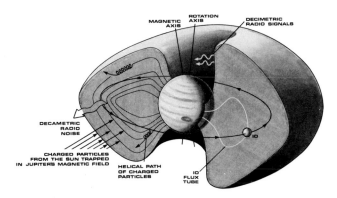

Eclipse Seen from Io. Io can spend as long as two hours in the shadow of Jupiter. Some observers have noticed that Io seems to be brighter for a few minutes following eclipses, and they have suggested that Io's surface may become cold enough to freeze out a thin "snow" of atmospheric sulfur dioxide, which sublimes when warmed by the Sun. *(Art by author)*

Left

The Io Flux Tube. Io's motion through the Jovian magnetic field causes a current of some 5 million amps to flow through the conducting loop formed by Io's ionosphere and the cloud of charged particles trapped in Jupiter's radiation belt, making the Moon-sized satellite a natural generator. This electromagnetic interaction also triggers decametric radio bursts that can be detected on Earth.
(Diagram by Michael Standlee Design)

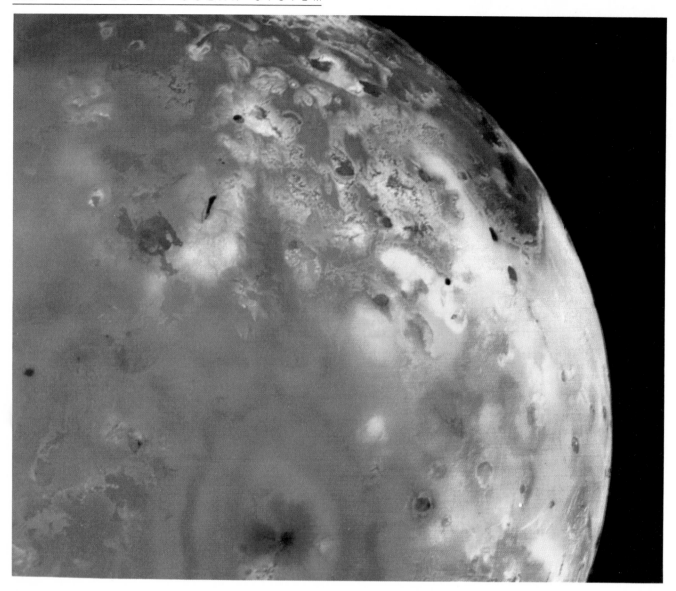

The reddish, white, and black areas are surface deposits of salt, sulfur, and volcanic ash. The lack of impact features on Io indicates that the surface is quite young and is continually being reshaped by internal forces. Surface features changed noticeably in the four-month interval between the *Voyager* visits. *(NASA photo)*

Facing page, top
Volcanic Vapor. The green blue patch at the upper right seems to be a cloud of gas, probably sulfur dioxide, venting from a volcanic caldera. Particles of this gas are likely to condense quickly and fall to the surface as snow. Black areas in the floors of some calderas are probably pools of molten sulfur. *(NASA photo)*

Facing page, bottom
As Europa formed, it was so strongly heated by the heat of Jupiter's collapse that it may have briefly experienced Earthlike conditions, permitting shallow and temporary seas to develop. *(Art by author)*

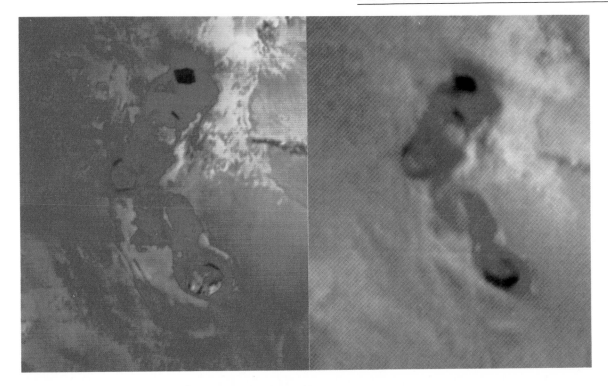

Map 5

PRELIMINARY PICTORIAL MAP OF EUROPA

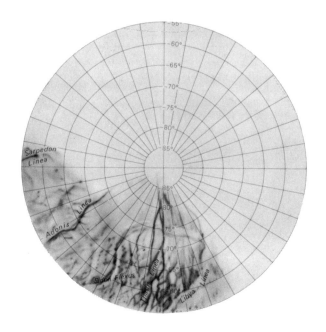

SOUTH POLAR REGION

NORTH

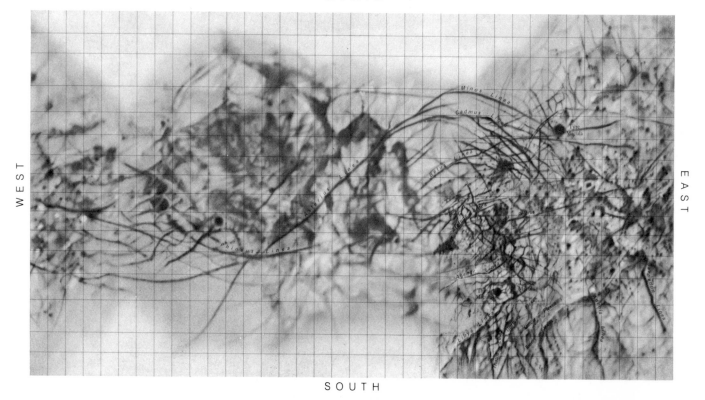

WEST

EAST

SOUTH

Map 6

PRELIMINARY PICTORIAL MAP OF GANYMEDE

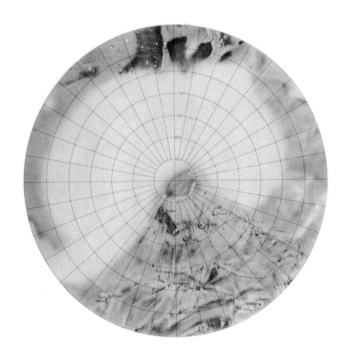

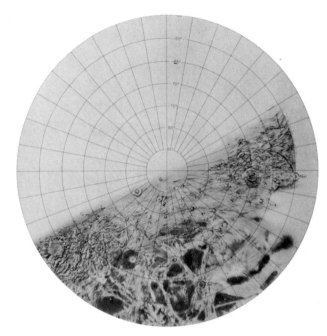

NORTH POLAR REGION

SOUTH POLAR REGION

NORTH

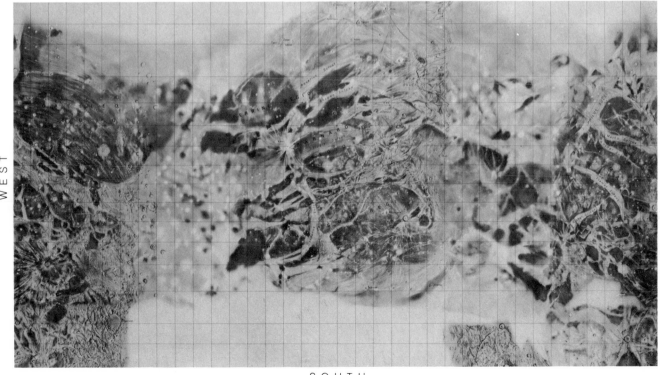

WEST

EAST

SOUTH

Ganymede, the largest Galilean satellite, is shown at left in a photograph taken by *Voyager II* at a range of 1.2 million kilometers. The bright dots on the surface are relatively recent impact craters, while lighter circular areas may be older impact areas. The light, branching bands are ridged and grooved terrain that is probably younger than the more heavily cratered dark regions. The nature of the bright area covering the northern part of the dark circular feature is uncertain, but it may be some type of condensate. Most of the features seen on the surface of Ganymede have probably been created by internal and external forces acting on the thick icy layer that comprises the crust of the satellite. *(NASA photo)*

Facing page, top
Europa, smallest of the Galileans, is here imaged in a photograph taken by *Voyager II* on July 9, 1979, from a range of 241,000 kilometers. Europa is the brightest of the satellites and has a density slightly less than that of Io, which suggests that it has retained a reasonable amount of water. The water probably forms a mantle of ice, with interior slush that is perhaps 100 kilometers deep. The network of cracks in Europa's icy surface differs from the pattern of fault systems found on Ganymede, where pieces of the crust have moved in relation to one another. Europa's crust apparently fractures, but the sections remain in their original positions. *(NASA photo)*

Facing page, bottom
Viewed from the bottom of one of the thousands of icy fissures that crisscross the second large Jovian moon, Europa, a waning Jupiter looms larger than 200 full Moons, while the volcanic satellite Io transits.
(Art by author)

Map 7

PRELIMINARY PICTORIAL MAP OF CALLISTO

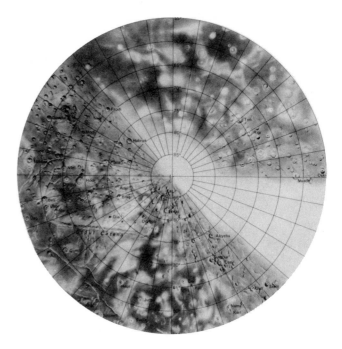

NORTH POLAR REGION

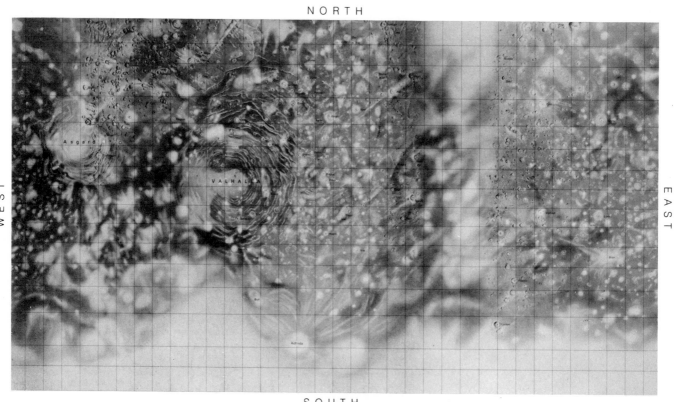

floats on a mantle of water that is kept liquid by the heat of radioactive decay in the rocky core. The slow convection of the slushy interface between crust and mantle causes slippage along cracks and forces the flow of fresh "clean" ice from below, giving Ganymede its piebald aspect. Occasional impacts expose the bright subsurface ice.

Callisto seems to be the most heavily cratered body in the solar system. Its icy crust is apparently very thick and very ancient, and has been shaped primarily by impacts. Even the violent collision that formed the huge, bull's-eye feature that dominates one hemisphere apparently failed to fracture the crust at a level deep enough to permit the flow of new ice from below. Though contrast-enhanced photos of Callisto suggest a rugged surface, its limb and terminator are very smooth. Its crust, like that of Europa and

Close-up of Ganymede. Several bright, young impact craters are shown in this photo of the region 30°S, 180°W. The light-colored terrain may be the result of shearing of the surface along fault lines. The dark areas are ancient cratered terrain. The smallest features shown here are only about 6 kilometers across. *(NASA photo)*

Tiny red Amalthea whizzes around Jupiter every 12 hours, only 110,000 kilometers above the cloudtops. This partially illuminated satellite appears to be about 130 kilometers high and 170 kilometers long. Amalthea only reflects about 10 percent of the incident light, making it darker than the larger satellites. The little moon's irregular shape bespeaks a history of cratering, and its brick-red color may be a coating on the surface. *(NASA photo)*

Ganymede, does not support massive structures, so surface contours would tend to be soft and flowing.

Fascinating as the Galileans are, the harsh Jovian radiation environment will probably preclude the manned exploration of any but Callisto. One would hope that in the not too distant future we can dispatch *Surveyor*-type spacecraft to land on them, however. These icy planets are totally unlike anything in our experience, and they deserve further study.

Of the other satellites, only tiny Amalthea, which orbits a scant 100,000 kilometers above Jupiter's clouds, was photographed in any detail by the *Voyager* spacecraft. This lumpy, roughly 200-kilometer-wide body probably has a rocky composition, but its distinct brick-red color is suspiciously reminiscent of the Red Spot and Io. Whether Amalthea's color, too, can be attributed to organic sulfides remains to be seen.

Unlike Saturn, which seems to have given birth to a litter of fair-sized satellites, Jupiter has only five or six satellites (the innermost ones) that seem to be native to the Jovian system. The rest are apparently captured asteroids, only a few kilometers across. Stray asteroids and comets must wander into Jupiter's immense gravitational well quite often, but they tend to be temporary guests; satellites more than 20 million kilometers from Jupiter will eventually resume independent orbits, because of perturbations caused by other planets.

An observer on tiny Amalthea, Jupiter's inner satellite, would have a view of the giant planet's weather that is unmatched elsewhere in the Jovian system. *(Art by author)*

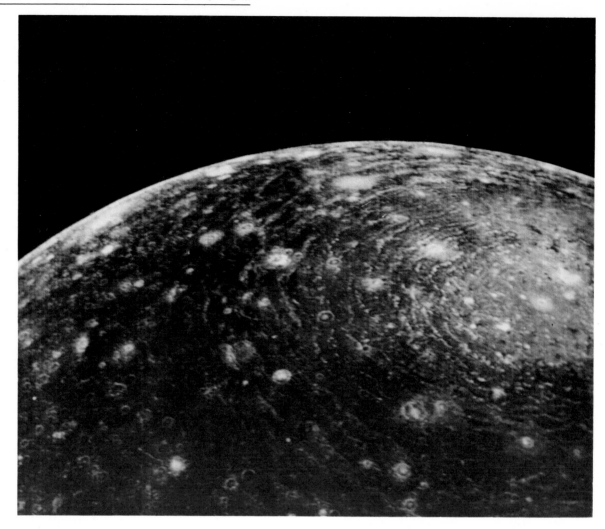

Callisto. The outer Galilean satellite is only
slightly smaller than Ganymede and is
apparently composed of a mixture of ice and
rock. The darker color of Callisto suggests that
its surface is either dirty ice or water-rich rock
frozen by the low temperatures (120°K) that
prevail in this part of the solar system. The
prominent bull's-eye feature is believed to be an
impact basin similar to the Mare Orientale on
the Moon, or Mercury's Caloris Basin.
(NASA photo)

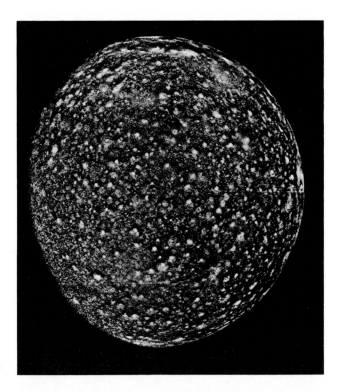

Craters on Callisto. The impact-crater distribution on Callisto is uniform across the disk. The bright-rayed craters are probably quite young, and the large, circular impact feature near the limb has about 15 concentric rings surrounding the bright central region. In keeping with Callisto's icy, plastic crust, the limb is very smooth. *(NASA photo)*

Below
Callisto's Icy Landscape. The surface of Jupiter's outermost Galilean satellite seems to be a mixture of pulverized ice and rock.
(Art by author)

BECAUSE ITS THIRTY-YEAR-LONG ORBITAL period carries it slowly among the constellations, Saturn was probably the last of the five classical planets to be discovered in antiquity. Its plodding motion must have suggested the infirmities of old age to early astronomers, for Saturn has generally borne this pessimistic association in astrological lore. As is usually the case with astrology, more data might have changed the conclusions; had an astronomer of Ptolemy's time been vouchsafed a glimpse through a telescope, he probably would have promptly renamed Saturn after the prevailing goddess of beauty. Saturn's glorious system of rings makes it the jewel of the solar system.

Although Saturn is only about twice as distant from Earth as is Jupiter, it is much more than twice as difficult to study telescopically. Virtually everything we can learn about a planet comes from analysis of the sunlight reflected from its surface or cloudtops, and because Saturn is so far from the Sun, it is very dimly lit. Each square centimeter of the Sun's surface radiates some 1.6×10^{22} photons into space every second.* After the 90-minute journey to Jupiter's clouds and back to Earth, this flux has been reduced to 5.8×10^7 photons per square centimeter per second — an attenuation factor of 280 trillion. Yet this is still 16 times more light than we receive from Saturn.

If we may compare the amount of information carried by Jupiter's light to a cup of chicken soup, then light from Saturn is like a cup of soup stock that has been "stretched" with 15 cups of water — not a particularly nourishing broth. Nevertheless, a great deal had been learned about Saturn even before the space age. In 1611, Galileo's fairly primitive telescope revealed that there was something odd about Saturn, and he speculated that Saturn might have "handles," or two very large nearby satellites. By observing Saturn with a superior instrument, the Dutch astronomer Christian Huygens was able to discover, in 1655, that the planet is encircled by "a thin, flat ring, not connected to the globe at any point." Later observers, such as Gian Cassini, found that the ring system was actually composed of at least three concentric rings, the outer two of which were separated by a narrow, apparently empty gap.

The multiplicity of these rings, together with the fact that they are semitransparent, suggested to some observers that the rings were not solid, and in 1857 James Clerk

---

Facing page
Arching like a rainbow, Saturn's ring system — seen here from just above Saturn's clouds, at 30 degrees north latitude — provides one of the most spectacular sights in nature. During the course of each revolution about the Sun, a given point on Saturn's surface may be darkened for years at a time by the shadow cast by the rings. This point will again see sunlight only when the changing orientation of Saturn's rotation axis with respect to the Sun causes the immense shadow to move ponderously northward or southward. But once every 15 years, on the average, the Sun shines briefly through Cassini's division, providing a respite from the long eclipse. Wispy clouds of frozen methane, high in Saturn's atmosphere, may refract sunlight to produce prismatic halos. *(Art by author)*

---

* In order to deal more conveniently with numbers that are, appropriately, astronomical in size, scientists use a kind of shorthand called scientific notation. A moderately sized number, such as the radius of the asteroid Pallas — 600 kilometers — could be expressed as $6 \times 10 \times 10$, or, by using exponents, as 6.0×10^2 (read: six-point-zero times ten-to-the-second). A larger number, 6000 for instance, is equal to $6 \times 10 \times 10 \times 10$ or 6.0×10^3 (six-point-zero times ten-to-the-third). By convention, the decimal point is moved enough places to leave one significant figure to its left. Thus a really big number, such as the number of kilometers in a light-year, 9,460,000,000,000 — more than 9 *trillion* — could be written 9.46×10^{12}.

Scientific notation works well in dealing with the very small, also. The wavelength of the hydrogen-alpha emission band is 0.0000006563 meter. To express the number in scientific notation, we move the decimal point seven places to the *right* and make the exponent negative, thus: 6.563×10^{-7}.

Saturn, sixth and most spectacular of the Sun's planets, was 5.3 million kilometers away from *Voyager 1* when this photo was taken on November 16, 1980 — four days after the spacecraft's closest approach to Saturn. The planet's shadow falls across the rings, while the rings themselves cast a shadow near Saturn's equator. The illuminated hemisphere of the planet can be glimpsed through all but the densest parts of the ring system. *(NASA photo)*

Maxwell demonstrated that no known substance would be able to withstand the tidal stresses that existed between the outer and inner portions of the system. In 1895, J. E. Keeler observed that the inner portion of the rings completed a revolution about Saturn in 4 hours, while the outer edge required 14 hours. These periods correspond exactly to the orbital periods of satellites at the respective distances of the inner and outer ring boundaries, proving that the rings are, in fact, composed of billions of tiny satellites, each following its own orbit about Saturn. The brightness of the rings in both radar and optical wavelengths strongly suggests that these myriad satellites are composed of ice, and the fact that the rings essentially disappear when we view them edge-on indicates that the system is probably less than 2 kilometers thick. This is 1/200,000 the diameter of the ring system. Above the microscopic level, no other structure in nature exhibits such geometrical perfection as Saturn's ring system. A scale model of the rings, cut from the paper of this book, would be 20 meters in diameter — approximately the distance from home plate to the pitcher's mound on a baseball diamond.

Perhaps what is most curious about Saturn's rings is the fact that they exist at all. If the rings were the result of a

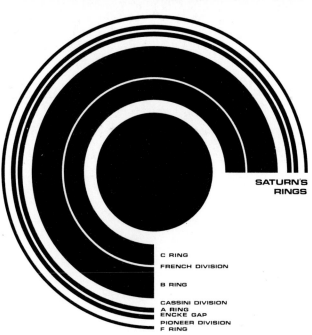

SATURN'S RINGS

C RING

FRENCH DIVISION

B RING

CASSINI DIVISION
A RING
ENCKE GAP
PIONEER DIVISION
F RING

Seen from Earth, only the largest features in Saturn's ring system can be photographed. *Voyager I* gathered more information during the few weeks it was in the vicinity of the planet than had been acquired in all of human history. *(Naval Observatory photo)*

Saturn's Rings Seen in Bird's-eye View. Six major rings, discovered through three centuries of telescopic observation and a preliminary reconnaissance by the spacecraft *Pioneer XI* in September 1978, have been named. Not shown here are the very tenuous *D* ring, which reaches to the planet's cloudtops, and the virtually invisible *E* ring, outside the *F* ring. *(Diagram by Michael Standlee Design)*

geologically recent tidal disruption of a satellite, or of a collision between satellites, their existence would be understandable. But the fact that Jupiter and Uranus also have rings suggests that Saturn's rings have existed since the beginning of the solar system. This is puzzling, because although such ring structures are probably inevitable concomitants of planetary formation, there are many processes that over the course of time should tend to destroy them. If, for example, the tiny icy satellites that comprise the rings began their careers with diameters smaller than a few centimeters, 4.5 billion years of solar ultraviolet radiation would have caused so many water molecules to sputter away from their surfaces that the particles would have, by

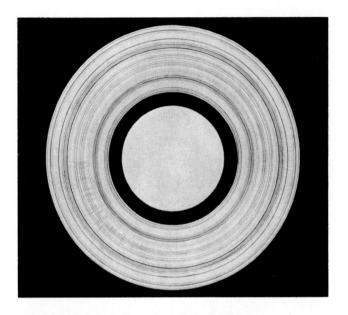

A thousand more rings were discovered by *Voyager 1.* Contrast has been exaggerated in this diagram, to bring out the finer ring divisions. *(Art by author)*

A two-image mosaic of the rings, taken by *Voyager 1* at a range of 8 million kilometers, shows at least 95 concentric features. The newly discovered fourteenth satellite of Saturn is visible just above the "tip" of the ring, as is the irregular 150-kilometer-wide *F* ring. *(NASA photo)*

now, eroded to nothing. Long before this happened, however, the pressure of sunlight and the electromagnetic forces exerted on the rings as they spin through Saturn's magnetic field would have forced the ring particles to spiral into the planet. Even though the ring particles are large (the absorption of *Voyager*'s radio signal as it passed behind the *C* ring suggested that most of the particles were on the order of a meter in diameter), the slight deviations from perfectly circular orbits, and the resulting collisions, should have caused the rings to slowly spread outward, diffusing into space. But despite all these arguments against their durability, the rings are amazingly still there.

The photographs taken by *Voyager 1* provided a clue to solving this mystery. Only three major rings, identified by the letters *A, B,* and *C* (*A* being the outermost), can easily be observed or photographed from Earth. Although skilled observers using large telescopes under excellent conditions have charted many finer divisions within the major rings, these observations are difficult to confirm. As *Voyager* closed on Saturn, however, the rings exhibited a wealth of detail, right down to the resolving limits of the camera system. Bradforth Smith, the *Voyager* imaging team leader, reported that he tried to count the new rings and gave up at 500. The rings were found to resemble a long-playing phonograph record, complete with gaps between the selections.

This unexpected complexity, together with the fact that the "classical" rings and divisions manifested very sharp boundaries, suggested that the accepted theory of tidal resonances was not entirely adequate to explain the structure of the rings. According to this theory, the positions of ring divisions are dependent on simple, whole-number relationships between the orbital periods of ring particles and those of the other satellites. For example, a particle orbiting at the distance of the famous Cassini's division, between the *B* and *A* rings, will complete two revolutions about Saturn in the same amount of time that Saturn's moon Mimas completes one. This means that every other orbit, the ring particle in question will experience a slight gravitational tug from Mimas at the same point in the particle's orbit. The periodic tugging will eventually clear most particles out of this zone, and indeed Cassini's division is one of the least densely populated parts of the ring

The Orbiting Ice. Saturn's rings are composed of billions of chunks of ice, ranging in size from a few centimeters to several kilometers, each following an independent orbit about the planet. Large, irregular ring particles probably have their longest axis tidally locked toward Saturn, so that they complete a rotation in the same amount of time required for an orbit. The largest ring particles (10–100 kilometers in diameter) apparently play an important role in maintaining the structure of the ring system. (*Art by author*)

Computer enhancement of this photo taken by *Voyager I* on November 13, 1980, looking back toward the crescent Saturn, brings out fine structure in the tenuous *C* ring, the ring nearest the planet (save for the *D* ring, which is invisible in this image). Note how sunlight reflected from the rings illuminates Saturn's Night Side. *(NASA photo)*

system. But it is not completely empty; *Voyager*'s photos revealed no fewer than five minor rings within Cassini's division, and these were neither hazy nor diffuse, but sharp-edged, as if something quite substantial were keeping each ring precisely in place.

A possible explanation has been provided by the discovery that the *A* ring is bounded by a small satellite, designated S-15, that is approximately 800 kilometers in diameter. The *F* ring also has two tiny satellites associated with it. These ring-satellite associations could be attributed to coincidence, but the permanence and complexity of the rings can be explained quite nicely if we assume that these satellites are representative of a class of similarly sized bodies, several thousand of which are embedded in the rings. Such moons could act as gravitational "sheepdogs," worrying escaping ring particles back into their proper paths.

To understand how this process works, we must bear in mind that the farther out in the rings a particle orbits, the more slowly it will move. Particles in the *A* ring move with only about 30 percent the velocity of those in the *C* ring. But just as a boulder poised at the top of a hill has greater potential energy than one at the base, so satellites in high orbits have greater gravitational potential energy than those in lower orbits. If we add energy to a satellite

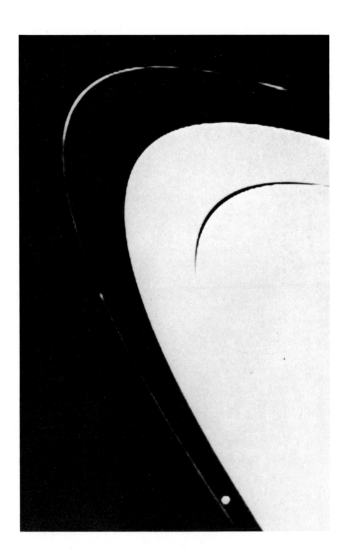

— by strapping a rocket engine to it, for instance — it will speed up and move to a higher orbit, where it moves more slowly. If we apply thrust in the opposite direction, the satellite will lose energy and drop to a lower orbit, where it moves more quickly. In either case, the energy scales will balance; the tendency of the satellite to "want" to fly off at a tangent, like a stone tossed from a sling, is exactly counterbalanced by the gravitational pull of the primary at a given altitude. Now suppose that a ring particle, through collisions or gravitational perturbations, has been nudged into a high-energy path that will carry it upward — away from Saturn. As it rises along its now-eccentric orbit, the ring particle will eventually overtake one of the "sheepdog" satellites, which will be moving more slowly. The sheepdog has its own gravitational field, albeit a weak one, and it will pull the fugitive ring particle toward itself. Since the embedded satellite is moving more slowly, the effect of this interaction is to slow the progress of the ring particle by robbing it of some energy. Its escape plans dashed, the ring particle then drops back. Now falling along an orbit that carries it closer to Saturn, it eventually will be overtaken by an embedded satellite moving more quickly in a lower orbit. This satellite's gravitational field will in effect add energy to the ring particle, nudging it into a higher orbit. Trapped in a game of gravitational Ping-Pong, the ring particle oscillates eter-

Left
"Clumping" in the *F* ring is revealed in this overexposed photograph. The *F* ring orbits near the outer boundaries of the Roche limit, within which it is believed that large satellites cannot form. Local clumping of material in this ring may represent a stage in the formation of satellites (although it is unlikely that the process proceeds much farther than this). S-14 is visible near the bottom of the picture, just inside the *F* ring. *(NASA photo)*

Right
High resolution of Saturn's *C* ring reveals that at least one of the minor ringlets has an eccentric orbit. The narrow, horizontal line marks the juxtaposition of two photos of different parts of the ring system that are approximately 180 degrees apart. While most of the fine ring divisions mate perfectly to their antipodal counterparts, the fine, bright ring contained within the first broad, dark division on the left does not; on one side of Saturn the ring is brighter and orbits approximately 100 kilometers farther out than on the other side. *(NASA photo)*

The thinnest of Saturn's rings resemble grooves in a phonograph record, in this photo taken eight hours after *Voyager*'s encounter with Saturn, when unique lighting conditions revealed the greatest amount of detail in the ring system. Major features are, from top to bottom, the bright, narrow *F* ring; the *A* ring (containing the narrow, dark Encke division); the dark Cassini's division; the bright, wide *B* ring; and the dark grayish *C* ring. The radial spokes, which before encounter appeared dark, are now bright, indicating that they are good forward scatterers of light and therefore composed of very fine particles. *(NASA photo)*

nally between the two embedded moons. Although *Voyager* was moving too rapidly during its closest approach to the rings to permit photography of any embedded satellites, postulating their existence is perhaps the best way to explain the durability of the rings.

Saturn's strong magnetic field also influences the appearance of the rings. As long ago as 1896, the great French visual astronomer E. M. Antoniadi sketched diffuse, dark, spokelike features in the rings, and time-lapse movies taken by *Voyager* during its approach indicate that these spokes indeed rotate through the morning side of the rings, giving the system the general appearance of a wagon wheel. While local inhomogeneities and clumping of the ring particles clearly mapped the differential orbital motion of the rings, the inner portions overtaking the outer, the spokes were puzzling in that they maintained their structures for periods of several hours — a fact seemingly at variance with the laws of orbital motion. The shear effect of differential

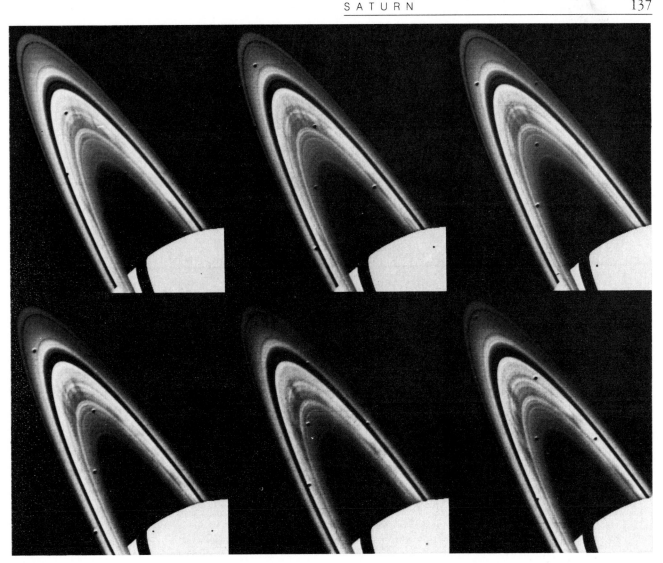

rotation should have broken up each spoke within a few minutes.

One clue to the mystery is the fact that the spokes are most prominent in the *B* ring, where particles orbit Saturn in approximately ten hours, the same amount of time as the rotational period of Saturn. This region is analogous to the 24-hour synchronous orbit favored for communication satellites 36,000 kilometers above Earth's equator; a satellite placed here will stay over the same point on the rotating planet's surface. A ring particle in the co-rotating position not only orbits over the same point on Saturn's globe, but within the same region of Saturn's magnetic field, and it is subject to whatever time-variant effects the field produces as it spins around the planet. When the "spoke" movie was computer-rectified to give a plain view of the rings, and then was permitted to run in the 10-hour-per-revolution, co-rotating mode, it was apparent that the spokes were indeed moving in accordance with the magnetic field.

Knowing this allows us to speculate on the physical nature of the spokes, although it will probably be years before the phenomenon is clearly understood. Charged subatomic particles in the solar wind, electrons in particular, are trapped by Saturn's magnetic field, and forced to

Dark, radial spokes rotate through the Morning Side of the rings in this sequence of *Voyager* images, taken at 15-minute intervals. (The sequence progresses from top left to bottom right, and the dark circles are calibration marks, not features.) Because the inner portions of the rings rotate more quickly than the outer, the durability of the spokes over a period of an hour or more is difficult to explain, unless it is assumed that they are an effect generated by the rotation of Saturn's magnetic field.
(NASA photo)

The braided *F* ring is here imaged at high resolution. The ring is apparently composed of three very tenuous rings that intertwine in three dimensions. Scientists suspect that electrostatic attractive and repulsive forces, generated by the motion of the ring particles through Saturn's magnetic field, may be responsible for this bizarre behavior. *(NASA photo)*

move between the poles of the planet, following tight spiral paths along each "line" of magnetic force. But the rings are in the way of these speeding particles. Large chunks of ring material are little affected by absorption of this plasma, but small, dust-size bits of the ring can pick up a significant electrical charge from their interaction with this ionizing radiation. Particles in the co-rotating *B* ring may receive more than their fair share of this radiation and thereby pick up enough of a static charge to be propelled above the ring plane, where they will cast a shadow on the ring particles below. These shadows may be the spokes we observe. The spokes are most prominent only for a few hours after emergence from Saturn's shadow, and then they fade away, so some occurrence apparently related to sunlight — either warming or perhaps further ionization by solar ultraviolet radiation — seems to cancel the effect. Or it is possible that a thin atmosphere of water vapor sublimed from the warming ring particles acts to ground out the suspended dust.

Effects associated with Saturn's magnetic field may also be responsible for the curious structure of the *F* ring. Satellites orbiting close to Saturn, the ring particles being a case in point, are constrained by the geometry of Saturn's gravitational field to orbit in the planet's equatorial plane. A particle that is launched, by a collision, for example, into a high inclination orbit will quickly be brought back to the equatorial plane by the inertial drag exerted by Saturn's rotating gravitational field. In addition, satellite orbits in general follow a simple curve known as the ellipse. Deviations from this closed curve must be the result of gravitational perturbations caused by a body other than the primary. All of Saturn's myriad rings, save one, obey these basic laws of celestial mechanics. Apparently the *F* ring never studied celestial mechanics. Not only do the three rings of which it is comprised follow complex, wavy paths about Saturn, but they dip several hundred kilometers above and below the ring plane. In fact, they seem to intertwine, like strands in a braided rope.

This discovery does not mean that something is wrong with our understanding of celestial mechanics. If it were, the *Voyager* navigation team could hardly have guided the spacecraft to Saturn in the first place. What it does suggest is that more than gravitational forces are at work in the *F* ring. The particles in the *F* ring (or, more precisely, *F* ring*s*) are strong forward scatterers of sunlight. That is, they appear brightest when lit from behind. This is interpreted to mean that the particles are small. Small particles are most easily affected by electromagnetic forces, so it is probable, though not certain, that the braided structure of the *F* ring is the result of electrical repulsion or attraction between the strands. This phenomenon, like the spokes, will provide years of study for scientists. Saturn is the first world we have explored in which forces other than gravity may play a significant role in shaping the satellite system.

Exaggerated but real color differences within the ring system are shown in this enhanced photo. The blue tint of Cassini's division and the *C* ring may be due to Rayleigh scattering by fine particles of dust, while the yellowish tint of the other rings may be caused by chemical impurities within the icy ring particles.
(NASA photo)

In much the same way that Jupiter and its Galilean satellites serve as a scale model of the solar system, the rings of Saturn may prove to be a replica in miniature of the solar accretion disk; and a detailed understanding of the rings may lead to a new understanding of the processes by which planets, and indeed solar systems in general, form. Not only did *Voyager*'s encounter with the rings provide us with a wealth of new knowledge; the encounter also drove home Hamlet's lesson that "there are more things in heaven and in Earth, Horatio, than are dreamt of in your philosophy." We went to Saturn thinking we knew, and came away puzzled, delighted, and awed.

The planet Saturn bears a superficial resemblance to Jupiter. Both worlds are gas giants, consisting primarily of hydrogen and helium. Both worlds take about 10 hours to rotate. Saturn, however, has only about 30 percent of Jupiter's mass, and this results in significant differences in its physical makeup. Although Saturn has more than 100 times the volume of Earth, it contains only 95 times as much matter, with the result that despite Saturn's great bulk, its gravity near the equator is actually slightly less than that of Earth. Saturn is so loosely held together that its density is actually less than that of water. Were there a bathtub big enough to hold it, Saturn would float. (It would, of course, leave a ring.)

Like Jupiter, Saturn is a source of heat, radiating some 2.9 times the amount of heat it receives from the Sun, in comparison to Jupiter's reradiation factor of 1.7. Allowing for Saturn's greater distance from the Sun, this means that Saturn radiates about 40 percent as much heat as does Jupiter. If, as is currently believed, this heat is the result of the conversion of gravitational energy to thermal energy, brought about by the continued slow contraction of these giant, gaseous worlds, then the larger planet, Jupiter, should be a greater source of heat, as indeed it is. What is puzzling to scientists is the fact that, gram for gram, Saturn is actually one-third more efficient at generating heat than is Jupiter. Prior to the *Voyager* encounter with Saturn, some scientists suggested that an additional source of thermal energy on Saturn might be the slow settling toward the core of the slightly more dense helium gas; and the predicted lower abundance of helium in Saturn's upper atmosphere was indeed observed in the *Voyager* data.

As is also the case with Jupiter, Saturn's internal heat source plays a more important part than solar radiation in warming the upper atmosphere and generating weather. Because of Saturn's lower gravity, the scale height of the atmosphere — that is, the distance between levels of similar pressure or density — is greater than on Jupiter. This produces not only denser clouds but also a much thicker layer of methane haze in the upper atmosphere, which obscures our view of Saturnian weather systems. In comparison to Jupiter's swirling, colorful belts and storms, Saturn appears quite bland. Only the major light zones and dark belts are easily discernible on the light-ocher disk. Saturn is not without complex weather systems, but contrasts and colors must be greatly enhanced to make them visible in photographs. Although Saturn boasts nothing as

Facing page, top
Lit from behind, the rings seem like a photographic negative of their appearance as seen from Earth: dark rings become bright and bright ones are dark. Under backlit conditions, the lower the population density of a given ring, the brighter it appears. The sparsely populated Cassini's division transmits and scatters much more sunlight than its denser neighbors, the A and B rings, while the C ring, which from Earth is barely detectable, becomes dazzling. (*NASA photo*)

Facing page, bottom
Another backlit view, showing the outer portions of the ring system, also demonstrates the grainy nature of the rings. While no individual ring particles can be resolved in this image, color enhancement brings out clumping in the major rings that is similar to that seen in the *F* ring. (*NASA photo*)

Two Views of Saturn. Although Saturn's rings provided a wealth of detail for *Voyager's* cameras, the planet itself appears quite bland. Saturn bears some resemblance to Jupiter in that, like Jupiter, it is banded, its weather systems having been stretched out by rapid rotation. And like Jupiter, it is generally brownish in color. But while Jupiter's atmosphere is clear enough to permit a view of its turbulent clouds, a dense haze of methane ice crystals obscures Saturn's lower atmosphere.

The photo at left, taken October 30, 1980, at a range of 18 million kilometers, shows Saturn as it actually appears, while the right-hand image, taken 12 days earlier, has been enhanced by computer to bring out more detail. The violet (actually brown) belt above the ring shadow is the Northern Equatorial belt, and the wide, dark belt above it is the Northern Temperate belt, within which can be glimpsed a number of light-colored spots. Similar spots can be observed on Jupiter, and they are thought to be convective storms towering above the average cloud level, similar to Earthly thunderstorms but much bigger; the spots are about 300 kilometers across. Since Saturn is highly oblate, and *Voyager's* viewpoint from north of the equator meant that it was looking through a greater thickness of atmosphere in the Southern Hemisphere than in the Northern, the southern part of the planet appears quite blue in this picture. *(NASA photos)*

Facing page, top left
Saturn and two satellites, Tethys *(above)* and Dione, are shown in this *Voyager* image. Note the shadows cast by the three major rings on Saturn's cloudtops, as well as the shadow cast by Tethys. Cassini's division is so sparsely populated by ring particles that the limb of the planet, tinted blue by the scattering of the atmosphere, is clearly visible through it. *(NASA photo)*

Facing page, top right
Viewed from near the equatorial plane, Saturn's rings assume an appearance of solidity quite at variance with their actual nature. The low contrast of Saturn's cloudbands suggests that little of interest is happening in the way of weather, but closer study reveals subtle details that hint at Jupiter-like turbulence in the atmosphere. The brown spot at left center and the bright oval below it were observed for several weeks by *Voyager*. Wind speeds in this latitude may be as high as 60 meters per second. The black spot at the bottom is the shadow of Dione. *(NASA photo)*

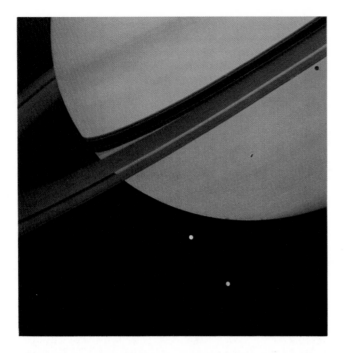

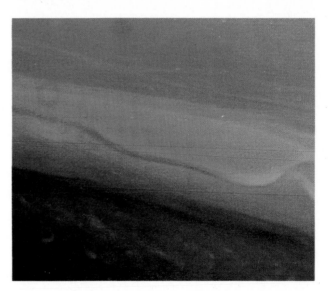

Brown ovals, apparently similar in nature to Jupiter's Great Red Spot, are visible in the upper right portion of this *Voyager* image. Each is about 1000 kilometers across. *(NASA photo)*

Saturnian clouds in the temperate latitudes of the Northern Hemisphere show a ribbonlike wave structure. The smallest features resolved in this photo are about 65 kilometers across. Comparison with photographs of Jupiter made at similar resolution suggests that weather systems on the two planets are quite different. *(NASA photo)*

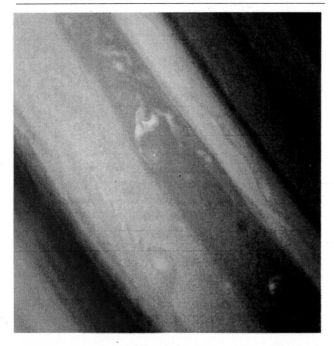

Enhanced color reveals Saturnian features as spectacular as any on Jupiter. In the upper photo, bright, convective cloud formations a few hundred kilometers in extent swirl in the brown belt that runs diagonally through the picture. Near bottom center, in the light-brown zone, there is an eye-shaped convective storm that shows a hint of hurricanelike spiral features. A longitudinal wave ripples down the center of the light blue band at the upper right. The lower photo shows what has been dubbed Saturn's Red Spot — a cloud formation some 1200 kilometers long, visible near the lower right of the planet's disk. The feature was observed for a period of several months by *Voyager 1*. The shadow of Dione is at the top of the frame. *(NASA photos)*

spectacular or permanent as the Great Red Spot of Jupiter, numerous observers have charted large white oval features from time to time, and several small, light-colored ovals were photographed by *Voyager 1*. These are probably giant, thunderhead-like storm systems towering high in the atmosphere. Enhanced images show dark, streaming cloud features thought to be evidence of very high winds, but these streamers are most prominent near the centers of white zones, rather than near the edges as they are on Jupiter. Whether this indicates a basic difference in the weather patterns of the two worlds, or an error in interpretation, remains to be seen.

TITAN

Saturn bears the distinction of having more satellites than any other planet. Most of these, of course, are the billions of icy moonlets that comprise the rings. These probably range in size from pebbles to boulders. An additional 1000 or so moons, ranging in diameter from 10 to 100 kilometers, are probably embedded in the rings. Orbiting outside the rings are at least 15 other satellites. Five of these — Dione, Tethys, Iapetus, Rhea, and Titan — are more than 1000 kilometers in diameter. The first four of these large moons are balls of ice. But unlike the icy Galileans, the Saturnian satellites are so cold that their surfaces behave like solid rock and are able to retain extremely rugged topography. Titan, however, is in a class apart.

In 1944, Gerard Kuiper discovered the spectroscopic signature of the gas methane (CH_4) in the sunlight reflected from Titan. Titan was known to be smaller than Mars, but it is so much more distant from the Sun, and consequently colder, that it seemed quite reasonable that Titan could retain a thin, Mars-like atmosphere, despite its lesser mass. Titan's reddish coloration was further reminiscent of Mars, so for nearly three decades following Kuiper's discovery most astronomers believed that Titan was a similar desert world, cloaked in a cold, wispy, unbreathable atmosphere. In the popular mind, Titan's main appeal was the dramatic view of Saturn supposedly afforded by its surface. Perhaps the most evocative image in the field of space art is Chesley Bonestell's 1944 painting of Saturn seen from Titan, depicting a crescent Saturn poised above a frosty landscape, shining through a deep blue sky. More than one space scientist attributes the development of a youthful interest in astronomy to this image.

A flood of information, starting around 1972, has led us far from the early model of Titan as a smaller, colder version of Mars. Micrometer-wavelength observations of Titan by David Morrison and other researchers suggested that Titan's atmosphere was probably much denser than had been believed, and possibly warmer. In 1973, Bishun Khare and Carl Sagan showed that Titan owed its red color not to a desertlike surface but to a haze of organic compounds suspended high in the atmosphere. Until *Voyager 1*'s flyby of Titan, there was even speculation that the

 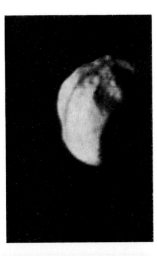

Satellite number 11, yet unnamed, shares an orbit just outside Saturn's rings with number 10, Janus, which was discovered in 1966. S-11 seems to be involved in a game of gravitational leapfrog with Janus; both satellites are approximately 100 kilometers in diameter, but their orbits are only 50 kilometers apart. At the time of the *Voyager I* encounter, the two tiny satellites were approximately 105 degrees apart in their orbits, with S-11 gradually overtaking the other moon. Scientists consider it unlikely, however, that the two moons are on a collision course. As the trailing satellite approaches, its gravitational field will tend to slow the leading satellite, forcing it to move into a slightly lower orbit. The trailing satellite gains energy from this interaction and speeds up, moving into a higher orbit, thus avoiding a collision.

The pair of images shown here were taken 13 minutes apart, and they show the passage of a thin ring shadow across the irregular face of the satellite. The jagged shape of this satellite and the peculiar orbit it is in have suggested to some scientists that the two co-orbiting moons may once have been a single body that was later shattered. *(NASA photo)*

A huge crater, some 130 kilometers in diameter, dominates the leading face of the 390-kilometers-in-diameter satellite Mimas. The satellite's low density indicates that it is composed mainly of ice, but Mimas (along with the other moons of Saturn) is so cold that the ice behaves like the strongest of rocks, still retaining a record of the last wave of cratering some 4 billion years ago. *(NASA photo)*

Tethys, another icy satellite, is about 1050 kilometers in diameter, which is about one-third the size of our Moon. The long, curving fault valley near the right side of the image may be evidence of some sort of internal activity. *(NASA photo)*

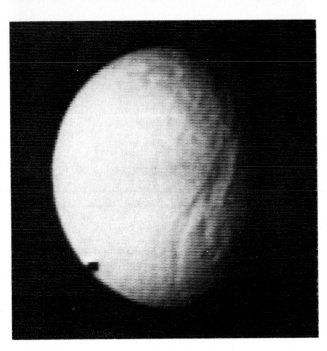

The other hemisphere of Mimas *(above)* is saturated with craters and has probably remained unchanged since the beginning of the solar system. *(NASA photo)*

Dione's brightness is evident in this view of the 1120-kilometer satellite, seen here in transit against the clouds of Saturn, which are 377,000 kilometers farther back. The trailing hemisphere of Dione *(left)* contains fairly dark material crisscrossed by wispy streaks, while the leading hemisphere is uniformly covered with impact craters. *(NASA photo)*

Facing page
A closer view of Dione shows several rills or fault lines snaking through the icy crust, perhaps indicating internal activity. The largest crater is about 100 kilometers in diameter and has a central peak that is much higher, proportionately, than any other peak yet observed in the solar system. *(NASA photo)*

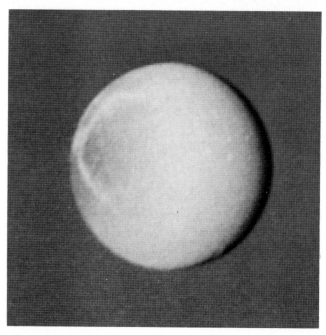

Saturn's rings, seen from the surface of Rhea *(above)*, would fill half the sky; but because Rhea orbits in essentially the same plane as the rings, giving an edge-on view, the rings would appear only as a thin line bisecting Saturn's disk. *(Art by author)*

Flashing like a cosmic heliograph, the 1440-kilometers-in-diameter satellite Iapetus has long puzzled astronomers, for it is six times brighter on one side of its orbit than on the other. Although this *Voyager* photo, taken from a range of 3.2 million kilometers, seems to show a crescent Iapetus with the sunlight shining from the upper right, the moon was actually fully lit, with the light coming from behind the viewer. The darkness at the lower left portion of the disk represents a real difference in surface brightness. This leading hemisphere may have been covered with dust excavated by impacts. *(NASA photo)*

Facing page
Rhea is one of the largest of Saturn's moons, some 1530 kilometers in diameter, and it is the most heavily cratered, preserving impact scars from the earliest period of the solar system. Many craters have central peaks formed by the rebound of the crater floor following impacts. Multiple ridges and grooves, seen in best relief near the terminator, are similar to features on the Moon and Mercury. *(NASA photo)*

greenhouse effect of Titan's atmosphere might raise surface temperatures sufficiently to permit life.

As *Voyager* drew near Titan on the evening of November 11, 1980, transmitting a new picture every few minutes, scientists strained to glimpse details on the globe that was growing steadily on the TV monitors, but Titan remained essentially featureless. The aerosol haze in the atmosphere was unbroken, preventing any glimpse of the surface. Only images taken through ultraviolet filters showed any details, the most prominent of which was a dark hood of clouds or haze in the Northern Hemisphere. It remains to be determined whether this polar hood is a permanent feature in the Titanian atmosphere or an effect that appears only during the onset of Northern Hemisphere spring. The only other features revealed in the photos were discrete layers of haze seen along Titan's limb, extending from the polar hood.

Usually the most dramatic returns from the first flyby of a planet are the photographs, but in the case of Titan, results from the radio occultation experiment were far more revealing. Years before encounter, *Voyager I*'s trajectory had been chosen to carry the spacecraft behind Titan, as it is seen from Earth. When *Voyager* began to slip behind Titan, the radio signal from the spacecraft gradually faded, because of absorption by Titan's atmosphere. Painstaking analysis of the pattern of this fading permitted scientists to measure composition, temperature, and pressure at various levels in the atmosphere. While the results were certainly discouraging to those who still harbored hope of finding life elsewhere in the solar system, Titan was revealed to be a truly alien and fascinating world.

Titan is cold. The atmosphere near the surface is at a temperature of about 90°K, some −300° F. The atmosphere is far denser than Earth's: Titan's surface pressure is some 1.6 bars — more than twice that at terrestrial sea level. And methane, far from being the primary constituent, accounts for only 8 percent of Titan's atmosphere, the rest being nitrogen, which is the prime component of Earth's atmosphere. In many respects, Titan is a terrestrial planet in perpetual deepfreeze.

An atmosphere of 1.6 bars at 90° is interesting, for this is the so-called "triple point" of methane — the temperature and pressure at which that substance can exist simultaneously as a solid, liquid, and gas. Apparently methane on Titan plays the same geophysical role that water does on Earth. Titan's poles may be blanketed by glaciers of methane, and perhaps during the summer they thaw to form streams and lakes. Whether or not there are actual seas of liquid methane near Titan's equatorial regions is a question whose answer must await more detailed exploration by landers or orbiting radar probes.

Titan's resemblance to a very cold version of Earth is only superficial. Visitors to the surface would not see anything resembling a terrestrial landscape, if indeed they could see anything by the feeble sunlight that penetrates the hazy atmosphere. The action of solar ultraviolet radiation over the course of billions of years has broken the molecular bonds of the molecules, such as methane, ammonia, hydrogen cyanide, and other gases, that originally

Facing page, top
The most heavily cratered area of Rhea's surface is shown in this photo. Other areas of Rhea's surface are deficient in large craters, indicating a change in the nature of the impacting bodies, and an early period of internal activity. White areas on the edges of several craters in the upper right of the photo may be fresh ice exposed on steep slopes, or deposits of refrozen volatiles that leaked from fractures. *(NASA photo)*

Facing page, bottom
The surface of Iapetus may provide a view of the rings unmatched elsewhere in the Saturnian system. Since Iapetus is an outer satellite, its orbit is not confined to the ring plane but rises above and dips below it, permitting an open view of the rings. *(Art by author)*

Changing perceptions of a distant world are
depicted in these three paintings of Titan's
surface. The figure above is based on the Mars-
like model, originally propounded in the late
1940s. A tenuous atmosphere of methane
permits a view of Saturn. The figure on the
facing page, top, is based on observations made
during the 1970s that suggested a dense,
cloudy atmosphere. The image at lower right
shows the most current ideas on the nature of
Titan's surface: cliffs of methane ice flow like
glaciers across a surface blanketed by frozen,
asphaltlike sludge hundreds of meters thick.
The lowering, smog-filled sky does not permit a
view of Saturn, or even of the Sun.
(Art by author)

Titan, seen from a distance of 4.5 million kilometers, shows little detail, but even at close range there is very little to see. The 5140-kilometers-in-diameter moon is shrouded by an orange aerosol "smog" that prevents any view of the surface. The gradual darkening toward the terminator at the right of the disk is consistent with a thick, hazy atmosphere. The only definite feature revealed by this photo is a dark hood of haze that seems to cover the Northern Hemisphere. *(NASA photo)*

Facing page
Distinct haze layers are evident in this greatly enhanced view of Saturn's atmosphere. The layers of haze seem to spread out from beneath Titan's North Polar hood. *(NASA photo)*

comprised Titan's primordial atmosphere. Not only was nitrogen freed by this process, but the other dissociated atoms eventually recombined to form a plethora of complex organic compounds such as polyacetylene, which is thought to be the main ingredient in the photochemical "smog" that gives Titan its brownish color. In turn, these polymers have probably further combined to produce heavier, tarlike substances that precipitate to the surface. By estimating the rate of this organic synthesis over the past 4.5 billion years, some scientists have speculated that Titan's surface is covered to a depth of one-half kilometer by an asphaltlike sludge that has been chilled hard as rock.

Curiously enough, this model of the Titanian environment may have a bearing on our current quest for energy. The conventional theory that geologists use to account for the deposits of coal and oil upon which the world's energy economy is based suggests that coal and oil are the fossil remains of lush forests that existed a few hundred million years ago. These ancient forests, according to the theory, lived, died, and decomposed, layer upon layer, and were ultimately buried deep below Earth's surface by geologic upheavals. There they were transformed to coal and oil by heat and pressure. There is a minority view, however, which suggests that oil is completely abiologic in origin and was produced, like Titan's aerosols, by photodissociation of Earth's original atmosphere. The discovery that Titan's atmosphere, like Earth's, is composed predominantly of nitrogen lends some credence to this idea, and raises the tantalizing possibility that another prediction of this maverick theory may be correct: deep within Earth's crust there may remain, untapped, immense reservoirs of primordial methane — also known as natural gas.

This possible parallel between Earth's ancient environment and Titan's present one is an example of the sort of practical information that occasionally derives from space exploration. But Titan is a world that deserves study in its own right, and its thick atmosphere, while a hindrance to remote investigation, will facilitate exploration by lander probes. Such probes could use heat shields and then parachutes to reduce their high entry velocity, and then perhaps deploy balloons to sample different levels of the atmosphere, eventually dipping low enough to photograph the surface and select a landing site. On the ground, the probes could analyze whatever strange compounds may blanket Titan. Clues to our own world's early history may lie preserved in deepfreeze beneath Titan's smoggy clouds.

Perhaps someday, a generation or two hence, human explorers will follow the *Voyagers* to Saturn, and behold firsthand the glory of the rings and the mysteries of Titan. Unlike the Jovian system, which is poisoned by deadly radiation, Saturn and its satellites present a benign environment for humans.

URANUS IS MORE THAN TWICE AS DISTANT from Earth as Saturn is, and Neptune is half again as far, making both very difficult to study. Because the two planets are similar in size, color, and density, they are usually treated together, although it is likely that they will ultimately prove to have characters as distinct as any other two planets. Both are gas giants, about four times larger than Earth. They differ from Jupiter and Saturn in that their masses may have been insufficient to compress their hydrogen atmospheres to the exotic metallic state found deep within those larger planets. And it is possible that Uranus and Neptune have solid surfaces, perhaps of ice, some 10,000 kilometers beneath their cloudtops. The greenish color of these two worlds is characteristic of methane at very low temperatures, and indeed this ubiquitous molecule has been spectroscopically detected.

An important difference between the two worlds is that Neptune has a strong internal heat source, permitting it to radiate some 2.1 times the energy it receives from the Sun. In this respect it is similar to Jupiter and Saturn. Uranus, however, has little or no internal source of heat, which is puzzling. Also, Uranus seems to have about twice the amount of methane in its atmosphere that Jupiter and Saturn have (relative to the more abundant hydrogen and helium constituents), while Neptune has approximately the same amount as those planets.

URANUS

Uranus's chief claim to glory is that its rotation axis is tilted approximately 98 degrees, so that it more or less

Facing page
The Rings of Uranus. Uranus is encircled by a system of nine dark, narrow rings. Although the rings are extremely difficult to observe from Earth, the shadow they cast on Uranus's cloudtops has been photographed by *Stratoscope II*. (*Art by author*)

Uranus Seen from Oberon. Even from the vantage point of one of Uranus's satellites, the planet's rings might be virtually invisible. (*Art by author*)

rolls around on its side during its 84-year orbital period. This has the effect of alternately pointing the planet's North and South Poles toward the Sun, at 42-year intervals. In fact, the polar regions absorb more solar energy during the course of a Uranian "year" than do the equatorial latitudes. It is unfortunate that we can resolve no atmospheric details, for weather systems in such a situation are likely to be interesting.

Uranus's five known satellites orbit in the planet's equatorial plane, with the result that we can see them in virtually bird's-eye view at appropriate points in Uranus's orbit. The highly tilted aspect of the Uranian system presents an interesting problem in the theory of planetary formation. It is generally assumed that all the planets formed in essentially the same plane, out of a comparatively thin disk of gas and dust, and that they all moved counterclockwise around the Sun and rotated counterclockwise on their axes in a very orderly fashion. With the exception of Venus, whose rotation is retrograde (clockwise when viewed from solar North), the children of the Sun are quite well behaved, and the tilts of their rotation axes can be explained if we assume that all the planets were struck during the latter stages of their accretion by large planetesimals coming from more or less random directions. Venus's anomalous rotation can be accounted for by this hypothesis. The tilt of the Uranian system is more than a right angle, suggesting that the planet sustained either a monumental impact at some point, or, less likely, a series of smaller but systematic impacts. A less favored explanation is that the conditions during the formation of Uranus and its satellites were different from those of the other planets, and that the proto-Uranus accretion disk was, for some reason, already tilted with respect to the rest of the solar system.

In addition to its satellites, Uranus is attended by a system of dark rings. These were discovered when the planet occulted a star in 1977. Such occultations can be as fruitful as they are rare. If the planet is airless, the abrupt cutoff and reappearance of the star's light can enable observers to set limits on the planet's size. If the planet has an atmosphere, as does Uranus, the changing characteristics of the star's light can provide useful information about the density, composition, and structure of the atmosphere. To the surprise of astronomers, the star blinked on and off several times well before it vanished behind the globe of Uranus, and exhibited a similar pattern of brightening and dimming following its emergence. This observation indicated that Uranus is encircled by nine narrow rings. These rings are very dark and have been photographed only with very long exposures.

NEPTUNE

Discrepancies in Uranus's position in its orbit led John Couch Adams and Urbain Leverrier to independently predict the existence of an eighth planet. The subsequent discovery of Neptune in 1846 was considered the ultimate confirmation of Newtonian mechanics.

Neptune As It Might Appear from Triton. We might expect rugged topography on Triton, as a result of the tidal interaction that altered its orbit. Its surface apparently has a thin coating of methane frost. *(Art by author)*

Neptune seemed to be similar in general nature to Uranus. It is somewhat oblate and may be faintly banded, but this is uncertain. The planet's disk subtends only 3 seconds of arc. The larger of Neptune's two satellites, Triton (4000 kilometers in diameter), is of interest because it moves in a retrograde orbit inclined about 20 degrees to the plane of Uranus's equator. It seems to violate the rule that close satellites tend to orbit in the equatorial planes of their primaries. This suggests that Triton's motion may have been violently interfered with in the past. If the planet Pluto is a former satellite of Neptune, as some scientists have suggested, Triton's unusual orbit may be a result of the drastic tidal interaction that cast Pluto into the outer darkness.

Paradoxically, even though in time-exposure photographs Triton appears to be little more than a star, more is known about it than Neptune. Its density is very nearly the same as our Moon's, suggesting that it may have a similar rocky composition. This is somewhat surprising, for satellites in the cold outer regions of the solar system have generally been found to be low-density amalgams of rock, water, and ice. Triton's peculiar composition may be another bit of evidence pointing toward a violent past. A tidal interaction capable of altering Triton's orbit from its presumed original equatorial path to its current highly inclined one would generate a considerable amount of heat within the body of the satellite (just as Jupiter's moon Io is heated by tides raised by its primary). Such heating could easily have boiled away Triton's supply of ice, leaving behind the rocky core. If this is the case, we might expect Triton's topography to be relatively new, and shaped more by its brief period of volcanism than by impacts.

Dale Cruikshank has spectroscopically detected what appears to be a thin atmosphere of methane on Triton. It should be borne in mind, however — as our experience with Titan demonstrated — that methane is one of the more easily observed gases and may exist as a small component of an atmosphere consisting mostly of less easily detected gases. Triton's diameter is not much less than Titan's, and it may yet prove to be a fairly dynamic world.

Facing page
Pluto (*bottom*) and its satellite Charon orbit at the icy fringes of the solar system, so far away that virtually nothing is known about them. (*Art by author*)

IN ADDITION TO HIS STUDIES OF MARS, Percival Lowell attempted to duplicate the Adams/Leverrier coup of discovering a new planet through pure mathematics. While his calculations were ultimately in error, his persistence paid off. On February 18, 1930, a young astronomer named Clyde Tombaugh, who had painstakingly carried on the search for "Planet X" following Lowell's death, discovered a dim object that seemed to be moving as slowly as a trans-Neptunian planet might be expected to. Initial determinations of its orbit showed it to be at an astonishing distance of 6 billion kilometers from the Sun, with an orbital period of 248 years. The new planet was subsequently named Pluto, in keeping with its position as guardian of the Stygian depths at the frontier of the solar system. By a happy coincidence, the first two letters of its name are also the initials of the man who initiated the search.

The usual frustrations inherent in the study of distant planets apply in spades to Pluto. Even the largest Earth-based telescopes are unable to resolve the disk of the planet, so as basic a datum as its size has to be determined by a variety of indirect methods, including the observation of stellar occultations. Pluto is small — far too small to have caused the supposed perturbations in the orbit of Neptune that led astronomers to search for it. Recent observations suggest that Pluto is only about 3000 kilometers in diameter, which is about the size of our Moon. In addition, Pluto has an unusual orbit, inclined more than 17 degrees to the ecliptic plane and so eccentric that from 1979 to 1999 it will actually be closer to the Sun than Neptune is. These factors have led some astronomers to theorize that Pluto is not a proper planet at all, but a "lost" moon of Neptune.

The peculiar orbit of Neptune's satellite Triton lends credence to this idea. Computer-generated "replays" of the various orbital configurations of Pluto and Neptune show, however, that the two planets never approach within 18 astronomical units of each other, and this poses problems for the lost-satellite theory. If Pluto was gravitationally cast out of the Neptunian system, it should pass much closer to Neptune than it does.

In 1978, a new discovery was made that may add a countering weight to the objections many astronomers have to the lost-moon hypothesis: Pluto was found to have a satellite. It is a small body, named Charon (over the objections of some who felt that it would have been more appropriately named Proserpina, after Pluto's consort). Charon is perhaps 1500 kilometers in diameter and orbits only 20,000 kilometers from Pluto, making the Pluto-Charon system a closer binary planet than the Earth-Moon system, which not only has a smaller size ratio (4:1) but also has a separation that is, in scale, nearly five times as large. If Pluto formed in its own accretion disk at its present distance from the Sun, it has no business having a satellite so large. But if Pluto was torn into two or more chunks when it was ejected from Neptune's system, it could easily have satellites that followed it into exile.

All of this is, of course, speculation. Unfortunately, so is nearly everything else we might say about Pluto, except for a description of the parameters of its orbit. We do know that Pluto must be very cold: the distant Sun shines with only 1/1600 its terrestrial intensity, and its disk would be too small to be resolved with the unaided eye. Variations in Pluto's brightness indicate a rotation period of about six-and-a-half days, which is within the usual range of large satellites of gas giants. Methane frost has been detected on its surface, but this is likely to sublime into a gaseous state as Pluto nears the Sun, producing a very tenuous atmosphere that has perhaps one-thousandth the pressure of Earth's. Pluto's density is on the same order as that of Jupiter's satellites Ganymede and Callisto, suggesting that it too may be an icy, rather than rocky, body.

As Pluto reaches perihelion in 1989 *(top)*, the methane frost that has been detected on its surface may thaw to provide a tenuous and temporary atmosphere. Crystals suspended high in the atmosphere may produce prismatic halos about the Sun, which, viewed from Pluto, is merely a very bright star. *(Art by author)*

Discovery Plates of Pluto *(bottom)*. Clyde Tombaugh examined hundreds of thousands of star images before isolating the faint moving point of light that was Pluto, on February 18, 1930.
(Lowell Observatory photo)

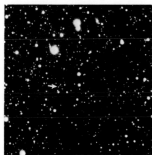

We are a star's way of finding out about stars.
Carl Sagan

THROUGHOUT HISTORY, THE SUN HAS BEEN recognized as the prime driving force in nature. If not considered a god itself, it was at least viewed as a manifestation of whatever gods might prevail. Stars were seen as such lesser lights in the metaphysical heavens that their creation could be dismissed with the offhand comment in Genesis that "He made the stars also." The prescient Greek scholar Aristarchus is credited with being the first to suggest that the Sun itself was a star that was just closer than the rest. Support for this point of view languished until the seventeenth century, when early telescopic observations showed that the Sun had blemishes (sunspots), rotated, and thus was clearly part of the material realm.

We know today that the Sun is a fairly typical star, although the word *typical* as applied to stars is misleading; stars vary as much as people do, and generalizations are difficult. But we can say that a star is essentially a ball of gas, composed primarily of hydrogen, with traces of helium and, in the case of older stars, heavier elements ranging up to iron on the Periodic Table. Stars are typically hundreds of thousands to billions of kilometers in diameter, and the character of an individual star is almost entirely determined by its mass. Very massive stars lead bright, brief lives, only a few tens of thousands to millions of years long, while stars of lower mass are less brilliant and can last billions of years. Our own Sun is in the latter category.

The initial driving force of a star's furnace is gravity. As the gas that goes into forming a star collapses, the tremendous kinetic energy of the infalling particles is given up as heat, and the star begins to glow. The intense temperatures at the core of the forming star tend to strip atoms down to their constituent particles. In particular, electrons are removed from hydrogen atoms, leaving behind the positively charged protons. The pressure within this superhot plasma is strong enough to overcome the electrical repulsion between the protons, initiating a fusion reaction called the proton-proton cycle:

$$^1H + {}^1H \longrightarrow {}^2H + neutrino + e^+$$

$$^2H + {}^1H \longrightarrow {}^3He + photon$$

$$^3He + {}^3He \longrightarrow {}^4He + {}^1H + {}^1H$$

In the first part of the reaction, two protons fuse to form a nucleus of heavy hydrogen (deuterium), which consists of a proton and a neutron; and two additional particles are liberated: the neutrino, a chargeless particle of very low mass; and the electron's antiparticle, the positron. The newly created deuterium nucleus can then react with a proton to form a Helium-3 nucleus, releasing a photon (usually of the high-energy sort known as a gamma ray). Helium-3 nuclei can then fuse to form a Helium-4 nucleus and two protons, completing the cycle.

Not only does this reaction allow new types of atomic nuclei to be cooked up in the heart of a star, but it converts matter into energy. There is less mass at the end of the

Facing page
Our Sun is a fairly typical star, but until the advent of atomic energy in 1945 it was our sole source of energy. Early societies recognized the Sun's importance and constructed elaborate and sometimes monumental astronomical computers, such as the one found at Stonehenge in southern England, to mark its seasonal comings and goings.
(Composite photo courtesy of H. J. P. Arnold of Space Frontiers, Ltd.)

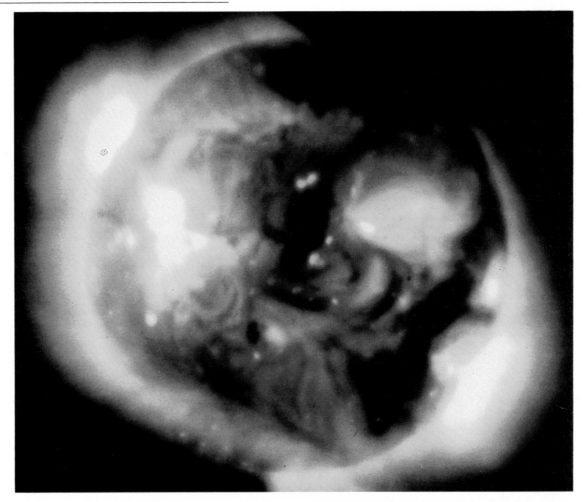

reaction than at the beginning, a condition that is accounted for by the photon. Though massless, the photon's energy is equivalent to a very small amount of mass, in accordance with Einstein's famous equation $E = mc^2$, in which E is energy, m is mass, and c is the speed of light. This means that a very small amount of mass is equivalent to a great deal of energy. In the proton-proton reaction, less than 1 percent of the mass involved is converted to energy, but because of the huge bulk of the Sun, approximately 4 million tons of matter are being converted to energy every second. Even at this rate, however, more than 10 trillion years would pass before the Sun shriveled into nothing. But other processes control the Sun's destiny, so its lifetime will be nowhere near that long.

The density of matter near the Sun's core is so great that even a photon has a hard time getting away. Its mean free path, or average distance between interactions with atomic or subatomic particles, is on the order of 1 centimeter. This means that each second, a given photon (or its re-emitted successors) risks 30 billion collisions. Far from traveling in the arrow-straight lines we usually associate with light, solar photons must move in a kind of "drunkard's walk," in short, random steps that take them ever farther from their starting point. At this rate, it will take an individual photon about a million years to reach the Sun's surface and freedom.

As these photons gradually move outward, they impart momentum, or thermal energy, to the gases between the core and the surface. This energy has to go somewhere, and, in accordance with the laws of thermodynamics, it tends to move toward a cooler region, toward space. It does this principally through the process of convection; hot masses of gas tend to be less dense than their surroundings, and they rise in a gravitational field just as bubbles rise in water, or, more accurately, as "cells" of hot water rise in a seething cauldron. In essence, the outer layers of the Sun are boiling. Cells of hot gas, called *granulae,* rise to the surface, radiate their heat into space, cool, and fall back into the Sun to continue the cycle. Such convection cells, which are characteristically 1000–2000 kilometers across, cover the Sun's face, giving it a grainy texture.

The Sun is approximately 1.4 million kilometers in diameter and more than 300,000 times more massive than Earth. It rotates on its axis about once a month, but since it is not a solid body and there are other than purely mechanical forces governing the motion of plasma inside it, not all parts of the Sun rotate at the same angular rate. As is also the case on Jupiter, regions at higher latitudes rotate more slowly. The dynamo effect of solar rotation creates an intense magnetic field that plays an important role in regulating the appearance and activity of the photosphere (the bright "surface" of the Sun). A given line of magnetic force may start out rotating in a plane with the solar rotation axis, but because ionized gases within the Sun rotate at slightly different rates, according to latitude, the field line gradually becomes distorted: that part of the line near the equator overtakes the rest, and eventually the field line wraps around the Sun like a doughnut. With many field lines doing this, the Sun's magnetic field even-

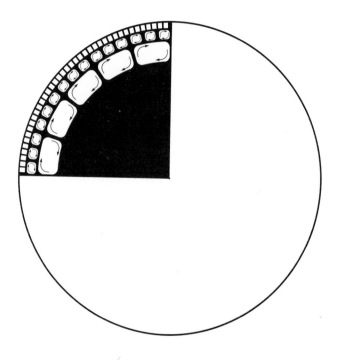

Heat flows out of the Sun's core primarily through the mechanism of convection. Pockets of hot gas rise, imparting thermal energy to the upper levels and breaking up into even smaller cells. Such convection cells account for the grainy appearance of the Sun's surface. Arrows suggest the churning motion of solar convection cells as they boil toward the photosphere. *(Diagram by Michael Standlee Design)*

Facing page, top
An x-ray image of the Sun, taken by *Skylab* astronauts, shows intense bursts of hard radiation erupting from the vicinity of flares and sunspots. *(NASA photo)*

Facing page, bottom
In the light of ionized helium gas, which can be observed only above the Earth's atmosphere, the Sun shows a wealth of features, such as the granulation of the photosphere and the dark, wavy shock waves in the chromosphere — that region of the solar atmosphere just above the surface.
(Photo courtesy of U.S. Naval Research Laboratory)

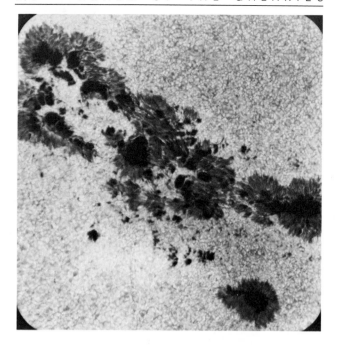

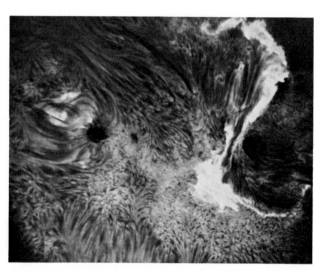

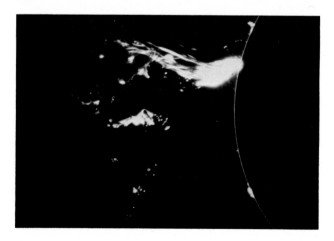

tually ends up a scrambled mess, quite unlike the symmetrical toroids that surround planets.

When the magnetic field approaches the maximally random state, plasma in the photosphere flows in a turbulent manner, "mapping" the field. The resulting magnetic storms are called sunspots, and since they are usually about a thousand degrees cooler than the surrounding areas, they appear dark. After the solar magnetic field is totally scrambled, it gradually re-forms in an orderly pattern, beginning a new cycle in which the magnetic poles have flipped. The period between the occurrence of maximum sunspot activity is on the order of 11 years, but it takes 22 years to complete the pole-reversal cycle.

This "sunspot cycle" has important effects on Earth — and off it. During maximum activity, high-energy particles are spewed into space and eventually reach the vicinity of Earth, where they are channeled into the upper atmosphere by Earth's magnetic field and produce the shimmering curtains of light known as auroras, best observed at high latitudes. In addition to the release of these essentially harmless particles, there may be especially violent outbursts called flares. Radio emissions from flares can disrupt communications, and x-ray and gamma-ray bursts could kill astronauts, who are unprotected by Earth's atmosphere and magnetic field. During the *Apollo* missions, a close watch was kept on solar activity, and it was even suggested that deep space missions be postponed during high-risk periods. (This advice was ignored, fortunately with no known ill effects on the astronauts.) Permanent bases or space colonies will probably have to have either magnetic screens or "flare shelters," to which residents can retire during a flare alert.

It can be said, then, that the Sun's atmosphere extends at least as far as Earth, and deep space probes have observed this "solar wind" beyond the orbit of Saturn. That part of the solar atmosphere which is actually visible is less extensive, however. The region just above the photosphere is called the chromosphere, because of its red color as seen during eclipses (primarily caused by the glow of hydrogen alpha emission), and this region merges into the corona, which has all the colors of mother-of-pearl. We are fortunate to have a Moon that is not only 400 times closer than the Sun but 400 times smaller as well. It can fit snugly over the solar disk at all-too-rare intervals, permitting us to enjoy a fleeting glimpse of the corona, surely one of the most awesome and beautiful sights in nature.

Our Sun is therefore not the static ball of ethereal fire the ancients believed it to be, but a dynamic, ever-changing entity. Since for the foreseeable future our continued comfort, if not existence, depends on a certain degree of constancy in the Sun's behavior, we may wonder whether it changes in ways that have not yet been observed during the century or so of serious solar astronomy. There is reason to believe that it does.

In considering the delicate balances necessary to support life, we have seen that small changes in basic factors such as orbital distance or the concentration of atmospheric carbon dioxide can produce profound effects. Even a small variation in solar radiation, if continued for a long enough time, could lead to major climatic changes. During the

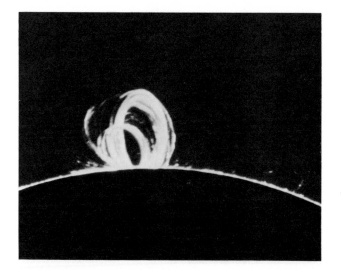

Facing page, top
Sunspots are magnetic storms in the Sun's photosphere, dark only in comparison to the slightly hotter surrounding gases.
(Photo © Association of Universities for Research in Astronomy, Inc., Sacramento Peak Observatory)

Facing page, middle
Solar flares are particularly violent outbursts of plasma. Since these ionized particles — primarily protons and helium nuclei — are constrained to move along the magnetic lines of force, they sometimes assume very tortuous shapes.
(Photo © Association of Universities for Research in Astronomy, Inc., Sacramento Peak Observatory)

Facing page, bottom
A spray prominence erupts to nearly 500,000 kilometers above the Sun, in this coronograph photo taken by Stan Cain on March 1, 1969.
(Photo courtesy of Institute for Astronomy, University of Hawaii)

Top, left
A loop prominence demonstrates the strength of the solar magnetic field by returning to the Sun instead of pursuing a ballistic trajectory.
(Photo © Association of Universities for Research in Astronomy, Inc., Sacramento Peak Observatory)

Top, right
In the far ultraviolet, a spray prominence reveals a variety of finer structures. This photograph was electronically enhanced so that different contours of brightness are imaged in different colors. Thus the regions of greatest ultraviolet emission are white, and the faintest are red.
(Photo courtesy of U.S. Naval Research Laboratory)

The solar corona, the Sun's outer atmosphere, is a beautiful phenomenon that can be observed without special instruments only during the rare and fleeting moments of a total solar eclipse. *(Art by author)*

latter half of the seventeenth century, there was an exceptionally low number of sunspots, and the coronas were much fainter. This period is called the Maunder minimum (after an astronomer of the time who observed sunspots). Such periods seem to correlate to changes in the growth rate of plants, as determined by tree rings. There is a very strong correlation between droughts in central Africa and periods of sunspot minimum. On a much larger time scale, certain rocks found near the centers of lunar craters (which could act as reflector ovens) have glazed patches on their upper surfaces, as if they had been partially melted by a particularly strong burst of sunlight.

A star's existence depends on maintenance of the balance between the pressure of its nuclear furnace and the weight of its gases. Some stars, such as the red supergiant Mira, maintain this balance by pulsating in the manner of a heat engine. Cyclic changes in the opacity of Mira's interior cause temperatures to periodically rise, which causes an expansion of the outer gases. This expansion in turn permits the added heat to dissipate into space. Mira then contracts to begin a new cycle. This case is extreme, but it is probable that no star ever achieves an absolutely static sort of balance. Our Sun may be a very-long-period variable, with a cycle of millions of years. In fact, there has been speculation lately that our Sun's furnace may occasionally shut off. Experiments designed to discover neutrinos — particles produced in the first step of the proton-proton reaction — have detected nowhere near as many as should be streaming from the Sun, suggesting that the solar furnace may even now be shut down. Temporarily, one hopes, or in a million years, when the last batch of photons makes its way to the photosphere, things could get chilly.

Whatever variations the Sun may exhibit, however, it is a remarkably stable star in comparison to most.

THE SUN'S COLLEAGUES

On a clear, moonless night away from city lights, a person with average eyesight can see approximately 3000 stars. Beyond counting and perhaps mapping them, however, little can be learned about stars without telescopic aid. Indeed, the history of astronomy is marked primarily by a quest for ever more light, in the literal as well as figurative sense. Most astronomical instruments are essentially devices that collect and analyze photons, those tiny messengers from the cores of distant suns. The more photons, the better!

The most obvious characteristic of stars is that some are brighter than others. Ancient astronomers established a scale of brightness, or magnitude, that is still used, although it is cumbersome. A first-magnitude star, such as Spica, is not twice as bright as a second-magnitude star, such as Mirzam, but 2.512 times brighter; and it is 6.3 times brighter than a third-magnitude star. Each magnitude is 2.512 times brighter than the next. This system is a result not of perversity but of physiology: a first-magnitude star really does *look* 3 times brighter than a third-magnitude star, not 6.3 times brighter. Human senses do not respond to stimuli in direct proportion to the degree of the stimulus, as do instruments such as photometers, but in a logarithmic fashion: two pinpricks fortunately do not hurt twice as much as one, but approximately 1.4 times as much. The advantages of such a system are obvious.

The first question that might be asked is, Do differences in stellar magnitude reflect intrinsic differences in luminosity, or are some stars just closer than others? To answer this, we have to measure stellar distances, and the only direct means we have of doing that is by observing the parallax, or apparent displacement against the background, that a star seems to exhibit when viewed from two widely separated points in space. The diameter of Earth's orbit provides a convenient baseline for measuring the nearer stars, but even the closest star shows a parallax of less than 1 second of arc. (The word *parsec* derives from this method. A parsec is the distance from Earth a star must be in order to show a *parallax* of one *second* of arc. A more familiar unit is the light-year, the distance a beam of light, moving at 300,000 kilometers per second, covers in a year. A parsec is equivalent to 3.26 light-years.)

Once the stars in the immediate neighborhood of Earth were surveyed, it was obvious that they had differing brightnesses. For example, Sirius, though more than 8 light-years away, is more than a full magnitude brighter than Alpha Centauri, which is only half as distant.

Another characteristic of stars is their color, which is particularly apparent in photographs. Stars with hotter surface temperatures tend to be blue, while those with cooler surfaces are red. The color index of a star, however, reflects only the surface temperature, not the total emissivity of radiation. A red supergiant such as Betelguese has a cooler surface than the bluish Sirius, but radiates far more energy.

A star's spectrum provides the most insight into its nature. Atoms in the atmospheres of stars absorb starlight at specific wavelengths, so their presence can be deduced by observing the position of dark bands, called Fraunhoffer lines, against the continuous spectrum of colors produced when the star's light is dispersed with a prism or a diffraction grating. Thus we can tell what stars are made of: mostly hydrogen and helium.

The final and most difficult quality to determine is a star's mass. Fortunately, most of the stars we see in the night sky are not actually solitary, but are multiples so close together that telescopes must be used to resolve them into discrete entities. Quite a few are binaries, such as the beautiful orange and blue pair known as Albireo, but as many as four stars have been known to form a stable system. Epsilon Lyrae is a pair of binaries orbiting a common center of mass (called the barycenter), making it a double-double star. The nice thing about binary stars is that once they have been observed long enough to determine their orbits, we can calculate their masses.

Once we know these basic properties — intrinsic luminosity, temperature, spectral characteristics, and mass — we can attempt to classify stars and speculate about their evolution.

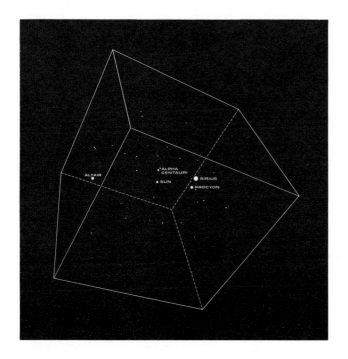

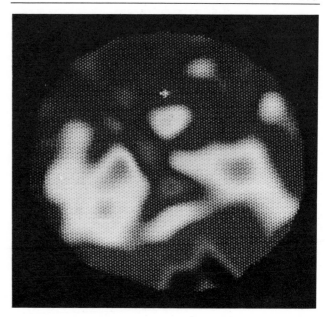

SPECTRAL TYPES

Stars are classified on the basis of their spectra, which are primarily dependent on their surface temperatures. The spectral sequence is O, B, A, F, G, K, M, from hottest to coolest, and can be remembered by the mnemonic sentence, "Oh, be a fine girl, kiss me." Below are some examples:

O Type: Typical surface temperatures of 30,000–60,000° Kelvin; blue-white in color; usually a white dwarf.

B Type: Surface temperatures of 12,000–25,000° Kelvin; blue-white; very massive; helium-burning. Spica is a B type.

A Type: Surface temperatures of 8000–11,000° Kelvin; white; massive; burns hydrogen and produces some light metals. Vega and Deneb are members of this class.

F Type: Surface temperatures of 6200–7200° Kelvin; yellow-white; hydrogen-burning; many metals evident. Procyon is an F type.

G Type: Surface temperatures of 4600–6000° Kelvin; yellow; hydrogen-burning; iron is evident. The Sun and Capella are G types.

K Type: Surface temperatures of 3500–4900° Kelvin; orange; hydrogen-burning, but starting to burn helium; contain many metals, and calcium is prominent. Arcturus is a K type.

M Type: Surface temperatures of 2600–3500° Kelvin; orange-red; leaving the main sequence of stellar evolution. Antares and Betelguese are M types.

There are many subdivisions and special categories, but most stars during their normal lives fit into one of these categories.

Facing page and above left
A model of the solar neighborhood, showing those stars within approximately 16 light-years of the Sun, suggests that particularly bright stars comprise an ethnic minority in our neck of the galaxy. Although our Sun has been disparagingly referred to as a "yellow dwarf," there are locally only four stars that are brighter: Alpha Centauri A, Sirius, Procyon, and Altair. Most of the other stars are faint red dwarfs barely detectable from Earth by the unaided eye. In this orientation, terrestrial North is along the axis pointing toward the upper right. *(Art by author)*

Above right
This photograph of the supergiant star Betelguese is the first image showing surface features on another sun. Although atmospheric distortions make it impossible to resolve the disk of a star with Earth-based telescopes, very short exposures are distorted in a pattern that can be unscrambled by a computer. This technique, known as speckle interferometry, was developed by A. Labeyrie. It allows us to observe what may be flares or sunspots on giant stars. *(Kitt Peak National Observatory)*

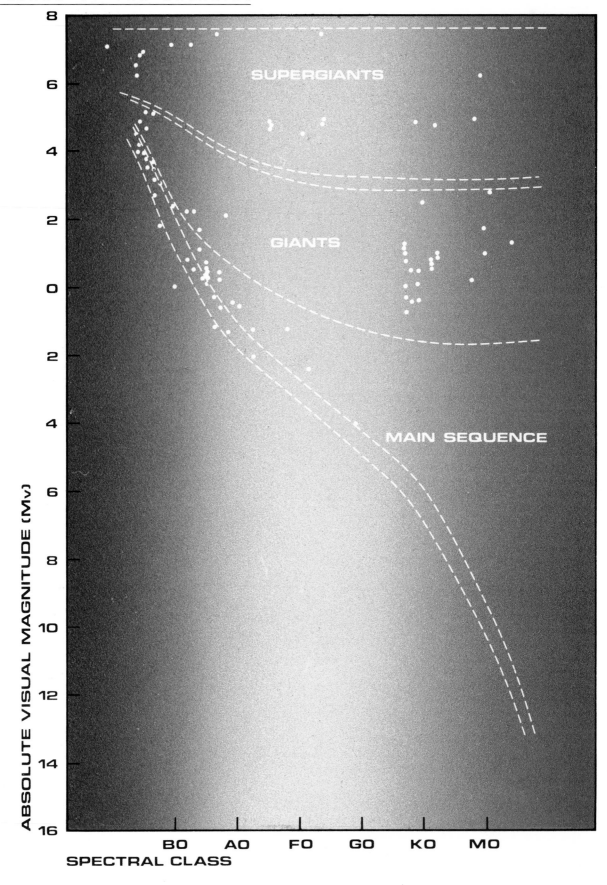

ENDINGS

Although a star's lifetime seems eternal in human terms, it is not. At any given moment, at least 5 percent of all stars are nearing the end of their lives. As we have noted earlier, a star, during the first part of its existence, burns hydrogen; but as the concentration of that original fuel becomes diluted with helium, the reaction flickers. The central regions of the star collapse. If the star's mass is approximately that of the Sun, the collapse leads to the burning of helium, and the subsequent burning of hydrogen in an outer shell causes the star to swell into a giant. It shines for a few hundred million years and then begins to cool and shrink, gradually becoming a white dwarf. If such a white dwarf is in a close binary system with a massive, swelling companion star, it may become a type of variable star known as a *nova*. Although shrunken in size, the white dwarf may still have a sufficiently strong gravitational field to enable it to pull streams of gas away from the companion star. This gas then accumulates in an accretion disk about the white dwarf, and, when it finally reaches the surface, sizzles like grease striking a hot griddle. When enough of this hydrogen accumulates, it detonates, permitting the white dwarf to shine with renewed glory for a few days or weeks. We see these occasional explosions as the outbursts of a nova. The accumulated hydrogen may drive the mass of the white dwarf past a critical limit of 1.44 solar masses. When this happens, the white dwarf suddenly implodes. The resulting energy released far exceeds that of a nova, and such a star shines briefly but brilliantly as a supernova of Type I. A Type II supernova is even more dramatic and powerful. It occurs when a massive star evolves beyond the stage of helium burning and forms a core of carbon. The star may then try to initiate carbon burning, but the carbon core is unstable and can detonate, shattering the entire star.

Stars more than three times more massive than the Sun may explode so violently that the concussion causes their cores to collapse — and keep collapsing. As these stars grow ever smaller, their surface gravity becomes stronger. If the star's matter is able to withstand the gravity, the collapse eventually stops at the point when atoms have been crushed out of existence. At that time, the star is composed of neutrons and free electrons. Such neutron stars are so dense that a cubic centimeter of their material could weigh as much as 100 million tons. If the collapse of the core is too rapid, however, even subatomic forces cannot halt it, and it will continue forever. When the radius of the collapsing star decreases to a few kilometers, the escape velocity exceeds the speed of light; nothing can get out. Our current understanding of physics does not enable us to predict what happens within such warps in space-time.

Facing page
The Hertzsprung-Russell diagram is an attempt to find a pattern that can relate several stellar characteristics, such as spectral class, temperature, and luminosity. When absolute magnitude (the magnitude a star would be observed to possess at a standard distance of 10 parsecs) is plotted against spectral type, several definite trends are apparent, and these may be interpreted in terms of stellar evolution. During the bulk of a star's lifetime, it burns hydrogen fuel. Such stars lie along the Main Sequence and are called dwarfs. Our Sun is of spectral class G2 (each spectral temperature class has ten subdivisions) and is near the middle of the Main Sequence. As it evolves, it will grow more luminous, swelling in diameter, and will move off the Main Sequence, becoming a red giant. After spending a few hundred million years in this stage, possibly as a variable star, it will cool, collapse, and become a white dwarf. Generally speaking, the farther a star is toward the right-hand tail of the Main Sequence, the longer its lifetime.
(Diagram by Michael Standlee Design)

Zeta Aurigae is a supergiant similar to Betelguese, so huge that if it replaced the Sun, Earth's orbit would be contained within it. The red giant is attended by a bluish star, probably of spectral type A, that is approximately three times more luminous than our Sun. The interaction of colors could produce interesting effects on the surface of any world that orbited in such a system. *(Art by author)*

Right
The Pleiades, sometimes called "The Seven Sisters," are a cluster of young stars fairly close to the solar system. The nebulosities that surround these stars are remnants of the cloud of gas that gave them birth. Note how the gas seems to have a structure of parallel filaments, probably the effect of local magnetic fields. *(Photo © Association of Universities for Research in Astronomy, Inc., The Kitt Peak National Observatory)*

Facing page
Pleione, a star in the Pleiades, spins so rapidly that not only is its shape distorted by centrifugal force, but it is also encircled by a ring of gas spun off from its outer layers. It is much hotter than the Sun, and a planet orbiting at 1 astronomical unit away would be roasted by ultraviolet radiation. *(Art by author)*

Even the ancient Greeks noticed that a faint star in the constellation of the whale seemed to change its brightness, and so they named it Mira, meaning "wonder." Mira, or Omicron Ceti, is a giant star with an internal oscillation that causes it to pulse like a fiery heart, taking 332 days for each "beat." It is attended by a white dwarf star that has about a million times the mass of Earth, but is the same size.
(Art by author)

Right
Light curve of Mira (Omicron Ceti), produced by averaging nightly observations of the variable star's magnitude every ten days. At minimum, Mira is too faint to see without a telescope, while at maximum it is of average brightness.
(Diagram by Michael Standlee Design)

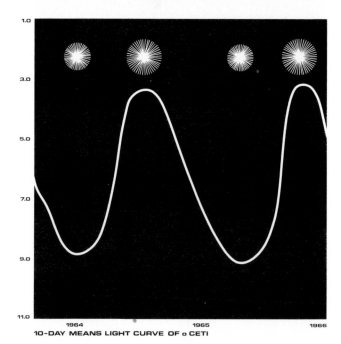

10-DAY MEANS LIGHT CURVE OF o CETI

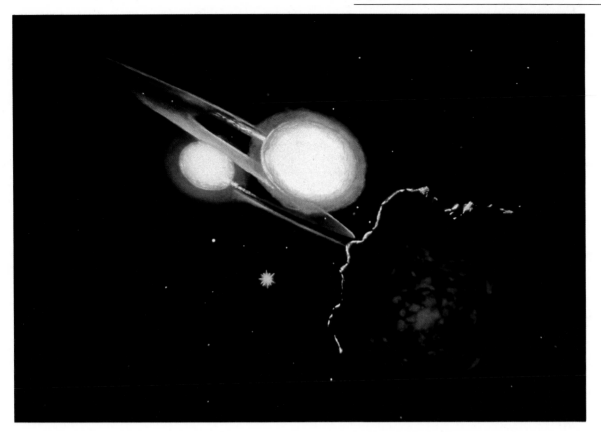

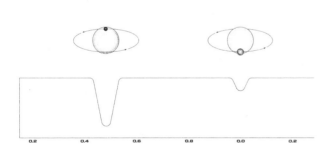

Algol *(above),* which is Arabic for "Demon" (reflecting the Aristotelian abhorrence of changeability in the heavens), is another variable that was detected in ancient times. Unlike Mira, however, its variation does not stem from intrinsic properties but is a result of geometry. As the two stars comprising the Algol system orbit their common center of mass, they eclipse one another. The two components are so close that tidal forces distort their shape, and there may be an exchange of material between them. The asteroid passing in the foreground is 30 million kilometers from this yellow G-9 star, and a third component, a K type, is seen about a light-year away. *(Art by author)*

Light Curve of Algol. An eclipsing binary may exhibit two minima, as does Algol during its three-day cycle. Maximum brightness occurs when both components are off the line of sight, while minimum takes place when the small darker star transits the brighter star, and, to a lesser extent, when it goes behind it. Dips represent minima. Numbers indicate fractions of a cycle. *(Diagram by Michael Standlee Design)*

Nebulae mark the births and deaths of stars. In the heart of the Great Nebula in Orion, seen here from the vicinity of a hypothetical solar system 5 light-years away, are 4 newborn stars known as the Trapezium. *(Art by author)*

Facing page, top
Beta Lyrae represents another variety of eclipsing binary, except for the fact that the components are so close they are essentially touching, and share a common envelope of gas. Such "ellipsoidal binaries" may be regarded either as two stars in very close proximity or as one misshapen star with two cores. Viewed from any planet that might be in orbit about them, the two suns in the B-Lyrae system would perform a stately dance about one another every 12 days. *(Art by author)*

Facing page, bottom
Antares, a type M supergiant, rises ponderously over the horizon of a world orbiting 13 billion miles away, at which distance temperatures would be comparable to those on Earth. During Antares's cooler youth, this world would have been locked in ice, but as its sun expanded in its old age, conditions might have become suitable — for a geologically brief period — for the development of life. A blue companion star is also visible. *(Art by author)*

To escape the limitations imposed by Earth's atmosphere, astronomers have built observatories at ever-increasing altitudes. The icy, wind-swept, rarified summit of Mauna Kea, on the island of Hawaii, rises 4.2 kilometers above sea level and is such a particularly favored site that five countries have established observatories there. *(Photo by author)*

NASA's Infrared Telescope Facility atop Mauna Kea can observe low-frequency parts of the spectrum that at lower altitudes are filtered out by water vapor. Infrared wavelengths are of particular interest in the study of stars that are in the latter stages of formation and beginning to commence nuclear processes.
(Photo by Dale P. Cruikshank, University of Hawaii Institute for Astronomy)

Facing page
The Trifid nebula is a particularly beautiful stellar factory that glows with the blue light of scattered starlight as well as the red light of hydrogen emission. The pressure of light from young stars pushes lanes of dusty matter together to form new stars.
(Photo © Association of Universities for Research in Astronomy, Inc., The Cerro Tololo Inter-American Observatory)

Supernova. Stars significantly more massive than the Sun do not merely bloat up in their old age and then quietly fade away, but erupt in cataclysmic explosions that would destroy any planets they might have. *(Art by author)*

Right
The Crab nebula is the still-expanding remains of a star whose supernova explosion was observed by Chinese astronomers, and perhaps American Indians, in A.D. 1054. At the heart of the Crab is a bizarre stellar remnant known as a neutron star.
(Photo by J. C. Brandt, Kitt Peak National Observatory)

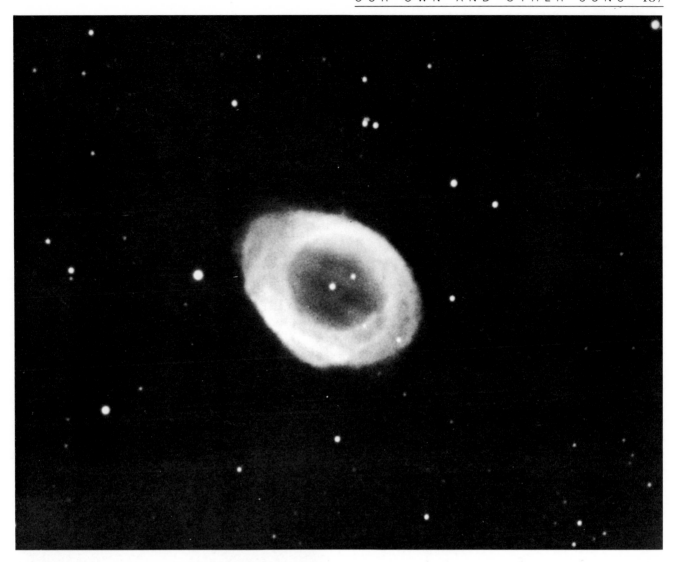

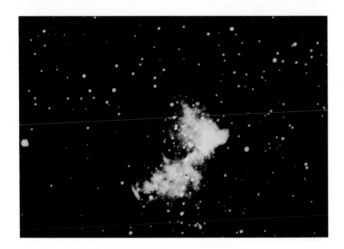

The Ring nebula in Lyra *(above)* is actually a spherical shell of gas blown off by the central star. The ring effect is caused by the greater optical density of gas viewed through the outer edges of the shell.
(Photo © Association of Universities for Research in Astronomy, Inc., The Cerro Tololo Inter-American Observatory)

The Dumbbell nebula *(left)*, approximately 1000 light-years away, surrounds a hot blue star in its death throes. *(Naval Observatory photo)*

The Veil nebula in Cygnus is probably a fragment of a highly dispersed supernova remnant. *(Naval Observatory photo)*

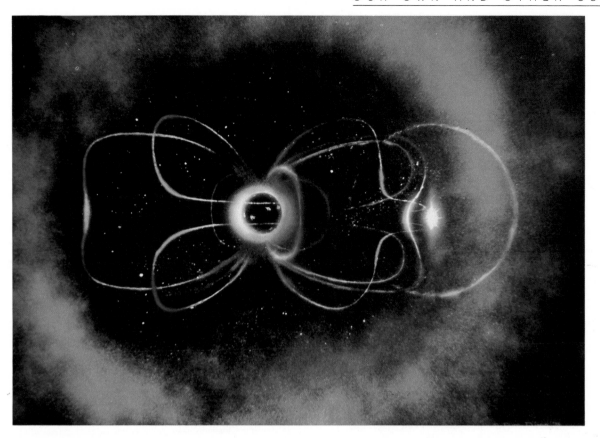

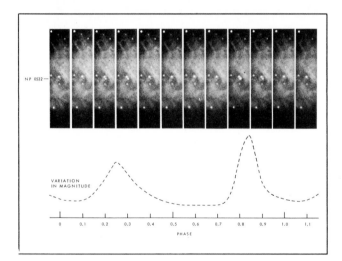

Pulsar. This diagram of a neutron star depicts the superdense stellar remnant at the center of the Crab nebula. It is under 20 kilometers in diameter, and yet contains approximately one solar mass and rotates 30 times each second. The neutron star's intense magnetic field rotates with it, but at a radius of approximately 2000 kilometers it is sweeping through space at the speed of light, and beyond this it cannot go. The field is swept back at this point to form a cylinder. Protons and electrons from "hot spots" on the star's surface are accelerated out to this light cylinder, and cast into space at high velocity, like a beam from a lighthouse. These high-energy particles cause the Crab to glow with synchrotron radiation. The scale of this illustration has been compressed to include all elements. *(Art by author)*

Left
Light Curve of the Crab Pulsar. The photos at the top show the appearance of the pulsar (the star near the center) as it flashes through a complete cycle. The phase scale represents fractions of a revolution by the pulsar; for example, 0.5 is half a revolution, while 1.0 indicates a complete cycle.
(Diagram by S. Maran, Kitt Peak National Observatory)

Cygnus X-1, a powerful source of x-rays, may be a black hole. When a star larger than 3 solar masses goes supernova, the implosion of the core is so violent that it continues to collapse indefinitely, until its gravity becomes so great that nothing, not even light, can escape from it. In this model of the Cygnus X-1 system, a black hole orbits its erstwhile stellar companion, draining away the star's matter like a cosmic vacuum cleaner. X-rays are emitted by gas as it is compressed just before spiraling into this gravitational whirlpool. *(Art by author)*

White Dwarf Star. Representing the next-to-last stage in the evolution of an average star such as our Sun, a white dwarf is a rather fantastic object. Imagine a star the size of a planet, which nonetheless retains perhaps 90 percent of its original mass. Its density is so great that a chunk of white-dwarf material would fall through the Earth like a rock falling through air. Though its surface is fiercely hot, it is much too small to provide any warmth to whatever planetary corpses may still orbit it, and for the few millions of years left before its fires finally flicker and die, it hoards its energy like a vengeful miser, poisoning the space around it with ultraviolet radiation.
(Art by author)

GALAXIES

IT IS OF INTEREST TO NOTE THAT VIRTUALLY all representations of deep-sky objects such as galaxies, whether artistic or photographic, are to some extent misleading. Even though galaxies shine with the light of billions of stars, they are quite faint and diffuse. The galaxy M-31 in Andromeda, for example, subtends an angle of nearly 5 degrees, which is equivalent to ten full Moons lined up. One would think that such a vast object would dominate the night sky and present a magnificent spectacle, but even on the darkest, clearest nights, M-31 appears as little more than a dim, oval smudge of light, best seen by peripheral vision. Our eyes can detect only its nucleus. (An observer's initial disappointment may be eased, however, by the realization that he is looking more than 2 million years into the past when gazing upon M-31.) Long time-exposures are required to bring out the colors and spiral structure of the galaxy. Such photographs are spectacular, but one should bear in mind that if an astronomer could be transported to a vantage point beyond the Milky Way, the surrounding galaxies would appear to him only as softly glowing patches of fog, suspended in a perfect blackness empty of stars. Only the rare sparkle of a supernova could provide a focusing point for his straining eyes.

Because of this limitation, the nature of galaxies was not discovered until the 1920s, with the advent of fast photographic emulsions and large telescopes. Prior to that, galaxies were considered to be clouds of gas contained within the Milky Way, which was regarded as the whole of creation. From our viewpoint, the scope of the universe has

Facing page
The Local Group of galaxies, seen from a point 1 million light-years from our own Milky Way. Like stars, galaxies are born in litters and tend to cluster in loose, gravitational association. We are contained within a cluster of at least 25 galaxies known as the Local Group — *local* meaning within 1 million parsecs. The spiral near the lower left of the picture is the Milky Way, which appears large only because of its proximity. Its irregular satellite galaxies, the Magellanic Clouds, appear just below it. Beyond lie the Fornax and Sculptor galaxies, Maffei I and Maffei II, and the great spiral M-31 in Andromeda, located toward the upper right of the picture. *(Art by author)*

The galaxy M-81, approximately 3 million parsecs away, is probably very similar in structure to our own.
(Photo © Association of Universities for Research in Astronomy, Inc., The Kitt Peak National Observatory)

increased vastly since then. We know today that our own Milky Way is just one of hundreds of millions of galaxies, each containing billions of stars.

Like mice in the cathedral at Chartres, we are residents in one of the more beautiful structures in nature but are unable to appreciate it. A galaxy can assume one of many shapes, depending on temperature, mass, volume, rotation, and other conditions that are attendant to its formation out of the primordial gas created at the beginning of the universe. Some galaxies are ragged and irregular groupings of stars, like handfuls of sand tossed in the air. Some are ellipsoidal in form — orderly, but not very interesting visually. Others, however, are glorious whirlpools of stars and glowing gases, and it is within such a spiral galaxy that we live.

Because we cannot observe our galaxy from the outside (at the speed of light, we would have to travel at least 10,000 years to get a decent view), we must deduce its structure by means of a variety of observations. First, there is the Milky Way itself, that frosty river of stars that girdles the night sky. Even simple binoculars resolve it into many thousands of stars. In the late 1700s, Sir William Herschel estimated the population density of stars throughout the whole sky and concluded, correctly, that the Milky Way was a disk-shaped mass of stars formed more or less like a millstone. We see more stars when looking along the plane of the "millstone" than when looking toward the poles. Modern mercator projections of the sky reveal that the Milky Way is shaped rather like a double convex lens. Photographs of other galaxies whose disks happen to be edge-on to our line of sight, and that

The galactic core seems to be an area of violent activity, but intervening clouds of gas and dust prevent us from observing any but the most energetic events with our radio telescopes. It is possible that the rich clustering of stars at the core of the galaxy has led to the formation of a giant black hole. Streams of gas and stars that are observed to have been ejected from other galaxies can be accounted for by the mechanism of very massive black holes, although such ejections are probably far more violent than anything analogous that may be occurring within our own galaxy. We do know that the core of the Milky Way is surrounded by a halo of globular clusters, each containing hundreds of thousands of stars. Night on a planet near the core would be spectacular indeed, although the radiation environment within such dense populations of stars would probably prevent the development of life. (Art by author)

Top
Viewed from the periphery, the Milky Way begins to assume a lens shape. *(Art by author)*

Middle
From 200,000 light-years away, viewed from a point above the galactic plane, the Milky Way is revealed as a vast whirlpool of stars — at least 200 billion of them — 100,000 light-years across. The core of the galaxy glows with the ruddy hue of dying coals. Here are the ancients, the red giant stars, survivors of the vigorous early days of stellar evolution, when the galaxy was young. The spiral arms glow with fainter, cooler colors. Here creation is still proceeding, as new stars condense out of the clouds of dust and gas that swirl out from the core. Such clouds contain the ashes of stars long dead, and the heavy atoms common to worlds like Earth. *(Art by author)*

Bottom
The Milky Way provides a dazzling backdrop for the Earth and Moon. Seen from space, this frosty river of stars is revealed as a complex structure full of glowing nebulosities, star clusters, and dark rivers of obscuring gas and dust. *(Art by author)*

The Milky Way rises like a ghostly whirlpool over an Earthlike world 100,000 light-years above the galactic pole. From this distance, we can't even see the small yellow star that is the Sun, as it carries its family of planets along on its 200-million-year orbit in the galaxy; but it would be about two-thirds of the way outward along one of the spiral arms. *(Art by author)*

A globular cluster (*below*), as seen from a planet whose parent sun has been tidally ejected from the cluster. *(Art by author)*

are known to be spirals, suggest that these galaxies are similar to our own. More recently, it has become possible to use radio telescopes to map regions of hydrogen clouds that are obscured by intervening stars and dust. When this is done, a definite spiral pattern emerges.

There are at least two theories to account for our galaxy's form. A collapsing cloud of gas, if it has sufficient angular momentum, tends to assume a bar shape. (This is thought to be the primary mechanism involved in the birth of binary stars.) According to one theory, this rotating bar sends waves of varying gravity through the rest of the nebula, in the same way that a slowly rotating stick produces ripples on the surface of a pond. These waves then produce a spiral pattern. According to another theory, irregular or elliptical galaxies in close interaction may stretch one another into bar shapes by means of tidal forces. Since there do not appear to be any nearby galaxies interacting with our own, it is thought that the Milky Way probably took shape by the method advanced in the former theory.

It should not be assumed that the dark spaces that separate the glowing spiral arms are empty; they are filled with massive rivers of dust and gas, and can lay just as much claim to being legitimate spiral arms as can the more luminous streamers. These areas are dark because stars tend to form along the spiraling density wave as it rotates through the galaxy. The dark lanes represent potential stellar matter that is waiting for the next wave to sweep through. Since the bar-shaped galactic core rotates rapidly, the density wave tends to rotate at much higher velocity than the stars themselves move in their orbits about the

galactic core; but stars such as our Sun are indeed bound by Kepler's laws: the Sun takes approximately 230 million years to complete an orbit about the Milky Way. At the beginning of the present galactic year, dinosaurs were becoming ascendant.

Thus we have found that our Sun is one of perhaps 200 billion stars, which collectively comprise the Milky Way galaxy, or, immodestly, *the* Galaxy — a designation that may be an attempt to preserve a fading chauvinistic pride in our place in the scheme of things. We know today that we are not at the center of *anything*. Even our Sun is merely another mote, displaced some 8000 parsecs from the center of a galaxy that is 30,000 parsecs in diameter.

THE EXPANDING UNIVERSE

In the 1920s, Edwin Hubble, the astronomer who first proved that M-31 was a vast cloud of stars at immense distance rather than a local cloud of gas, discovered a curious phenomenon that was ultimately to revolutionize our understanding of the universe. Upon comparing the spectra of various galaxies, he noticed that spectral lines of more distant galaxies were consistently displaced toward the low-frequency, or red, end of the spectrum. The displacement of spectral lines had been used for years to determine properties of motion for celestial bodies. This

The Large Magellanic Cloud is one of two small galaxies that are satellites of the Milky Way. Both galaxies are small, 8000 and 5000 parsecs across, respectively, and both are irregular in shape, although they seem to have loosely defined barlike structures thought to be characteristic of gravitational associations in the early stages of formation. The Milky Way probably had a similar bar in its center that eventually generated spiral arms. The rosy patch of light at the left of the photo is the Tarantula nebula, thought to be the nucleus of the Large Magellanic Cloud. It contains at least 100 supergiant stars.
(Photo © Association of Universities for Research in Astronomy, Inc., The Cerro Tololo Inter-American Observatory)

Top
M-31, the Great Galaxy in Andromeda, is probably the closest galaxy that is similar in structure to our own. Since its rotation axis is tilted about 13 degrees toward us, we can see the central regions that are forever hidden from us in the case of our Milky Way. The main disk of stars is approximately 150,000 light-years across and probably contains more than 250 billion stars. M-31 is probably slightly over 2 million light-years away and is the most distant object that can be seen with the unaided eye.
(Photo © Association of Universities for Research in Astronomy, Inc., The Kitt Peak National Observatory)

Middle
Galaxy M-84 is ellipsoidal in shape. Before reaching their minimum size, such galaxies probably assimilate most of their initial supply of hydrogen gas into stars.
(Photo © Association of Universities for Research in Astronomy, Inc., The Kitt Peak National Observatory)

Bottom
Galaxy M-104 has an unusually large and diffuse central region reminiscent of elliptical galaxies, but it also has an apparent spiral structure. Note the dark lanes of dust and gas along the rim.
(Photo © Association of Universities for Research in Astronomy, Inc., The Kitt Peak National Observatory)

was a well-understood phenomenon commonly known as the Doppler effect: just as the pitch, or frequency, of a siren or train whistle rises and falls as it approaches and passes an observer, so light waves "pile up" as the source approaches an observer, and "stretch out" when the source recedes. When the slit of a spectrograph is laid across the equator of a rotating star or planet, the resulting spectral lines will be slanted — to a degree depending on the speed of rotation — because light from the approaching limb is shifted toward the blue end, while light from the receding edge shifts toward the red. Spectra of nearby galaxies had already shown that most of them were moving away from us and only a few toward us, usually at characteristic speeds of less than a hundred kilometers per second. Hubble found, however, that all galaxies farther away than 20 million light-years were moving away from us, and that the farther away they were, the greater their speed of recession.

This observation was quickly interpreted to mean that the universe as a whole was expanding, and that galaxies, like raisins in a rising cake, were moving away from one another at speeds directly proportional to their separation. Such expansion of the universe had been predicted by the general theory of relativity.

The discovery of the expansion of the universe made it possible, for the first time, to hazard a guess about the nature of the event that began it all: if we took a motion picture of the universe as a whole and ran it backward, the universe would seem to contract until, ultimately, all the galaxies would come together at one point. Logically, this must have been the situation at the beginning, in which case the expansion we observe today is the result of a monumental explosion that George Gamow graphically, if unpoetically, termed the Big Bang. (Unfortunately, the name stuck.)

There is other evidence to support this cosmogony. Just as a conventional explosion cools as it expands, so must the universe. By estimating the current density of the universe and determining the speed of expansion, physicists are able to calculate the initial temperatures that must have prevailed within the primordial fireball, as well as the subsequent rate of cooling. The universe as a whole must now have a temperature just slightly above absolute zero, approximately 3 to 4 degrees Kelvin. In 1965, Arno Penzias and Robert Wilson discovered in sensitive radio receivers a persistent hissing, or noise, that seemed independent of the direction in which the antenna was pointing and could not be attributed to the radio system itself. They concluded that they were detecting the microwave emission that would be characteristic of a "black body" at a temperature of 3°K — the predicted temperature of the universe. They were detecting photons, immensely red-shifted, from shortly after the moment of creation, and for this discovery they were awarded the Nobel Prize.

More recently, sensitive microwave detectors, flown in a NASA jet high above the radio noise of the lower atmosphere, have detected a slight directional variation in the Cosmic Background Radiation. It is most intense in the direction of the constellation of Leo, and less so in the opposite part of the sky. This can be explained if we assume, as seems likely, that the Milky Way has a proper motion of its own, with respect to all the other galaxies, and is moving in the direction of Leo. The Cosmic Background provides us for the first time with an absolute standard against which to measure velocities.

So the weight of theory and observation suggests almost conclusively that the universe was born in an explosion, probably 16 billion years ago, and is still expanding. But will the expansion continue? Will the galaxies continue to drift apart, each slowly exhausting its supplies of stellar fuel and growing colder, its stars winking out one by one? Or will the combined gravitational attraction of all the galaxies slow the rate of recession until the expansion stops, and then begins to reverse, causing the universe to return to its starting point, perhaps to start all over again in

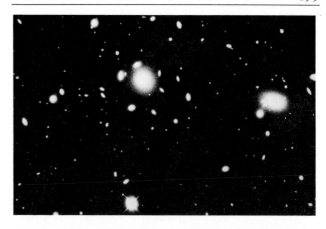

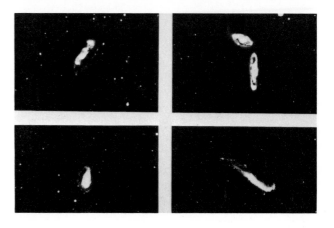

Top
More than one thousand galaxies are contained within this cluster in the constellation Coma Berenices. Most galaxies shown here are ellipticals. The sharp, pointlike objects are foreground stars in our own galaxy.
(Photo © Association of Universities for Research in Astronomy, Inc., The Kitt Peak National Observatory)

Bottom
Peculiar galaxies have structural distortions that can be caused either by close interactions with other galaxies or by internal explosions.
(Photo © Association of Universities for Research in Astronomy, Inc., The Kitt Peak National Observatory)

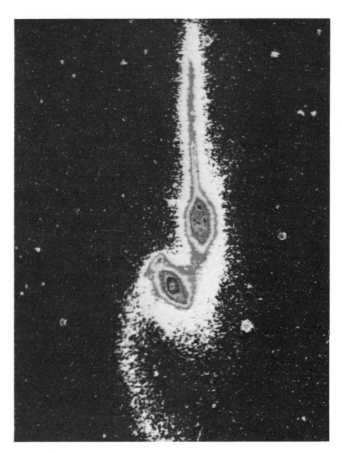

Left
Interacting Galaxies. Considering their size, galaxies tend to be almost frighteningly close to one another. Here, seen in the sky of an Earthlike planet, two galaxies drift ponderously past one another, drawing streamers of stars and gas across the intervening space. Computer simulations suggest that such encounters may be one mechanism by which peculiarly shaped streamers, vaguely resembling spiral arms, are formed. *(Art by author)*

Right
Contrast enhancement in this photo seems to show two elliptical galaxies that are either emerging to form a barred spiral galaxy or undergoing a grazing encounter that will draw out streamers of stars in both.
(Photo © Association of Universities for Research in Astronomy, Inc., The Kitt Peak National Observatory)

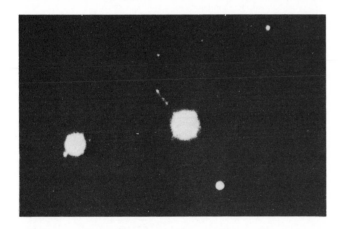

Colliding Galaxies *(top)*. Interactions between galaxies can occasionally be even more direct. Here a small, compact spiral is shown passing through a larger but more loosely structured galaxy. The little galaxy may emerge virtually unscathed, but the larger one shows considerable disruption. Individual stars within the galaxies would rarely collide, since they are comparatively tiny, but the high-velocity collision of gas clouds would generate radio emissions. *(Art by author)*

This quasar in Virgo is one of hundreds of quasi-stellar objects that seem to be at immense distances and apparently radiate more energy each than do hundreds of ordinary galaxies. The luminous jet that seems to have been ejected from the quasar may be 150,000 light-years in length and is possibly a stream of stars cast out by an interaction with a gigantic black hole. *(Photo © Association of Universities for Research in Astronomy, Inc., The Kitt Peak National Observatory)*

Quasars may be galaxies that are in the process of being torn apart by particularly massive black holes at their cores. Whereas a "conventional" black hole, such as the one suspected in Cygnus X-1, may take millions of years to consume a companion star, supermassive black holes may eat whole stars on a daily basis, squeezing them, in their final moments, to such densities that prodigious amounts of energy are released. *(Art by author)*

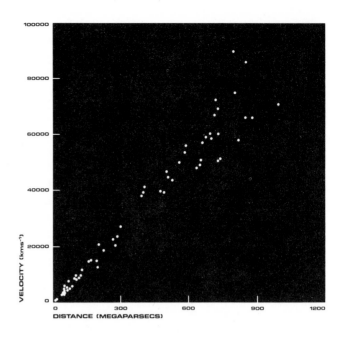

Right
Hubble's constant was determined by plotting
the apparent velocity of recession of distant
galaxies, as determined by their red shifts,
against their observed distance from Earth. The
slope of the graph, 57 km/sec/megaparsec,
reflects the rate of expansion of the universe.
Scattering of data near the upper part of the
curve is due to uncertainty in determining the
distance to the more distant galaxies.
(Diagram by Michael Standlee Design)

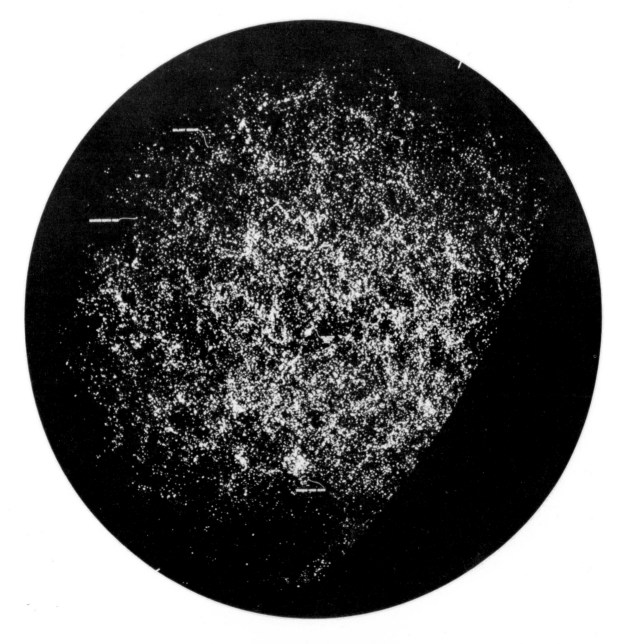

another explosion — one more in an infinite series of cycles of birth, death, and rebirth? The answer depends on the density of the universe as a whole. Below a certain concentration of mass, gravity will not be able to stop the expansion. Current estimates of mass density suggest that the universe is "open" — that is, that it will expand indefinitely. This answer is philosophically unsatisfying to many scientists, however, and efforts are under way to locate the "missing mass" that would be needed to "close" the universe. Perhaps it will be found in clouds of gas drifting between galaxies, or in black holes. In addition, it is known that the universe is rich in neutrinos, and it has recently been proposed that these have a small but definite mass. Such mass-carrying neutrinos in themselves would suffice to close the universe.

QUASARS

One consequence of an evolving universe is that it does not look the same at all times. Since we are looking back into time when we look out into the immensity of space, we should see objects different from those we observe closer in space-time. There is a particularly puzzling class of objects called quasars, which appear in photographs as very small, starlike points. These objects show red shifts that would seem to indicate recessional velocities that are significant fractions of the velocity of light. Most quasars are assumed to be at least 10 billion light-years away (and 10 billion years back in time). What is intriguing is that if quasars are indeed as far away as their red shifts suggest, each of them is radiating more energy than hundreds of normal galaxies — a phenomenon difficult to explain in terms of conventional physics.

It has been suggested that quasars are early galaxies that are being torn apart by black holes. This idea has merit, since it has been observed that some quasars have "jets" coming from them, similar to those seen in galaxies that are suspected of harboring black holes in their cores. Another theory suggests that quasars are not as far away as their red shifts indicate. The red shifts may be caused by intense gravitational fields, rather than by recession. Whatever the case, quasars represent just one of the problems of modern astrophysics. Attempts to explain such exotica as black holes and quasars will almost certainly lead to a new understanding, and appreciation, of the subtle laws governing the universe.

Facing page, bottom
The large-scale structure of the universe is seen in this map that was made by counting the number of galaxies within each $\frac{1}{6}° \times \frac{1}{6}°$ area of the sky and then assigning values on a gray scale, in accordance with galaxy population density. Thus black represents no galaxies and white represents ten or more. Note the tendency of galaxies to form not only in clusters, but in groups of clusters. Note also the filamentary structures that are reminiscent of those seen in supernova remnants such as the Crab nebula, suggesting that the universe is indeed the result of a titanic explosion, as other observational evidence suggests. (The map is based on a 12-year survey by Donald Shane and Carl Wirtanen at Lick Observatory, and was prepared by Bernie Siebers, Mike Seldner, and Ray Soneira.)

SINCE 1960, WHEN ASTRONOMER FRANK Drake turned a radio telescope toward the stars Tau Ceti and Epsilon Eridani in an effort to detect signals, the science of exobiology has evolved from a part-time pursuit hovering at the fringes of academic respectability to a full-blown discipline competing for NASA funds. Papers on interstellar travel and communication appear regularly in scientific journals, and the success of films such as *Close Encounters of the Third Kind* reflects a growing acceptance of the premise that we are not alone in the universe. This intellectual revolution has been fueled by several recent discoveries that have resulted in a new understanding of the processes that gave birth to the solar system and, ultimately, to ourselves. Perhaps more influential, however, is the example of our own thrust into space; if we can do it, after a scant 10,000 years of civilization and a mere century of advanced technology, why couldn't other, perhaps older races in the immensity of time and space have made a similar outward reach? This question has been asked for centuries, but only during the last few years have we developed a technology that provides a realistic hope of answering it.

Before embarking on such a quest, which could entail great expenditures of time and resources, it is of value to calculate the odds for success. In particular, we would like to have some idea of the number of technological civilizations in the galaxy. If there are only a few, then they would be considerably more difficult to find than a needle in a haystack. If there are a million, a search might be worthwhile. The Drake equation permits such a calculation.

The Drake Equation: $\qquad N = R_* f_p n_e f_l f_i f_c L$

N is the number of technological civilizations.

R_* is the number of new stars formed each year.

f_p is the fraction of stars that have planets.

n_e is the average number of Earthlike planets per system.

f_l is the fraction of such planets that bring forth life.

f_i is the fraction of such planets on which intelligence

evolves.

f_c is the fraction of races with high technology.

L is the average lifetime of technological civilization.

As written above, the parameters of the equation are listed in order of the extent of our ignorance about them. We know something about R_* and can make reasonable guesses about f_p and n_e, but our knowledge is woefully deficient beyond that. The best we can do is establish optimistic and pessimistic ranges for each of the parameters, and proceed on that basis. Nevertheless, the computation of N is an interesting exercise that enables us to explore the problems related to the search for extraterrestrial intelligence.

Our galaxy is on the order of 10 billion years old and contains about 200 billion stars. If stars formed at a steady rate, it could be expected that 20 would be formed each

Large radio telescopes, such as the 65-meter dish at Goldstone, in California's Mojave Desert, were built primarily to monitor deep-space missions and conduct astronomical research; but they can also be used to detect any signals that might be transmitted toward us from other civilizations. Note the comparative size of the bus, next to the antenna.
(Photo by author)

Facing page
Sagittarius. Nearly 10 million stars are imaged in this photograph of the dense star clouds that lie in the direction of the galactic center. It is possible that even after the elimination of all those stars that are too bright or short-lived, 100,000 still remain that shine upon life-bearing worlds. And perhaps two of them serve as suns to civilizations more advanced than our own.
(Photo by David L. Talent, © Association of Universities for Research in Astronomy, Inc., The Cerro Tololo Inter-American Observatory)

Project Cyclops, a study conducted at NASA's Ames Research Center in the mid-1970s, suggested that very large radio telescopes might be required to detect extraterrestrial signals. Shown here is a 2000-meter radio telescope that has been constructed out of lightweight materials in the weightlessness of orbit. In the background, 36,000 kilometers away, is the Earth, seen eclipsing the Sun. Spacecraft are used to maneuver receiving equipment at the antenna's focus. (Art by author)

year. The rate of star formation was probably much greater during the early history of the galaxy, however, so this value is probably too high. Within clouds of gas such as the Orion nebula, star formation is proceeding apace, and since there are many such stellar factories scattered throughout the spiral arms of the galaxy, it is probable that at least one new star is formed each year, and possibly even more. Let us assume that R_* is greater than one star per year and less than five. Thus, $1 < R_* < 5$.

Until we have a large telescope in orbit, it will be impossible to directly observe any planets that might attend other stars. The only evidence we have for extrasolar planets consists of highly controversial observations of "wobbles" in the proper motion of nearby stars. These are thought to be caused by the gravitational perturbations of giant unseen companions. In 1963, Peter Van de Kamp announced the discovery of a dark body, several times the mass of Jupiter, in orbit about Barnard's star, a red dwarf approximately 6 light-years away. More refined analysis of the star's wavy path suggested that the wobble might be caused by two roughly Jupiter-sized bodies. Such masses would qualify as planets rather than marginal stars. These deviations from a linear proper motion are very tiny, however, and are at the limits of optical resolution and the precision of the instruments used to measure the position of Barnard's star, so not all astronomers accept these observations as evidence of extrasolar planets.

Without direct evidence, we must fall back on theory. Prior to a few decades ago, it was thought that our solar system was the result of a very close and highly unlikely tidal interaction between our Sun and another star, which pulled out globs of stellar matter that later cooled to form the planets. In this scenario, solar systems would be very rare indeed. Observations of interstellar grains and accretion disks around young stars suggest, however, that planets are probably near-inevitable by-products of stellar formation. We have no reason to believe that there is anything exceptional about our solar system, and we now have fairly refined theories of planetary formation that predict the formation of planets out of nebulas rich with heavier elements. It seems a good bet that all solitary stars formed in, say, the last 8 billion years (after the first generation of stars cooked up the heavier atoms) are attended by planets, and there seems no reason to exclude very close or very distant binary stars, since planets could have stable orbits near them. Probably the only stars that do not have planets are very old, first-generation stars and those multiple systems whose components are separated by distances characteristic of the inner solar system — distances on the order of tens of millions of kilometers. Such systems would be too turbulent, gravitationally, to permit Earthlike planets to form. This still leaves about 100 billion stars, a number that we will accept as our upper limit. In lieu of other data, let us assume that the wavy proper motions observed by Van de Kamp do indeed indicate the presence of planets. If this is true, then at least 8 of the 59 stars within 5 parsecs of Earth have planets. Thus, $0.14 < f_p < 0.50$.

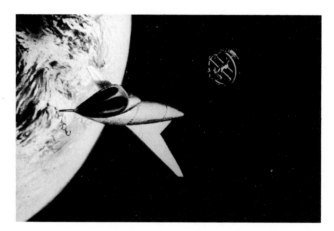

Left

Interstellar Probe. An alternative to passively listening for information about other solar systems is to go there ourselves, or at least send automated probes. One design, called Daedalus, that was proposed by the British Interplanetary Society, could attain approximately 10 percent of the speed of light by detonating pellets of nuclear fuel within a massive thrust chamber, thus making possible one-way trips to the nearer stars in less than half a century. Such a probe would have to carry a very sophisticated computer that would not only be able to alter its flight plan to meet unforeseen contingencies, but would also be able to diagnose and repair spacecraft malfunctions by using remote-control "wardens." The main stage of such a probe is here shown being checked out over the Moon. (*Art by author*)

Right

The lifetime of a technological civilization may be extended indefinitely, if it survives to establish self-supporting colonies in space. Reusable spacecraft, such as the *Space Shuttle* and its successors, are keys to the development of the space environment. (*Art by author*)

One model of a space colony is that of a torus, 2 kilometers across, which is rotated at 1 rpm to produce a centrifugal force equivalent to Earth gravity. Sunlight is directed into the colony by means of mirrors. *(Art by author)*

In considering the number of Earthlike planets per system, we are again forced to extrapolate from very limited data. We could rely on the principle of mediocrity and assume that ours is an average solar system, in which case one out of nine planets is similar to Earth. This seems extravagant, however, in light of recent discoveries about our neighboring worlds Mars and Venus. It used to be thought that any planet of approximately the Earth's mass maintained a reasonably clement environment as long as it orbited within its parent sun's "ecosphere" — that is, the range of distances bounded by the boiling and freezing points of water. Thus if Earth were moved closer to the Sun than Venus is, for instance, the seas would boil; and beyond the orbit of Mars, they would freeze. By this criterion, the Sun's ecosphere was substantial — more than 150 million kilometers wide — and the odds were good that a planet would form in such a large gap. Indeed, three planets did. It turns out, however, that the situation is far more complicated than this, and that Earth is perched precariously between fire and ice. Michael S. Hart has calculated that moving the Earth just 5 percent closer to the Sun would produce a runaway greenhouse effect and the hellish temperatures we observe on Venus, while increasing the average distance to the Sun by a mere 2 percent would result in runaway glaciation — a permanent ice age. It would seem, then, that the ecosphere of a Sun-type star is comparatively narrow, and that the chances of a planet forming in this zone are rather slim.

In order to maintain Earthlike conditions, a planet must also have the proper mass. If it is too small, as is Mars, its gravity will not be strong enough to retain more than a very thin atmosphere. If it is too large, say 50 percent larger than Earth, the greenhouse effect of the commensurately thick atmosphere may keep temperatures too high for organic molecules to survive. In our solar system, two planets — Earth and Venus — are the right size. Let us assume that approximately 1 out of 25 solar systems has a planet with more or less the same mass and temperature as Earth.

On what percentage of these planets does life evolve? Each year, new fossil evidence pushes the origin of life farther back. At present, the oldest fossils date from at least 3.5 billion years ago. If life were a rare phenomenon produced by an unlikely combination of molecules, we would not expect it to have developed as soon as it did. Again using the principle of mediocrity, we feel safe in assuming that any planet with a supply of liquid water on its surface will eventually bring forth life.

Mediocrity aside, there is evidence that the chemicals of life are plentiful in the universe. Radio-telescope observations of interstellar clouds have shown that these nebulae are rich in organic molecules. Hydrogen cyanide, ammonia, formaldehyde, and even ethanol (the intoxicant in wine) have been detected drifting between the stars. To be sure, these molecules are sparsely distributed in space, and interactions must be rare, but one thing the universe has in good supply is time. Given millions of years, organic molecules adhering to interstellar dust grains will eventually encounter and combine with others. The fact that they exist proves this.

The discovery of interstellar organic chemicals has led to a resurrection of the old panspermia hypothesis that life drifted to Earth from elsewhere. In the late 1970s, N. C. Wickramasinghe and Fred Hoyle (a distinguished British astronomer and occasional science fiction writer noted for outré ideas) put forward the lifecloud theory, which suggests that life, in the form of viruses, originated in interstellar gas clouds or within comets, rather than in the primordial sea. While traditionalists can muster numerous arguments against the idea of chemical evolution proceeding in interstellar space (for example, hard radiation would tend to shatter the bonds of molecules above a certain level of complexity), the cometary hypothesis is not so easy to dismiss. Eugene Shoemaker has suggested that the oceans were probably produced when icy planetesimals from the outer reaches of the solar system impacted Earth during the final stages of its accretion. This process would supplement the ocean's origin through outgassing from the interior of the Earth. These late-arriving planetesimals were essentially comets, so the early ocean can be regarded as a broth of melted comets. There seems to be no reason why chemical evolution could not proceed in protected pockets of liquid water beneath the crusts of comets as they are warmed during perihelion passage. One can imagine chains of ever more complex organics, including simple replicators, building up on the porous surfaces of dust grains suspended within such mini-seas, and eventually being released into space as the cometary crust erodes to the edges of these celestial wombs. Hoyle and Wickramasinghe have even suggested that certain persistent diseases, such as influenza and the common cold, are caused by the continued influx of new life forms from space. Epidemiologists hold other views, however, and this latter speculation is generally discounted.

Perhaps the most compelling argument for the prevalence and inevitability of life is the fact that meteorites, those samples of interplanetary matter that occasionally fall to Earth, contain amino acids, the building blocks of proteins. Organic molecules such as amino acids show symmetry; that is, their structures can be either right-handed or left-handed. A description of the reader's hands as being composed of four fingers and a thumb might lead one to believe that both hands are alike; but a cursory examination shows that they are not: they are mirror images and cannot be superimposed. Organic molecules exhibit a similar "handedness." A beam of light passed through an organic compound in colloidal suspension will be polarized either to the right or left. All biologically produced amino acids on Earth are left-handed, perhaps indicating that all terrestrial life has evolved from replicator molecules that happened to the left-handed. Amino acids in meteorites have an equal proportion of right- and left-handed molecules, proving their nonbiological, extraterrestrial origins.

These arguments suggest that life is part of the natural order and will occur anywhere conditions are right. Let us

The interior of such a colony could be a pleasant place in which to live, particularly in one of the larger settlements. *(Art by author)*

be optimistic, then, and make f_l equal to 1.0, assuming that all Earthlike planets bear life. At this point, we can use the Drake equation to estimate the number of life-bearing worlds, eliminating f_i and f_c and making L equal to the lifespan of a biosphere, rather than to that of a technological civilization. Thus the number of living worlds is given by $N_l = R_* \times f_p \times n_e \times L_b$. Assuming that the average biosphere endures for at least 3 billion years, we obtain a pessimistic estimate of 16,800,000 life-bearing worlds for N_1, and an optimistic estimate of 300,000,000. These numbers are impressive, but we must bear in mind that there are 200 billion stars in the galaxy. Even when we take the optimistic estimate, only 1 star in approximately 67 has a life-bearing planet, in which case Earth is probably the only living world within a range of 16 light-years.

We are most ignorant about the last three terms of the Drake equation, which pertain to the evolution and survival of intelligent technological species. It can be argued that the trend of evolution on Earth has been toward nervous systems of ever-increasing sophistication, but it is by no means obvious that technological intelligence is inevitable. If it were, then we would expect to find the remains of several prehuman technological civilizations in the fossil record; but such is not the case. It seems that Earth managed quite happily for 4.5 billion years before bringing forth the first astronaut.

There is reason to believe that our sort of intelligence is a fluke, the product of an unlikely combination of environmental factors. Suppose the convection of magma within the Earth's mantle had not forced open the Great Rift Valley in eastern Africa 15 million years ago, when that continent was inhabited by a dense population of apelike creatures. Without the wide range of habitats created by that geological upheaval, could our hominid ancestors have survived the fierce competition for food and territory that must have prevailed then? What if Earth had not been subject to a general cooling trend that culminated in a series of brutal ice ages, trying our ancestors' survival skills to the limit? Would we be here today, in our present form? It seems unlikely. Recognizably human beings have existed for only the last 0.01 percent of geologic time. Whereas the family of the apes contains four main genera, only one species of hominid has survived the tribulations of the last few million years, and we really don't know why. If a large brain, upright stance, and manual dexterity were the only qualities required for human survival, there should be other species in the family of man; but we are alone. It is as if there were only one species of hawk, shark, or monkey. Some accident of genetics or environment allowed us to survive when our hominid cousins perished.

It seems that man is a most unusual animal, a true freak of nature rather than the logical end-product of a steady series of improvements on a good basic design. It is difficult to isolate the characteristics that have given us an edge in the battle for survival, and the plight of our nearest relatives, the apes, is not reassuring. Chimpanzees and gorillas have been shown to be capable of quite abstract reasoning and of communicating through sign language or computer interface, but neither species has prospered in the wild. Despite their intelligence and dexterity, most apes are confined to increasingly endangered habitats, and the mountain gorilla is on the verge of extinction. Apparently, being "a little bit human" is not enough; an animal must have the full measure of human characteristics in order to profit from them.

So far, we have taken the chauvinistic stance that an animal must be rather like us in order to be intelligent, but this is not necessarily true. Dolphins and other toothed whales have brains as large and complex as ours. There is a wealth of anecdotal evidence, dating back to Aristotle, that dolphins have an intelligence comparable to man's, and it is difficult to observe their behavior without concluding that they are more than mere animals. In experiments at oceanaria, dolphins have demonstrated an ability to process and communicate such abstract concepts as left and right, number, shape, and identity. For example, when a dolphin is confronted with a wooden triangle juxtaposed to the symbol that he has been taught means "the same as," he will select another triangle from an assortment of geometric forms. If a sense of humor is indicative of intelligence, the dolphins must rate high on the IQ scale. No other animal, including man, has such a highly developed sense of fun, and if captive dolphins stoop to practical jokes — admittedly a low form of wit — it may be only because their keepers are too dense to appreciate puns expressed in Delphinese.

Most marine biologists would caution against reading too much into dolphin behavior, however, if only because dolphins *are* such agreeable creatures. They point out that animals can be trained to perform quite elaborate routines and exhibit "almost human" behavior, but that this has little to do with reasoning ability. The present consensus is that dolphins and other cetacea indeed seem to be very bright and complex animals and apparently have a form of intraspecies communication, but that we know too little about them to speculate on the nature of their intelligence. Forthcoming attempts to use a computer interface to establish a common language with dolphins may provide some definitive answers. One such endeavor is Project Janus, sponsored by the Human-Dolphin Foundation.

We may indeed prove to be the most intelligent beings on Earth — a sobering prospect in many ways — but we are certainly not the only intelligent creatures. Large brains are prevalent among mammals, and the ability to learn from past experience and to solve novel problems has obvious survival value. It seems that there must be evolutionary pressure to select for intelligence, and that reasoning creatures will eventually appear on any life-bearing world. Such creatures appeared on Earth only during the last 100 million years, however, at a point when our planet might be regarded as "middle-aged." Let us assume, then, that any particular planet at a given moment has a 50–50 chance of having intelligent life. Thus, $f_i = 0.50$.

Mere intelligence is not enough, however. Sperm whales may ultimately prove to be marvelous poets and philoso-

Sunjammer. As our civilization acquires greater expertise in space, increasingly novel means of getting about will be attempted. A particularly appealing sort of spacecraft is the solar sailor. Sunlight has momentum — that is, it can exert pressure. A handful of sunlight "weighs" about a millionth of an ounce. Spaceships equipped with lightweight sails of aluminized plastic, similar to that used in the early *Echo* balloon satellites, could take advantage of this feeble but continual "breeze" to cruise the solar system, ultimately attaining quite respectable speeds. Such sails would have to be kilometers across to be effective, and they might be difficult to trim, but the idea has already been demonstrated in principle: when the *Mariner Venus/Mercury* spacecraft seemed in danger of running out of stabilizing gas, technicians used the sail effect of the solar panels to maintain the probe's attitude. A solar sailor could "beat to windward" by tilting the sail toward the direction of its orbit. This would slow the orbital speed, and the craft would spiral sunward. Orbits that would carry the craft toward the outer planets could be achieved by "running" with the Sun more or less astern. (*Art by author*)

phers, but they are not likely to ever build spaceships or radio telescopes. Nor are any beings that may dwell in the seas of Tau Ceti IV. In our search for extraterrestrial intelligence, we are interested in finding beings who, like ourselves, characteristically alter their environments through technology, rather than survive by adapting to some particular ecological niche, as the whales have done.

In estimating the number of cultures that develop our sort of civilization, we are again forced to extrapolate from one example. As the products of a technological culture, we tend to assume that this is the normal state for man. But throughout most of mankind's history, a hunting-gathering way of life was the norm. Civilization is a recent acquisition, only about ten thousand years old, and it was made possible by the invention of the advanced solar technology known as agriculture. The use of farms to tap the Sun's energy allowed early cultures to remain in one place long enough to build cities, and it freed enough of the labor force from the basic task of food production to enable people to engage in more speculative pursuits, such as art, trade, and manufacturing. Although there have been periodic and localized setbacks, the civilization that arose on the banks of the Indus and Euphrates ten millennia ago has spread across the Earth and even to the Moon.

It would seem that technology has survival value. Dreamers who talk of returning to an imagined pretechnological Golden Age fail to realize that agriculture is technology, and so is the vaccination of babies. It is difficult to imagine a culture such as ours consciously opting to return to the good old days of 50 percent infant mortality and an average life expectancy of thirty years. Nor is it reasonable to suppose that returning to a subsistence econ-

A base on Titan, Saturn's largest satellite,
might be established to mine the hydrocarbons
necessary to support manned exploration and
colonization of the outer solar system.
(Art by author)

omy will usher in the Millennium. When resources are scarce, people fight. It seems probable that despite its drawbacks, technology confers such benefits upon a people that they can do naught but expand it.

Given that technology helps a species survive, what are the odds that intelligent creatures will develop it? If we feel intimidated by the probability that we are the first Earth creatures to develop civilization, we might try a simple thought-experiment: Suppose mankind were to suddenly disappear; which of our fellow species might succeed us?

Even excluding the apes and monkeys, there are many animals that have at least rudimentary technological potential. Raccoons are notorious for their expertise in breaking and entering, and otters routinely use stones to crack open seashells. A prime "nonhumanoid" candidate is the elephant, visions of Dumbo notwithstanding. The evolution of the elephant closely parallels our own. It arose from a piglike ancestor some 10 million years ago, and its development has been marked by a steadily increasing cranial capacity, coupled with a lengthening and refinement of that remarkable manipulative organ, the trunk. Any circus aficionado can testify that elephants have great manual ability. They can pick up a single peanut with ease, and there is reason to believe that their intellectual capacities do not lag far behind. Elephants pressed into hauling mahogany logs in Southeast Asia have been known to stuff mud into the bells hung about their necks, in order to facilitate raids on food stores. While the decline in ape populations can be attributed to overspecialization and maladaptation to a changing climate, the decrease in elephant population has been largely the result of human predation, specifically the ivory trade. Nevertheless, elephants — at least in Asia — have managed to survive and maintain an impressive geographical range. Who knows what elephants might accomplish in another few million years, if left to their own devices and confronted with the proper environmental pressures.

It it not difficult to come up with other examples. The point is that human intelligence differs from that of other animals more in degree than in kind. It may be that at some point in the evolution of life on a planet, intelligence supersedes adaptability as the determining factor in survival. If this is the case, intelligences similar to our own may be the rule rather than the exception.

In evaluating f_c, therefore, we are faced with two contradictory sets of evidence: mankind's unusual evolution versus the observed trend toward intelligence coupled with manipulative ability. Either our sort of culture is very rare, or it is the norm. Let us establish a range of probabilities to reflect this uncertainty. Thus, $0.001 < f_c < 1.0$.

Estimating the final parameter in the Drake equation requires no less than that we predict the future. How long will our civilization endure? The answer to this question inevitably reflects one's philosophy of life. A pessimist will say that technological civilizations destroy themselves shortly after discovering nuclear energy, in which case L is less than a century and there are probably no other civilizations contemporary to ours. Optimists will suggest that if a culture like ours survives long enough to establish a foothold in space, it becomes essentially immortal.

If our civilization can build self-supporting space colonies, it seems that there will be no limit to its lifetime, save that imposed by the evolution of our Sun, and even that probably does not apply. By the time the Sun enters its red-giant phase, the children of man may have scattered to stars yet unborn, and our descendants billions of years hence will probably be as far beyond our understanding as we would have been to the Australopithecine. The movement into space is not hubris but an affirmation of life, a completion of the great cycle that began in the hearts of unknown stars eons ago. And while the colonization of space may not ensure immortality for our species, it certainly improves the odds.

For purposes of our calculations, then, let us assume that a technological civilization can last as little as 100 years and as long as 1 million. Thus, $10^2 < L < 10^6$. At this point, we can estimate the number of extraterrestrial civilizations. Substituting into the Drake equation, we obtain a pessimistic value of 0.0003 for N, and an optimistic value of 50,000. The former value suggests that we are the only technological civilization in the galaxy, while the latter suggests that roughly 1 star out of every 4 million shines upon a civilization similar to our own.

It is obvious that the final term, L, is the critical one. Using all the pessimistic parameters we have obtained, but assuming L to be on the order of 10^6 years, the result still ends up being approximately two other civilizations. And if L is assumed to be one or two orders of magnitude greater, N becomes 30 or 300, respectively.

Even assuming that the most optimistic estimate is correct, however, scientists engaged in searching for extraterrestrials by listening for their radio transmissions are faced with the formidable task of looking at millions of stars before they can have any reasonable expectation of success; and this supposes the optimum situation in which the "others" have high-powered acquisition signals aimed continuously toward Earth, which is not likely. Most current approaches to SETI (Search for Extraterrestrial Intelligence) are therefore based on observing a large number of stars simultaneously, in the hope of detecting very powerful transmissions. The choice of frequencies at which to listen is particularly ingenious. The absorption and re-emission of radiation by gases in Earth's atmosphere creates a wall of noise in the radio spectrum, making it difficult for radio telescopes to look out. There is a quiet area, however, between 1000 and 10,000 megahertz (MHz). Not only does this range contain the 1420 MHz band at which hydrogen, the major constituent of the universe, emits (thus serving astronomers as a particularly useful window into space), but at 1662 MHz it contains the emission frequency of the hydroxl ion — a hydrogen atom bound to an oxygen atom. Between these two frequencies is the quietest part of the radio spectrum as seen from the surface of the Earth. Since this radio window is bound by the dissociation products of the water molecule, it has been poetically dubbed the "water hole" — the traditional meeting place of different species. It seems reasonable to suppose that intelligent beings biologically similar to us

Binary Sun. The ultimate test of a technological civilization may well be interstellar travel, something that is beyond the range of present technology. It may be centuries before human eyes look upon worlds such as this one, in orbit about a close binary. *(Art by author)*

Facing page, top
Marginally habitable worlds may be found relatively nearby, in the planetary system of Barnard's Star, a red dwarf approximately 6 light-years from our solar system.
(Art by author)

Facing page, bottom
Earthlike planets may be exceedingly rare. It may be thousands of years before our descendants discover a planet upon which they can live without artificial support, and where the native biology is compatible with our own.
(Art by author)

would follow the same logic and choose to broadcast in this region.

So far, all SETI experiments have been designed to look for directed transmissions, rather than to eavesdrop on the routine communications traffic of other civilizations. This approach presupposes that someone is signaling. It would be the ultimate cosmic irony if the galaxy were teeming with advanced societies, but they were all listening. The success of current SETI programs is predicated on the assumption that somewhere a highly advanced people have set out a beacon to which emerging societies may tune in. An older civilization might do this out of altruism, or perhaps out of sheer loneliness. Given the current state of the art, and our budgetary constraints, however, such a beacon is probably all we can expect to find. As an adjunct to regular astronomical programs, we can attach filters to radio telescopes and use computers to search for anomalies near the "water hole." But the giant radio-telescope arrays that would be required for interstellar eavesdropping — an activity far more likely to be successful — are decades in the future, and building them would require a major economic commitment similar to that of Project Apollo.

Suppose such a beacon is found within the next year, or the next 20 years. What might be the effect on our society? The usual cinematic treatment portrays government officials clamping a lid of silence on the discovery, in order to prevent panic among the common folk. Such a cover-up would probably be as ineffectual as it was patronizing,

however. To quote Edward Teller, who should know, "You can't keep a secret more than two years." This is especially true when a large number of scientists are involved. Contrary to the Hollywood stereotype, the best scientists are a talky and exuberant lot, and a discovery of such magnitude would more than likely end up on the front pages within a few weeks. As for panic, the widespread belief in UFOs and extraterrestrial pyramid-builders seems to indicate that most people want to believe that there are smarter folks among the stars. A president who could announce the establishment of diplomatic relations between the United States and an advanced civilization would be a shoo-in for reelection. More than likely, the short-term effects of such a discovery would be in the nature of a nine-day wonder: for a time, the most popular topic of conversation would be the "star people," but then interest would revert back to the Dodgers' chances in the World Series. Whatever unease people might feel would be offset by the fact that the nearest civilization would probably be hundreds of light-years away. It is difficult to worry about people who take centuries to respond to your "hello."

Long-term effects are apt to be more profound, particularly if the acquisition signal contains instructions to tune to a "news" channel for more information about the transmitting civilization. In its initial blind communication, a society would probably take pains to send enough information to be interesting, but not so much that the receiving culture would be corrupted. It seems reasonable to assume that a prime motivation for establishing interstellar communication is the desire to savor the taste of alien minds and cultures, and to learn other ways of looking at things. Overwhelming a young culture with advanced science and philosophy would defeat this purpose by turning the receiving society into a parody of the transmitting one. Only after Earth replied by sending a detailed account of human history, art, and science would a technologically superior people feel safe to send more than general background information and some pointers on more advanced communication techniques. If both civilizations lasted long enough to continue the conversation beyond "Hello. How are you?" then true dialogue might begin.

A side benefit of SETI is that it is a truly international effort. Even those countries without the industrial base to support a space program can participate: all that is required is a radio telescope and information-processing systems. It has often been said that the only event that will ever unite mankind is confrontation with extraterrestrials. Perhaps "confrontation" is too harsh a word in this context. If the interstellar gulf is ever spanned, it will not be for purposes of war. But an encounter with true otherness, with strangeness, with minds born of other seas and other suns, could do much to drive home the lesson that we humans are of one species and one flesh, more alike than different, and that we may someday have to speak with one voice. Our counterparts among the stars may aim their radio telescopes toward Earth and hear a rich song of many themes and diverse contrapuntals, or they may hear an indecipherable babble, and turn elsewhere in their search for friends. The choice will be ours.

PLANETARY QUANTITIES

Compiled by T. A. Heppenheimer
Center for Space Science, Fountain Valley, California

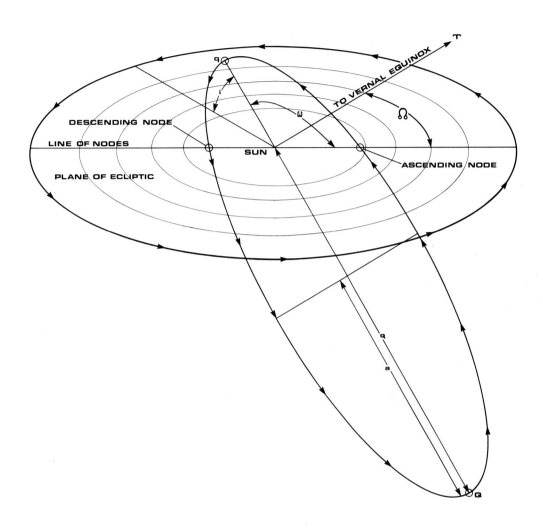

SOME NOTES ON ORBITS

Certain elements are of value in describing the orbital motion of a body such as a planet. Pictured in the above diagram (by Michael Standlee Design) are:

a, the semimajor axis of the ellipse.

q, the minimum distance from the primary (called *perihelion* in the case of the Sun, and *periapsis* in general).

i, the inclination of the orbital plane to the ecliptic (the plane of Earth's orbit).

Q, the maximum distance from the primary; "apoapsis."

T, "first point of Aries," a celestial benchmark defined by the intersection of the Sun's path southward, and the celestial equator.

Ω, positional angle of the line of nodes measured on the plane of the sky from North through East.

ω, longitude of the direction of periapsis (periastron) measured on the orbital plane from the ascending node to periastron.

Other symbols used in describing orbital motion include:

e, the eccentricity, given by $1 - \dfrac{q}{a}$. A perfectly circular orbit has an eccentricity of 0.0, while a highly elongated (but closed) orbit has an e that approaches 1.0. Eccentricities of 1.0 or more are characteristic of nonreturning parabolic or hyperbolic trajectories frequently followed by comets.

Y, the orbital period, or year, in the case of a planet.

FUNDAMENTAL AND DERIVED QUANTITIES

The following constants are useful:

Pole of ecliptic (equator and equinox, 1950.0): $\alpha = 270.0°$, $\delta = 66° 33' 29.22''$

$GM_\odot$ = gravitational mass of Sun = 1.327125×10^{26} cm^3/sec^2

G = gravitational constant = 6.673×10^{-8} cm^3 sec^{-2} g^{-1}

$M_\odot$ = solar mass = 1.9888×10^{33} g

AU = astronomical unit = $1.49597927 \times 10^{13}$ cm

$M_\oplus$ = mass of Earth = 5.976×10^{27} g

$M_\math{\mathbb{D}}$ = mass of Moon = 7.350×10^{25} g

$g_\oplus$ = surface acceleration of gravity for Earth = 980.665 cm/sec^2

Base of magnitude scale = $100^{1/5}$ = 2.511886431 taken as 2.512

The basic observed quantities are gravitational mass GM, photovisual magnitude V, and radius r. It is usual to reduce V to zero phase angle (corresponding to opposition) and 1 AU distance from both Earth and Sun. That is,

$$V = V(1,0) + 5 \log_{10} Rd \qquad (1)$$

V(1,0) = magnitude at unit distance from Earth and Sun (whether or not this configuration is physically possible). V(1,0) is a form of absolute magnitude for solar system objects.

R = distance from Earth, in AU

d = distance from Sun, in AU

Also useful is mean opposition magnitude V_o, given by

$$V_o = V(1,0) + 5 \log_{10} a(a - 1) \qquad (2)$$

a = semimajor axis, AU

Taking mean solar magnitude = -26.78, the radius r of a spherical body is

$$r = (2.512^{-V(1,0)/2}) / \sqrt{p_v} \cdot 660 \, \text{km} \qquad (3)$$

p_v = geometric albedo

The quantities V_o and V(1,0) are denoted respectively m_o and g in *Ephemerides of Minor Planets*.

In addition, there is the bolometric or Bond albedo, A, which is the fraction of incident solar flux that is reflected. The ratio $A/p_v = q$, a factor that depends upon the nature of the reflecting surface. The factor q can be found only by observation over a range of phase angles, and is frequently unknown. Then we often take q = 1 and have $p_v = A$.

If p_v is not known and the planet disk is not resolved in the telescope, then eq. (3) at least gives a constraint on r. If r is available from direct measurement, then p_v is found directly. Otherwise, r is available from visual and infrared photometry, using methods developed about 10 years ago.

If a planet rotates slowly or has little or no atmosphere, a reference subsolar temperature (on the equator at local noon) is available:

$$T_{ss} = 394.2 (1 - A)^{1/4} / \sqrt{a} \, °K \qquad (4)$$

If the atmosphere is thick and there is little temperature difference between day and night, then the received insolation is regarded as spread evenly across the entire planet, and we use the reference temperature:

$$T_{ref} = T_{ss} / \sqrt{2} \qquad (5)$$

Now, if we have planet mass M (= GM/G), equatorial radius r, and polar radius b, there is:

Density: $\rho = M/(\frac{4}{3}\pi r^2 b)$ g/cm^3 \qquad (6)

Ellipticity: $\varepsilon = \dfrac{r - b}{r}$ \qquad (7)

Let the planet have rotation period P. The acceleration due to gravity is

Equatorial: $g_e = \dfrac{GM}{r^2} - \left(\dfrac{2\pi}{P}\right)^2 r$ cm/sec^2 \qquad (8)

Polar: $g_p = GM/b^2$ \qquad (9)

where P is in seconds and b, r in cm. A value GM/r^2 may be used as a reference.

Of interest is the precession period — the time for an oblate planet to precess about the normal to the orbit plane. This is given by

$$T = \frac{2}{3} \frac{Y^2}{P} \frac{C}{J_2 \cos \phi} \, \text{days} \qquad (10)$$

Y = period of revolution about the Sun

P = rotation period, days

C = I/Mr^2 where I = moment of inertia about rotation axis. C = 0.4 for a uniformly dense sphere.

J_2 = dynamical oblateness

ϕ = obliquity of the planet on its orbital plane

Equation (10) holds for a planet without satellites and thus cannot be applied to Earth and Pluto. It is used for the other planets.

Finally, it may be of interest to give equations of use in orbit mechanics. The velocity v of a satellite in orbit about a body is given by the vis-viva formula:

$$v^2 = GM\left(\frac{2}{R} - \frac{1}{a}\right) \qquad (11)$$

$$R = \text{distance to planet center, cm}$$

$$a = \text{orbit semimajor axis, cm}$$

There are several cases of interest:

(a) Circular velocity for a close satellite: $R = r = a$

(b) Escape velocity: $a = \infty$, $R = r$

(c) Velocity at periapse: $R = a(1 - e)$

(d) Velocity at apoapse: $R = a(1 + e)$

If the planet rotation is not tidally locked to its revolution rate about the primary, the radius R_{syn} of a satellite having orbital period equal to the planet's rotation period P is

$$R_{syn} = \left((P/2\pi)^2\, GM\right)^{1/3} \text{ cm} \qquad (12)$$

and the satellite altitude is $R_{syn} - r$. Equation (12) holds even for Mercury (for which $P = 2/3\ Y$) and for Venus, which has a retrograde rotation period longer than its period of revolution. The reason is the enhanced stability of retrograde satellite orbits. But if the planet rotation is synchronous, then the concept of a satellite with $P_{syn} = P$ is replaced by the concept of the L_1 and L_2 libration points. To compute their distances from the planet center, define

$$\mu = GM/GM' \qquad \upsilon = \left(\mu/3(1-\mu)\right)^{1/3} \qquad (13)$$

where $GM' = GM$ for the primary. Then,

$$L_1: \ R_{L1} = a\upsilon(1 - \frac{1}{3}\upsilon - \frac{1}{9}\upsilon^2 - \frac{23}{81}\upsilon^3 + \frac{151}{243}\upsilon^4 - \frac{1}{9}\upsilon^5) + O(\upsilon^7) \qquad (14)$$

$$L_2: \ R_{L2} = a\upsilon(1 + \frac{1}{3}\upsilon - \frac{1}{9}\upsilon^2 - \frac{31}{81}\upsilon^3 - \frac{119}{243}\upsilon^4 - \frac{1}{9}\upsilon^5) + O(\upsilon^7) \qquad (15)$$

where a = planet semimajor axis. L_1 lies between primary and planet; L_2 lies beyond the planet orbit.

With these preliminaries, the presentation of planetary data will proceed. The data are as follows:

a, semimajor axis, AU
e, eccentricity
i, inclination
p_v, geometric albedo
q, perihelion, AU
Q, aphelion, AU

Y, period of revolution
Measured surface temperatures
T_{ss} or T_{ref}, °K
A, Bond albedo
P, rotation period
Pole of rotation, referred to mean equator and equinox of 1950.0; right ascension, declination.
Mass, grams, and fraction of $M_\odot$
J_2, dynamical oblateness
Radius, equatorial and polar, km
Density, g/cm³
Surface gravity (at equator), cm/sec³
Obliquity or axial tilt
Atmosphere: constituents by pressure at surface, if any
Magnetic field (equatorial strength at equator and pole offset)
Precession period

For satellites and some planets, an appropriate subset of these data are given in the planetary tables that follow.

MERCURY

Semimajor axis (a) = 0.387099 AU	Perihelion (q) = 0.307501 AU
Eccentricity (e) = 0.205628	Aphelion (Q) = 0.466697 AU
Inclination (i) = 7° 0′ 15″	Period of revolution (Y) = 87.9696 days
Geometric albedo (p_v) = 0.125	Rotation period (P) = 58.6457 days = $\frac{2}{3}$ Y

Subsolar temperature (T_{ss}) = 624.5°K

Measured surface temperatures 100°K to 700°K

Pole of rotation: right ascension (α) = 280.86°, declination (δ) = 61.40° (1950.0)

Mass (M) = 3.3020 ± 0.0018 × 10^{26} grams = Solar mass ($M_\odot$) / 6,023,700 ± 300

Dynamical oblateness (J_2) = 8 ± 6 × 10^{-5}

Radius: equatorial (r) = 2439 ± 1 km; polar (b) cannot be distinguished from r

Density (ρ) = 5.433 ± 0.012 g/cm³

Surface gravity, at equator (g) = 370 cm/sec²

Axial tilt (ϕ) < 1°

Atmosphere: ~ 10^{-10} millibar (1 bar = 1 kg/cm² ~ 1 atmosphere)

   He, H present

Magnetic field: 330 ± 18 × 10^{-5} gauss, tilted 14° ± 5° to pole

Precession period (T) ~ 1200 years

VENUS

Semimajor axis (a) = 0.723332 AU	Perihelion (q) = 0.718423 AU
Eccentricity (e) = 0.006787	Aphelion (Q) = 0.728241 AU
Inclination (i) = 3° 23′ 37.1″	Period of revolution (Y) = 224.701 days
Bond albedo (A) = 0.77	Rotation period (P): Retrograde, 243.019 ± 0.014 days

Reference temperature (T_{ref}) = 227.0°K

Measured surface temperatures: 741 ± 7°K

Pole of rotation: right ascension (α) = 272.8° ± 0.5°, declination (δ) = 67.2° ± 0.3°

Mass (M) = 4.8683 × 10^{27} grams = Solar mass ($M_\odot$) / 408,523.9 ± 1.2

Dynamical oblateness (J_2) = 4.0 ± 1.5 × 10^{-6}

Radius: equatorial (r) = 6050.0 ± 0.3 km; polar (b) differs by < 1 km

Density (ρ) = 5.269 g/cm³

Surface gravity, at equator (g) = 890 cm/sec²

Axial tilt (ϕ) = 177.22° ± 0.18°

Atmosphere: pressure 99 bars, density 0.066 g/cm³ at 750°K

CO_2, 96.4% ± 1.03%	Ar, 67.2 ppm ± 2.3 ppm	Data from *Pioneer Venus:*
N_2, 3.41% ± 0.0207%	Ne, 4.31 $^{+5.54}_{-3.91}$ ppm	Altitude, 21.6 km
H_2O, 0.135% ± 0.0149%		Pressure, 17.8 bars
CO, 19.9 ppm ± 3.1 ppm	SO_2, 186 $^{+350}_{-155}$ ppm	

Magnetic field: << 4x 10^{-5} gauss

Precession period (T) ~ 30,000 years

EARTH

Semimajor axis (a) = 1.0000 AU

Eccentricity (e) = 0.016722

Inclination (i) = 0.0000

Bond albedo (A) = 0.30

Reference temperature (T_{ref}) = 255°K

Mean surface temperature = 288°K

Pole of rotation: declination (δ) = 90°

Mass (M) = 5.976 ± 0.004 × 10^{27} grams = Solar mass $(M_\odot)$ / 332,995.9 ± 0.4

Dynamical oblateness (J_2) = 1.08264 × 10^{-3}

Radius: equatorial (r) = 6378.164 ± 0.003 km; polar (b) = 6356.779 km

Density (ρ) = 5.518 ± 0.004 g/cm³

Surface gravity, at equator (g) = 980.665 cm/sec²

Axial tilt (ϕ) = 23° 26′ 30.78″

Atmosphere: pressure, 760 mm Hg = 1.01325 bar

density = 1.2928 × 10^{-3} g/cm³ at 273.15° K = 0°C

Perihelion (q) = 0.983278 AU

Aphelion (Q) = 1.016722 AU

Period of revolution (Y) = 365.25636556 days

Rotation period (P) = 23^h 56^m 4.091^s

N_2, 78.084%	CO_2, 335 ppm	Kr, 1.14 ppm	N_2O, 0.27 ppm
O_2, 20.947%	Ne, 18.2 ppm	CO, 0.06–1 ppm	O_3, 0.01–0.1 ppm
Ar, 0.934%	He, 5.24 ppm	SO_2, 1 ppm	Xe, 0.087 ppm
H_2O, 0.1–2.8% (mean: 1.6%)	CH_4, 1.8 ppm	H_2, 0.5 ppm	NO_2, 0.0005–0.02 ppm

Magnetic field: 0.31 gauss; pole at 76°N, 101°W

Precession period (T) = 25,725 years

MOON

Semimajor axis (a) = 384,401 ± 1 km

Eccentricity (e) = 0.0549

Inclination (i) = 5° 8′ 43″ to ecliptic

Geometric albedo (p_v) = 0.112

Bond albedo (A) = 0.067

Subsolar temperature (T_{ss}) = 387.4°K

Dark-side temperature: 104°K

Perihelion (q), extreme = 356,400 km

Aphelion (Q), extreme = 406,700 km

Period of revolution (Y) = 27.3216614 days

Rotation: synchronous

Pole of rotation: 1° 32.5′ from pole of ecliptic, precessing with period 18.61 years

Ecliptic pole: right ascension (α) = 270.0°
declination (δ) = 66° 33′ 29.22″

Mass (M) = 7.350 × 10^{25} grams = Mass of Earth $(M_\oplus)$ / 81.3025

Dynamical oblateness (J_2) = 2.05 × 10^{-4}

Radii: toward Earth = 1738.9 km

along orbit = 1738.6 km

polar = 1737.8 km

Axial tilt: to ecliptic = 1° 32′ 30″

to plane of orbit = 6° 41′

Density (ρ) = 3.341 g/cm³

Surface gravity, at equator (g) = 162.2 cm/sec²

Atmosphere: ~ 10^{-10} mbar; H_2 (~ 10^7 H_2 molecules/cm³)

Magnetic field: < 0.05 × 10^{-5} gauss

MARS

Semimajor axis (a) = 1.523691 AU

Eccentricity (e) = 0.093377

Inclination (i) = $1° 51' 0''$

Geometric albedo (p_v) = 0.154

Reference temperature (T_{ref}) = 216.2°K

Measured temperatures: 145°K to 245°K

Perihelion (q) = 1.381413 AU

Aphelion (Q) = 1.665969 AU

Period of revolution (Y) = 686.980 days

Rotation period (P) = $24^h 37^m 22.663^s \pm 0.004^s$

Pole of rotation: right ascension (α) = 317.340° $\pm$ 0.006°,
     declination (δ) = 52.710° $\pm$ 0.004°

Mass (M) = 6.4181×10^{26} grams = solar mass ($M_\odot$) / 3.098,709 $\pm$ 9

Dynamical oblateness (J_2) = 1.9628 $\pm$ 0.0092 $\times 10^{-3}$

Radius: equatorial (r) = 3396.6 km; polar (b) = 3376.7 km

Density (ρ) = 3.933 g/cm³

Surface gravity, at equator (g) = 371.23 cm/sec²

Axial tilt (ϕ) = 25.12°

Atmosphere: 6.1 millibar, mean surface pressure

| CO_2, 95.6% | Ar, 1.6% | O_2, 0.1% |
| N_2, 2.7% | CO, 0.16% | H_2O, 0.01–0.1% |

Magnetic field: $< 6.4 \times 10^{-4}$ gauss

Precession period (T) = 178,000 years

	PHOBOS	DEIMOS
Semimajor axis (a)	9378.5 km	23,458.9 km
Eccentricity (e)	0.0135 $\pm$ 0.0001	0.0008 $\pm$ 0.0001
Inclination (i)	1.074° $\pm$ 0.012°	2.842° $\pm$ 0.02°
Rotation period (P) and period of revolution (Y)	$7^h 39^m 24.52^s$	$30^h 18^m 18.04^s$
Geometric albedo (p_v)	0.06	0.06
Subsolar temperature (T_{ss})	314.4°K	314.4°K
Mass (M)	9.9 $\pm$ 1.8 $\times 10^{18}$ grams	2.9 $\pm$ 0.4 $\times 10^{18}$ grams
Radii, km	13.5 / 10.5 / 9.0	8.5 / 6.0 / 5.5
Density (ρ)	1.9 $\pm$ 0.6 g/cm³	2.4 $\pm$ 0.3 g/cm³
Absolute magnitude (V[1,0])	11.9	13.0

JUPITER

Semimajor axis (a) = 5.202803 AU

Eccentricity (e) = 0.04845

Inclination (i) = 1° 18′ 17″

Bond albedo (A) = 0.35

Reference temperature (T_{ref}) = 109.7°K

Measured temperature: 125 ± 3°K

Perihelion (q) = 5.454879 AU

Aphelion (Q) = 4.950727 AU

Period of revolution (Y) = 11.86223 years

Rotation period (P) = 9^h 55^m 29.711^s ± 0.004^s

Pole of rotation: right ascension (α) = 267.998° ± 0.016°
            declination (δ) = 64.504° ± 0.004°

Mass (M) = 1.901 × 10^{30} grams = solar mass ($M_{\odot}$) / 1047.346 ± 0.004

Dynamical oblateness (J_2) = 0.014733 ± 0.000004

Radius: equatorial (r) = 71,398 km; polar (b) = 66,770 km

Density (ρ) = 1.333 g/cm^3

Surface gravity, equatorial (g) = 2268 cm/sec^2 (includes centrifugal term)

Axial tilt (φ) = 3.07°

Atmosphere:

H_2, 81% ± 5%	C_2H_6, 24 ± 6 ppm	C_2H_2, 0.054 ± 0.021 ppm
He, 19% ± 5%	H_2O, 1 ppm	CO, 0.002 ppm
CH_4, 0.16%	PH_3, 0.15 ± 0.05 ppm	GeH_4, 0.0006 ppm
NH_3, 200 ppm	HCN, 0.1 ppm	

Magnetic field: 4.25 ± 0.03 gauss; pole at 79.4° ± 0.7° N, 229° ± 2.4° E

Precession period (T) = 1,408,000 years

Ring

Outer limit: 128.300 km   Bright segment width: 800 km   Dim segment width: 5200 km

Io flux tube

Voltage: 200,000 volts   Current: 5,000,000 amperes

SATELLITES OF JUPITER

	1979 J1	J5 (AMALTHEA)	1979 J2	IO
Semimajor axis (a), km	128,500 ± 700	181,170	221,720	421,700
Eccentricity (e)	0.0	0.0028		0.0
Inclination (i)	0.0	0° 27.3′	1° 15′	0° 1.6′
Period of Rotation & Revolution (P & Y)	$7^h 8^m$	$11^h 57^m 22.70^s$	$16^h 11^m 21.25^s$ ± 0.5^s	$1^d 18^h 27^m 33.51^s$
Geometric albedo (p_v)	< 0.05	0.05 ± 0.01	~ 0.05	0.63
Bond albedo (A)	< 0.05	~ 0.05	~ 0.05	0.56 ± 0.12
Subsolar temperature (T_{ss})	120°K	120°K	120°K	141 ± 11°K
Mass (M) (Jupiter = 1)				4.684 ± 0.022 × 10^{-5}
Mass (M), grams				8.894 ± 0.042 × 10^{25}
Radius (r)	15–20 km	270 ± 15 / 170 ± 15 / 155 ± 10 km	40 km	1819 ± 5 km
Density (ρ)				3.53 g/cm³
Absolute magnitude (V[1,0])	10.8	6.3	9.3	− 1.68
Surface gravity (g)				179.4 cm/sec²

	EUROPA	GANYMEDE	CALLISTO
Semimajor axis (a), km	671,030	1,070,400	1,882,700
Eccentricity (e)	0.0003	0.0015	0.0075
Inclination (i)	0° 28.1′	0° 11.0′	0° 15.2′
Period of Rotation & Revolution (P & Y)	$3^d 13^h 13^m 42.05^s$	$7^d 3^h 42^m 33.35^s$	$16^d 16^h 32^m 11.21^s$
Geometric albedo (p_v)	0.64	0.43	0.17
Bond albedo (A)	0.58 ± 0.14	0.38 ± 0.11	0.13 ± 0.06
Subsolar temperature (T_{ss})	139 ± 12°K	154 ± 6°K	167 ± 3°K
Mass (M) (Jupiter = 1)	2.523 ± 0.025 × 10^{-5}	7.803 ± 0.030 × 10^{-5}	5.611 ± 0.019 × 10^{-5}
Mass (M), grams	4.791 ± 0.047 × 10^{25}	1.482 ± 0.057 × 10^{26}	1.075 ± 0.036 × 10^{26}
Radius (r)	1563 ± 5 km	2638 ± 5 km	2424 ± 5 km
Density (ρ)	3.03 g/cm³	1.93 g/cm³	1.79 g/cm³
Absolute magnitude (V[1,0])	− 1.41	− 2.09	− 1.05
Surface gravity (g)	130.9 cm/sec²	142.1 cm/sec²	122.1 cm/sec²

	J13 (LEDA)	J6 (HIMALIA)	J10 (LYSITHEA)	J7 (ELARA)
Semimajor axis (a), km	11,110,000	11,470,000	11,710,000	11,740,000
Eccentricity (e)	0.146	0.158	0.130	0.207
Inclination (i)	26.7°	27.6°	29.0°	24.8°
Period of Revolution (Y)	240^d	250.6^d	260^d	260.1^d
Geometric albedo (p_v)		0.03		0.03
Radius (r)		85 ± 10 km		40 ± 10 km
Absolute magnitude (V[1,0])	13.3	8.0	11.7	9.3
Radius, photometric ($r\sqrt{p_v}$)	1.44 km	16.5 km	3.02 km	9.1 km

	J12 (ANANKE)	J11 (CARME)	J8 (PASIPHAE)	J9 (SINOPE)
Semimajor axis (a), km	20,700,000	22,350,000	23,300,000	23,700,000
Eccentricity (e)	0.17	0.21	0.38	0.28
Inclination (i)	147°	164°	145°	153°
Period of Revolution (Y)	617^d	692^d	735^d	758^d
Absolute magnitude (V[1,0])	12.2	11.3	11.0	11.6
Radius, photometric ($r\sqrt{p_v}$)	2.40 km	3.63 km	4.16 km	3.16 km

A satellite J14 was observed by Kowal and Roemer in 1975, but has been lost. While this book was in page proofs, another Jovian satellite, 1979 J3, was discovered:

1979 J3

Semimajor axis (a), km	127,700
Period of Rotation & Revolution (P & Y)	7^h 4^m 30^s ± 3^s
Geometric albedo (p_v)	~ 0.05
Subsolar temperature (T_{ss})	120°K
Radius (r)	20 km
Absolute magnitude (V[1,0])	10.8

SATURN

Semimajor axis (a) = 9.53884 AU

Perihelion (q) = 9.00800 AU

Eccentricity (e) = 0.5565

Aphelion (Q) = 10.06968 AU

Inclination (i) = 2° 29′ 22″

Period of revolution (Y) = 29.4577 years

Bond albedo (A) = 0.54 ± 0.15

Rotation period (P) = $10^h 39^m 24^s$

Reference temperature (T_{ref}) = 74.3°K

Measured temperature: 96.5 ± 2.5°K

Pole of rotation: right ascension (α) = 38.43723°
            declination (δ) = 83.30761°

Mass (M) = 5.684×10^{29} grams = solar mass ($M_\odot$) / 3497.99

Dynamical oblateness (J_2) = $1.646 \pm 0.005 \times 10^{-2}$

Radius: equatorial (r) = 60,330 km; polar (b) = 55,021 km

Density (ρ) = 0.689 ± 0.015 g/cm³

Surface gravity, equatorial (g) = 880 cm/sec² (includes centrifugal term)

Axial tilt (ϕ) = 26.74°

Atmosphere: H_2, 89% ± 4% NH_3, 0.17% H_2S, 1.4 ppm

He, 11% ± 4% PH_3, 17 ppm C_2H_2, 0.26 ppm

CH_4, 0.64% C_2H_6, 75 ppm

Magnetic field: 0.21 + 0.005 gauss, tilted 0.7° ± 0.35° to rotation axis

Precession period (T) = 7.42×10^6 years

RINGS OF SATURN

Thickness of rings, 1.3 ± 0.3 km

FEATURE	DISTANCE FROM SATURN CENTER, KM	ALBEDO	PARTICLE SIZE	OPTICAL DEPTH
Cloud tops	60,300			
D ring	~ 67,000 to 73,200			
C ring	73,200 to 90,000	0.21 ± 0.05	~ 2 meters	0.1 ± 0.02
French division	90,000 to 92,200			
B ring	92,200 to 117,500	0.63 ± 0.08		> 1
Cassini division	117,500 to 121,000	0.32 ± 0.05	~ 8 meters	$\sim 0.08 \pm 0.02$
A ring	121,000 to 136,200	0.63 ± 0.08	~ 10 meters	0.4 ± 0.08
Encke gap	133,500 km; width, ~ 200 km			
Pioneer division	136,200 to 140,600			
F ring	~ 140,600 km (three narrow components)			
G ring	~ 170,000 km (seen only in forward-scattered light)			
E ring	~ 210,000 to ~ 300,000			
E ring maximum	~ 230,000 km (near orbit of Enceladus)			

SATELLITES OF SATURN

	1980 s28	1980 s27	1980 s26
Semimajor axis (a), km	137,670	139,353	141,700
Eccentricity (e)	0.002 ± 0.003	0.003 ± 0.003	0.004 ± 0.003
Inclination (i)	$0.3° \pm 0.2°$	$0.0° \pm 0.15°$	$0.05° \pm 0.15°$
Period of Rotation & Revolution (P & Y)	$14^h 25^m 46.2^s$	$14^h 42^m 43.2^s$	$15^h 5^m 4.8^s$
Geometric albedo (p_v)	~ 0.25	~ 0.08	
Subsolar temperature (T_{ss})	$\sim 119°K$	$\sim 125°K$	
Radius (r)	20/10/10 km	110 km	100 km
Absolute magnitude V(1,0)	9.7	6.6	

	1980 s3	1980 s1	MIMAS
Semimajor axis (a), km	151,422	151,472	185,800
Eccentricity (e)	0.009 ± 0.002	0.007 ± 0.002	0.0201
Inclination (i)	$0.34° \pm 0.05°$	$0.14° \pm 0.05°$	$1° 31.0'$
Period of Rotation & Revolution (P & Y)	$16^h 39^m 49.5^s$	$16^h 40^m 18.96^s$	$22^h 37^m 5.3^s$
Geometric albedo (p_v)	~ 0.4	~ 0.4	0.6 ± 0.1
Subsolar temperature (T_{ss})	$\sim 112°K$	$\sim 112°K$	$101.5 \pm 5.8°K$
Mass (M) (Saturn = 1)			$6.58 \pm 0.16 \times 10^{-7}$
Mass (M), grams			$3.74 \pm 0.09 \times 10^{22}$
Radius (r)	45/20 km	50/45/40 km	195 ± 5 km
Density (ρ)			1.21 ± 0.1 g/cm^3
Absolute magnitude V(1,0)	7.7	6.6	3.3
Surface gravity (g)			6.57 cm/sec^2

	ENCELADUS	TETHYS	DIONE
Semimajor axis (a), km	238,300	294,900	377,900
Eccentricity (e)	0.00444	0.0000	0.00221
Inclination (i)	$0° 1.4'$	$1° 5.6'$	$0° 1.4'$
Period of Rotation & Revolution (P & Y)	$1^d 8^h 53^m 6.8^s$	$1^d 21^h 18^m 26.1^s$	$2^d 17^h 41^m 9.5^s$
Geometric albedo (p_v)	1.0 ± 0.1	0.8 ± 0.1	0.6 ± 0.1
Subsolar temperature (T_{ss})	$\lesssim 70°K$	$85.3 \pm 30°K$	$101.5 \pm 5.8°K$
Mass (M) (Saturn = 1)	$1.3 \pm 0.6 \times 10^{-7}$	$1.09 \pm 0.02 \times 10^{-6}$	$1.85 \pm 0.06 \times 10^{-6}$
Mass (M), grams	$7.2 \pm 3.3 \times 10^{22}$	$6.22 \pm 0.12 \times 10^{23}$	$1.05 \pm 0.03 \times 10^{24}$
Radius (r)	250 ± 10 km	525 ± 10 km	560 ± 10
Density (ρ)	1.1 ± 0.6 g/cm^3	1.03 ± 0.06 g/cm^3	1.43 ± 0.09 g/cm^3
Absolute magnitude V(1,0)	2.2	0.7	0.88
Surface gravity (g)	7.69 cm/sec^2	15.06 cm/sec^2	22.39 cm/sec^2

	1980 S6	RHEA	TITAN
Semimajor axis (a), km	378,060	527,600	1,222,600
Eccentricity (e)	0.005 ± 0.003	0.00098	0.029
Inclination (i)	$0.15° \pm 0.2°$	$0° \, 21'$	$0° \, 20'$
Period of Rotation & Revolution (P & Y)	$2^d \, 17^h \, 44^m \, 18^s$	$4^d \, 12^h \, 25^m \, 12.3^s$	$15^d \, 22^h \, 41^m \, 27.1^s$
Geometric albedo (p_v)	0.04 ± 0.01	0.6 ± 0.1	0.21
Subsolar temperature (T_{ss})	$126.3°K$	$101.5 \pm 5.8°K$	$120.3°K$
Reference temperature (T_{ref})			$85.1°K$
Measured temperature			$93°K$ (at surface)
Mass (M) (Saturn = 1)		$4.38 \pm 0.26 \times 10^{-6}$	$2.3664 \pm 0.0008 \times 10^{-4}$
Mass (M), grams		$2.49 \pm 0.15 \times 10^{24}$	$1.3451 \pm 0.0005 \times 10^{26}$
Radius (r)	80 km	765 ± 10 km	2570 ± 26 km
Density (ρ)		1.33 ± 0.10 g/cm^3	1.89 ± 0.06 g/cm^3
Absolute magnitude V(1,0)	8.0 ± 0.3	0.16	-1.20
Surface gravity (g)		28.37 cm/sec^2	135.9 cm/sec^2
Magnetic field			$<3 \times 10^{-4}$ gauss
Atmosphere			Pressure, 1.6 bars
			$N_2, \gtrsim 93\%$ C_2H_2, 3 ppm
			$CH_4, \lesssim 7\%$ C_2H_4, 1 ppm
			C_2H_6, 20 ppm HCN, 0.2 ppm

	HYPERION	IAPETUS	PHOEBE
Semimajor axis (a), km	1,484,100	3,562,900	12,960,000
Eccentricty (e)	0.104	0.02828	0.16326
Inclination (i)	0.4°	14.72°	150.05°
Period of Revolution	$21^d \, 6^h \, 38^m \, 23.9^s$	$79^d \, 9^h \, 11^m \, 22^s$	$550^d \, 10.8^h$
Rotation	Tidally locked; state not known	Synchronous	Not known
Geometric albedo (p_v)	0.3 ± 0.1	0.49 ± 0.05 bright side 0.10 ± 0.01 dark side	~ 0.05
Subsolar temperature (T_{ss})	$116.8 \pm 4.0°K$	$107.9°K$ bright side $124.3°K$ dark side	$\sim 126°K$
Mass (M) (Saturn = 1)		$3.3 \pm 1.4 \times 10^{-6}$	
Mass (M), grams		$1.9 \pm 0.8 \times 10^{24}$	
Radius (r)	145 ± 20 km	720 ± 20 km	~ 120 km
Density (ρ)		1.2 ± 0.5 g/cm^3	
Absolute magnitude V(1,0)	4.6	0.6 bright side 2.3 dark side	6.9
Surface gravity (g)		35.65 cm/sec^2	

URANUS

Semimajor axis (a) = 19.1819 AU

Eccentricity (e) = 0.04724

Inclination (i) = 0° 46′ 23″

Bond albedo (A) = 0.37 ± 0.05

Perihelion (q) = 18.2757 AU

Aphelion (Q) = 20.0881 AU

Period of revolution (Y) = 84.0139 years

Rotation period (P) = 24 ± 3 hours

Reference temperature (T_{ref}) = 56.7°K

Measured temperature: 58 ± 3°K

Pole of rotation: right ascension (α) = 75.11467° ± 0.00247°
              declination (δ) = 15.04100° ± 0.00058°

Mass (M) = 8.6677 × 10^{28} grams = solar mass ($M_\odot$) / 22,945 ± 15

Dynamical oblateness (J_2) = 0.00343 ± 0.00002

Radius: equatorial (r) = 25,900 ± 300 km; polar (b) = 25,350 ± 300 km

Density (ρ) = 1.217 ± 0.042 g/cm³

Surface gravity, at equator (g) = 830 cm/sec²

Axial tilt (φ) = 97.93°

Atmosphere: H_2, probably ~ 90%

He, probably ~ 10%

CH_4, 0.4%

Precession period (T) = 8.0 × 10^8 years

RINGS OF URANUS

Albedo of Rings = 0.03

RING	SEMIMAJOR AXIS	WIDTH	ECCENTRICITY	MASS
Ring 6:	41,980 km	~ 5 km		
Ring 5:	42,360 km	~ 5 km		
Ring 4:	42,663 km	~ 5 km	1.14 ± 0.14 × 10^{-3}	
Ring α	44,839 ± 1 km	9 km	0.63 ± 0.03 × 10^{-3}	~ 4 × 10^{16} grams
Ring β	45,799 km	14–16 km	0.44 ± 0.03 × 10^{-3}	~ 4 × 10^{16} grams
Ring η	47,323 km	~ 50 km		

RING	SEMIMAJOR AXIS	WIDTH	ECCENTRICITY	INCLI- NATION	MASS
Ring γ	47,746 km	7 km	< 1.0 × 10^{-3}	< 0.08°	
Ring δ	48,423 km	~ 5 km	< 1.6 × 10^{-3}	< 0.13°	
Ring ε	51,284 ± 6 km	20–100 km	7.80 ± 0.12 × 10^{-3}	0.0°	~ 5 × 10^{18} grams

SATELLITES OF URANUS

	MIRANDA	ARIEL	UMBRIEL
Semimajor axis (a), km	129,800	190,900	266,000
Eccentricity (e)	0.012 ± 0.001	0.0033 ± 0.0007	0.0011 ± 0.0006
Inclination (i)	$4.0° \pm 0.3°$	0	0
Period of Rotation & Revolution (P & Y)	$1^d\ 9^h\ 55^m\ 24.78^s$	$2^d\ 12^h\ 29^m\ 20.77^s$	$4^d\ 3^h\ 27^m\ 36.82^s$
Mass (M) (Uranus = 1)	$0.032 \times$ Titania	$0.58 \times$ Titania	$0.17 \times$ Titania
Mass (M)	$\sim 2.8 \times 10^{23}$ grams	$\sim 5.1 \times 10^{24}$ grams	$\sim 1.5 \times 10^{24}$ grams
Absolute magnitude (V[1,0])	3.8	1.7	2.6
Radius ($r\sqrt{p_v}$), photometric	114.7 km	301.7 km	199.3 km

	TITANIA	OBERON
Semimajor axis (a), km	436,000	583,400
Eccentricity (e)	0.0018 ± 0.0003	0.0006 ± 0.0003
Inclination (i)	$< 0.1°$	$< 0.1°$
Period of Rotation & Revolution (P & Y)	$8^d\ 16^h\ 56^m\ 26.91^s$	$13^d\ 11^h\ 7^m\ 3.85^s$
Mass (M) (Uranus = 1)	$1.0 \pm 0.7 \times 10^{-4}$	$0.77 \times$ Titania
Mass (M)	$8.7 \pm 6.1 \times 10^{24}$ grams	$\sim 6.7 \times 10^{24}$ grams
Absolute magnitude (V[1,0])	1.3	1.5
Radius ($r\sqrt{p_v}$), photometric	362.7 km	330.8 km

NEPTUNE

Semimajor axis (a) = 30.0578 AU

Eccentricity (e) = 0.00858

Inclination (i) = 1° 46' 22"

Bond albedo (A) = 0.33

Perihelion (q) = 29.7999 AU

Aphelion (Q) = 30.3157 AU

Period of revolution (Y) = 164.793 years

Rotation period (P) = $19^h 35^m \pm 0.3^m$

Reference temperature (T_{ref}) = 46.0°K

Measured temperature = 55.5 ± 2.3°K

Pole of rotation: right ascension (α) = 294.91°, declination (δ) = 40.53°

Mass (M) = 1.0307×10^{29} grams = solar mass ($M_\odot$) / 19,296 ± 9

Dynamical oblateness (J_2) = 0.0050 ± 0.0005

Radius: equatorial (r) = 24,753 ± 59 km; polar (b) = 24,112 ± 126 km

Density (ρ) = 1.666 ± 0.016 g/cm³

Surface gravity, at equator (g) = 1100 cm/sec²

Axial tilt (ϕ) = 28.80°

Atmosphere: H_2, probably ~ 90% C_2H_6, ~ 1 ppm

He, probably ~ 10% C_2H_2, ~ 0.01 ppm

CH_4, 0.19 ± 0.01%

Precession period: 4.25×10^8 years

	TRITON	NEREID
Semimajor axis (a)	355,550 km	5,567,000 km
Eccentricity (e)	0.0	0.74934
Inclination (i)	159.945°	27.71°
Period of revolution (Y)	$5^d 21^h 2^m 39.3^s$	$359^d 21^h 9^m$
Geometric albedo (p_v)	≥ 0.19	
Subsolar temperature (T_{ss})	≤ 68.2°K	
Mass (M)	$1.36 \pm 0.24 \times 10^{26}$ grams	
Radius (r)	2200 ± 400 km	$r\sqrt{p_v}$ = 104.6 km (photometric)
Absolute magnitude (V[1,0])	− 1.2	4.0
Density (ρ)	3.0 ± 1.5 g/cm³	
Surface gravity (g)	187.5 cm/sec²	
Atmosphere	CH_4, $1 \pm 0.5 \times 10^{-4}$ bar	
Rotation	synchronous	unknown

PLUTO

Semimajor axis (a) = 39.439 AU

Perihelion (q) = 29.571 AU

Eccentricity (e) = 0.2502

Aphelion (Q) = 49.307

Inclination (i) = 17° 10′

Period of revolution (Y) = 247.686 years

Geometric albedo (p_v) = 0.36 ± 0.14

Rotation period (P) = 6^d 9^h 16^m 54^s ± 26^s

Subsolar Temperature (T_{ss}) = 56.1°K

Pole of rotation: Right ascension (α) = 285°, declination (δ) = 35°

Mass (M) = 1.5 ± 0.25 × 10^{25} grams = solar mass ($M_\odot$) / 130,000,000 ± 20,000,000

Radius: equatorial (r) = 1500 ± 200 km

Density (ρ) = 1.1 ± 0.5 g/cm³

Surface gravity, at equator (g) = 44.5 cm/sec²

Axial tilt (ϕ) = 55° to ecliptic

Absolute magnitude (V[1,0]) = −1.01

Atmosphere: CH_4; pressure highly variable with temperature, 0.01 to 1 mbar

CHARON

Semimajor axis (a) = 20,000 ± 1000 km

Eccentricity (e) = 0.0

Inclination (i) = 115° ± 5° to ecliptic

Rotation: synchronous

Absolute magnitude (V[1,0]) = 0.7

Radius, ($r\sqrt{p_v}$) ~ 420 km, photometric

GLOSSARY

albedo: The fraction of incident light reflected from a body, ranging from 0.0 (no light reflected) to 1.0 (all light reflected). The Moon's albedo is 0.067, meaning that it reflects 6.7 percent of the light that falls upon it.

aphelion: The farthest point from the center of the Sun attained by a body in solar orbit.

astronomical unit (A.U.): The mean radius of Earth's orbit. One A.U. is equal to 149,597,927 kilometers.

black body: Theoretical object that absorbs and re-emits energy with perfect efficiency.

convection: Transmission of thermal energy by physical motion of molecules within a fluid or gas, from a hotter region to a cooler, usually by means of small pockets or "cells" within the substance.

coriolis effect: Apparent deflection of an object moving with respect to a rotating reference frame. An air mass moving northward from the equator will rotate in a counterclockwise direction with respect to the Earth's surface, because the eastward rotational velocity of the surface decreases with increasing latitude, while the air mass retains the greater rotational speed of the lower latitude from whence it originated, permitting it to overtake the surface. Weather systems in the Southern Hemisphere curve in the opposite direction from those in the Northern.

corona: The Sun's tenuous, luminous upper atmosphere, visible during total eclipses.

Cosmic Background Radiation: A persistent "noise" observed by radio astronomers to be coming from all directions in space, equivalent to the radiation that would be expected from a black body at a temperature of 3° Kelvin — the predicted overall temperature of the universe, according to the Big Bang cosmology.

deferent: One of the larger circles upon which planets moved in the Ptolemaic, Earth-centered model of the universe.

diffraction grating: A mirrored, optically smooth surface that has been scored with as many as 20,000 parallel lines per linear inch, used to break up "white" light into a spectrum.

ecliptic: (1) The plane defined by Earth's orbit. (2) The projection of the ecliptic plane on the sky, or celestial sphere, along which the Sun, Moon, and planets seem to move.

emissivity: Measurement of the total energy output of a star at a given temperature.

epicycle: Smaller circle along which planets were thought to move in the Ptolemaic model of the universe. Used to explain the apparent change in direction, or "retrograde loop," that planets exhibited in their motion with respect to background stars.

escape velocity: The minimum velocity required to escape the gravitational field of a mass given by $V_e = \sqrt{\dfrac{2GM}{R}}$, where G is the gravitational constant (6.673×10^{-8} cm³/g $\times$ sec²), M is the mass in grams, and R is the distance from the center of the body in centimeters. Escape velocity at the surface of the Earth is about 11.2 km/sec. Escape velocity from the Moon is 2.4 km/sec.

field line: Line along which magnetic force acts, connecting opposite poles in a magnetic field. The more lines through each square centimeter, the greater the field's intensity.

flux tube: With reference to the Jupiter–Io electromagnetic interaction, the flux tube is that roughly toroidal, or doughnut-shaped, region of space connecting Io's ionosphere to the magnetic poles of Jupiter, through which charged particles flow.

galactic year: The time required for the Sun to complete one orbit about the center of our galaxy. Approximately 250 million years.

gas giant: Member of a class of planets in which there is an overwhelmingly large ratio of atmospheric constituents — gases and liquefied gases — to solid, rocky, or metallic core materials. Jupiter, Saturn, Uranus, and Neptune are gas giants.

heat sink: In thermodynamics, a sink is an energy reservoir, a region into which energy will tend to flow and accumulate.

impact ejecta: Material thrown out during the formation of craters, often to distances hundreds of kilometers from the site of impact. Bright "rays" emanating from young lunar craters, such as those from Copernicus and Aristarchus, mark regions of secondary cratering caused by the fall of ejecta.

lava: (1) Molten rock. (2) Magma, upon reaching the surface. (3) Rock produced by volcanic activity.

limb: The curved "edge" of a planet, seen against space. Atmospheric absorption causes the limb of Jupiter's disk to appear darker than the center.

main-belt asteroids: Those asteroids whose orbits lie between the orbits of Mars and Jupiter.

main sequence: The evolutionary path along which most stars spend the bulk of their lifetimes. In the Hertzsprung-Russell diagram, the diagonal band along which stars are most densely concentrated.

massif: A large, dense clustering of mountains.

mercator projection: Map generated by projecting surface features from a globe onto a cylinder in such a way that compass headings between geographical locations are not distorted.

mural quadrant: Device used by Tycho Brahe and others to measure with great precision the elevation of a star above the horizon, or the angular separation between stars — so called because the scale was often wall-sized.

nova: Star whose brightness increases due to explosive loss of material from outer layers; thought to be caused by gas falling into it from a companion star.

occultation: Eclipse of a small or very distant object by a relatively large or close one. Although the Moon occults several bright stars every month, occultations of stars by planets are much rarer.

opposition: Configuration in which a planet appears directly opposite the Sun, as seen from Earth. Mars comes to opposition approximately every two years.

organelles: Literally, "tiny organs," such as chloroplasts or mitochondria, that serve approximately the same purpose in one-celled organisms that stomachs, kidneys, and so forth do in larger creatures.

parallax: Apparent displacement of an object against a more distant background when viewed from two widely separated points. Useful in determining distance.

perihelion: Point of closest approach to the Sun.

planetesimal: Member of a class of small bodies, ranging in size from a few millimeters to several kilometers in diameter, from which the planets formed.

planetoid: "Planet-like." Etymologically more accurate than *asteroid,* but less commonly used to describe small bodies in solar orbit.

precession: The tendency of the rotation axis of a planet to move at right angles to a force applied to it, such as a gravitational perturbation. The Moon's gravity causes Earth's rotation axis to precess with a period of about 25,725 years.

quantum: Fundamental and indivisible packet of energy or mass. The photon is the quantum of the electromagnetic field.

radio occultation experiment: Any experiment that uses the pattern of fading of a radio signal to determine characteristics, such as size and atmospheric density, of the body responsible for occulting, or eclipsing, the radio source.

Rayleigh scattering: Preferential scattering of light of short wavelength by small particles, such as gas molecules, giving the sky its blue color.

red shift: Degree to which spectral lines from a receding object are shifted toward the low-frequency, or red, end of the spectrum. The fact that the more distant a galaxy is, the more its light is red-shifted, suggests that the universe is expanding. The greater the red shift, the higher the velocity of recession.

Roche limit: Minimum distance at which a rocky, natural satellite can orbit without being torn about by the tidal forces of its primary.

spiral arm: In galaxies, the bright curving streamers along which stars tend to form.

sublimation: Process by which a substance under appropriate conditions of temperature and pressure may go directly from the solid to gaseous stage, without first melting. On Earth, dry ice (frozen carbon dioxide) and camphor mothballs are observed to sublime.

subtend: To delimit, as in angular measure. The Moon subtends an arc of about one-half of a degree.

supernova: The most violent of stellar explosions, in which a massive star may expel as much as 50 percent of its matter and, for a period of a few weeks, outshine a galaxy.

synchronous orbit: An orbit, in the equatorial plane of a planet, whose period is the same as the rotation period of the planet, permitting the satellite to remain over the same point on the rotating globe. Satellites orbiting 36,000 kilometers from Earth complete an orbit in 24 hours. The radius for a synchronous orbit is given by $R_s = \sqrt[3]{MGT^2/4\pi^2}$, where M is the planet's mass, G the gravitational constant, and T the rotation period of the planet.

T-Tauri: A variety of variable star believed to be in the early stages of formation and expelling mass into space with its solar wind.

tectonic plate: A continent-sized slab of rock floating on a planet's mantle and being moved slowly about the face of the planet by the convection of magma in the mantle.

terminator: The line marking the boundary between the Day and Night hemispheres of a planet.

toroid: Form similar to a torus, the shape defined as the locus of points equidistant from a circle in space; a doughnut shape. Planetary magnetic fields are toroidal in form.

variable star: A star that changes in brightness, either because it is a member of a binary star system and subject to eclipses by its companion, or because it has an internal instability that causes fluctuations in its rate of energy production.

wave of darkening: Seasonal variation in the shape and reflectivity of Martian features, once thought to be evidence of biology but now known to be caused by seasonal winds moving dust about the surface.

INDEX